CAN THEATRE TEACH?

CAN THEATRE TEACH?

An Historical and Evaluative Analysis of Theatre in Education

by

Christine Redington, B.A., Ph.D.

PERGAMON PRESS

OXFORD · NEW YORK · TORONTO · SYDNEY · PARIS · FRANKFURT

U.K.	Pergamon Press Ltd., Headington Hill Hall, Oxford OX3 0BW, England
U.S.A.	Pergamon Press Inc., Maxwell House, Fairview Park, Elmsford, New York 10523, U.S.A.
CANADA	Pergamon Press Canada Ltd., Suite 104, 150 Consumers Rd., Willowdale, Ontario M2J 1P9, Canada
AUSTRALIA	Pergamon Press (Aust.) Pty. Ltd., P.O. Box 544, Potts Point, N.S.W. 2011, Australia
FRANCE	Pergamon Press SARL, 24 rue des Ecoles, 75240 Paris, Cedex 05, France
FEDERAL REPUBLIC OF GERMANY	Pergamon Press GmbH, Hammerweg 6, D-6242 Kronberg-Taunus, Federal Republic of Germany

Copyright © 1983 C. Redington

First edition 1983

Library of Congress Cataloguing in Publication Data

Redington, C.
Can theatre teach?
Bibliography: p.
Includes index.
1. Theater in education.   I. Title.
PN3171.R4   1983   371.3'32   83–11463

British Library Cataloguing in Publication Data

Redington, Christine
Can theatre teach?
1. Drama in education — Great Britain
I. Title
792'.0226'0941   PN3171
ISBN 0-08-024699-0 (Hardcover)
ISBN 0-08-024698-2 (Flexicover)

Printed and bound in Great Britain by
William Clowes Limited, Beccles and London

Acknowledgements

I am most grateful for the financial help I received from the Calouste Gulbenkian Foundation and from the Scottish Arts Council. In 1976 the Gulbenkian Foundation gave me a 3-month grant to travel around Britain observing the work of the various Theatre in Education teams. The Scottish Arts Council's Bursary for 1978–79 enabled me to write up my material and carry out the research project on the programme "Race Against Time".

I would like to express my gratitude to all those people who allowed me to interview them, to the Theatre in Education teams whose work I saw, and especially to the Greenwich Theatre in Education team for their help and co-operation.

My thanks also to Martin Heller for the loan of the photographs and information on the Compass Theatre; to Stuart Bennett and John Daniell of Greenwich Young People's Theatre; to the Cockpit, Coventry; and Leeds TIE teams for the photographs used in this book.

My grateful thanks to the late Professor James Arnott for his help and encouragement with the original research on Theatre in Education.

I am also greatly indebted to Tony Jackson, of Manchester University, for his incisive and constructive comments on this manuscript.

My grateful thanks to Mrs. R. Webb and the secretaries of Eliot College, University of Kent, for typing out the manuscript.

My special thanks to Giles Havergal, Grace Matchett, and to the many people in Glasgow, who offered their constant help and support whilst I was working at the Citizens' Theatre.

Contents

Acknowledgements   v

Introduction   1

1. The Origins of Theatre in Education   13

    Education   13
    Theatre   20
    Children's Theatre   30

2. Theatre in Education at Coventry, 1965–70   42

    Infant Programmes   58
    Junior Programmes   63
    Secondary Programmes   71

3. The Development of Young People's Theatre   84

4. Changes in Theatre in Education   111

    Changes in the theory and practice of TIE since 1965   111
    The Standing Conference of Young People's Theatre (SCYPT)   128
    Funding   134

5. The Evaluation of Theatre in Education   141

    Research Project in the Evaluation of a TIE Programme   164
    "Race Against Time"   164
    Problems Encountered   166
    Analysis and Classification of Material

6. The Evaluation Project on "Race Against Time"   168

Conclusion   201

Appendix A   215

Arts Council: Analysis of Drama Grants and Guarantees, YPTS and TIE

Appendix B 217
Spread of Personnel from Coventry TIE

Appendix C 219
Research on "Race Against Time"

Bibliography 249

Index 251

Introduction

The title of this book deliberately poses a question. Playwrights from Sophocles to Brecht have used their plays to teach, to convey facts, political attitudes or moral instruction to their audiences. But although the playwright's intention may be clear, the effectiveness of this teaching is much more difficult to assess.

This book is about Theatre in Education, a recent development in British Theatre which has taken the effectiveness of theatre as a teaching medium seriously. The aim of Theatre in Education (the title is usually abbreviated to TIE) is that its presentations in schools should educate, widen pupils' horizons, and lead them to ask questions about the world around them, as well as entertain. The purpose of this book is to analyse the effectiveness of TIE's work in schools, and to explore how it uses theatre to teach. This examination of TIE is placed in its historical context to explain how and why TIE developed.

For anyone involved in education this book provides resource material on TIE's past and present educational methods and experiments. The evaluation project described in Chapters 5 and 6 is an important part of the discussion on TIE's effectiveness as a teaching medium. For the student of recent theatrical developments the book attempts to fill in some historical gaps in the knowledge of TIE relating it to the "alternative" theatre movement, the British Repertory system and to Young People's Theatre.

What is Theatre in Education?

A TIE team — note the emphasis on shared effort in this description — is a group of actor–teachers who usually have experience in both professions. They devise, or write, "programmes" for very specific age groups, and take these out to schools. The use of the word "programme" avoids the limiting description of the work as a play or a lesson; in fact it is often both, using a complex mixture of theatrical forms and educational techniques.

Although closely related to Children's Theatre, TIE does not set out to offer a hall full of pupils an afternoon of "Hansel and Gretel", or a stage overflowing with weeping princesses and wicked witches. TIE teams are much more likely to offer pupils an aspect of a national or world problem, either contemporary or historical. The subject matter is frequently presented in a realistic manner, and involves the pupils within the action. To aid this contact with pupils, and to create a believable environment, TIE companies rarely use the stage in the school hall for their presentations, but work with the pupils using the classroom, the whole hall or even the school grounds. The pupils are not passive recipients of information, nor are they just an audience: they are active participants in the TIE programme, but their participation may vary from physical involvement in a drama session to watching a play and taking part in a discussion.

As a form in its own right TIE emerged at Coventry in 1965, with the setting up of the first team, which was attached to the Belgrade Repertory Theatre. Helped by the economic boom of the late 1960s and early 1970s other TIE companies were formed, many based on the Coventry model. These companies were set up in the same period as the growth of "alternative" theatre in Britain, a movement in which groups of performers began to experiment with new theatre forms performing in diverse venues. Many of these companies worked as co-operatives; a few eventually gained official funding from the Arts Council. TIE, however, usually received grant aid from the moment a company was established. The funding came from the Local Education Authority and from the Arts Council. Where these grants were generous enough, TIE could be offered as a free service to schools such as in Coventry and Leeds. When the grants were insufficient, then a TIE company would need to charge schools, such as Watford TIE.

TIE programmes

The subject-matter of a TIE programme has some basis in real life. It might, for instance, present the problems of gypsies and their treatment by the local council, or demonstrate the life of the nineteenth-century navvy building railways. The content of TIE work is often social and political, and in this respect it is similar to the content of Political Theatre. However, it does not baldly state a political message; it offers the pupils an experience of a socio-political problem without giving a pat answer.

The structure of a TIE programme will include a range of educational techniques from complex problem-solving to simple occupational mime. The theatrical elements of a programme are a means and not an end in themselves providing plot, suspense, dramatic climax and characterization. The actor–teachers usually stay in character throughout the programme, working with the pupils to help them solve the various problems they encounter in the course of the "plot".

Theatrical and educational elements in TIE programmes

An analysis of TIE programmes, suggesting some of the main elements which may appear, is, of course, no substitute for the experience of a TIE programme itself, and I would recommend that the reader first looks at the description of "Race Against Time" in Chapter 5, or at some of Coventry's programmes outlined in Chapter 2. To aid clarity I have split this section into two main headings: first the educational and then the theatrical elements; in a TIE programme, however, they are often inextricably mixed. The listing is not in order of importance, as all elements are important.

Educational elements

(a) Child centred:

Although TIE teams select subjects for programmes which particularly interest them, they always make sure that the subject-matter and the form of the programme centres on the child's needs, abilities and potential. The majority of programmes are based on the child's participation, both physical and intellectual, but unlike creative drama improvisations, the action does not stem entirely from the children; they do not make up the plot and invent the characters. Instead they are guided through a series of events in which the children have a definite role and an influence on what happens next. The programmes are carefully geared to the children's intellectual level and experience.

(b) Use of play:

The programmes use the child's natural enjoyment of play. Imaginary situations are created by the team, such as being down a coal-mine, and the children play at being miners. They work in the mine sharing the events with the characters they have met. The "playing at" is taken very seriously; it stimulates the pupils' imagination and involves them in the dramatic action.

(c) Learning by doing:

The essence of TIE work is that pupils learn by experiencing the events that occur within a programme. This experience is physical, mental and emotional, and through this total involvement the pupils learn by discovery.

(d) Project teaching:

Many Infant and Junior TIE programmes can provide the starting-point, or the climax to a Project in a school. Programmes such as Coventry's "Rare Earth" on pollution, or Edinburgh's "Opportunity Strikes" about the oil industry's effect on the Scottish countryside, offer a variety of possible follow-up work, and are genuinely cross-curricular.

(e) Drama in Education:

In the late 1960s and early 1970s there were a number of TIE teams which wished to promote Drama in Education, and even now, the drama teacher is often a TIE team's main point of contact in a Secondary school. Without the introduction of drama teachers it would have been much more difficult for TIE teams to begin work with older pupils, and some of the most imaginative follow-up work to a TIE programme is often done in drama lessons. TIE uses drama in education methods such as occupational mime, role-play and improvisation as an integral part of the work.

(f) Relation to age group:

In relating the form and content of their work to a particular age group, TIE teams are using the accumulated knowledge of child psychologists and pedagogues concerning mental, physical and emotional stages of development. The length of programme is an essential part of this thinking, and to ensure that they can work in some depth with pupils TIE teams usually play to one class of pupils at a time, perhaps for only half a day. Complex programmes often require one or two return visits a week or so later. For Secondary schools return visits are difficult to timetable, but a team often spends a whole day in the school.

(g) Problem-solving:

Within a TIE programme the use of problem-solving helps to stimulate the pupils' curiosity, retain their attention during the programme and motivate them to learn more about the subject afterwards. Pupils are introduced to a problem through the programme's characters, who ask the pupils to help them find a solution. In the process, the pupils must understand, and be able to analyse, the character's differing points of view. For instance, in Coventry TIE's programme for Infants, "Ifan's Valley", the pupils meet Glyn Ifan, the sheep farmer, and Armitage from the Water Board. They become involved in Ifan's problem of how to cope with the Water Authority, which wishes to use his valley as a reservoir.

(h) Language development:

Pupils' mental and physical involvement in a TIE programme, and their need to solve the problems encountered, often motivates them to ask questions, to argue with the characters and amongst themselves, and to discuss quite complex issues. This process can certainly help in the development of the pupils' vocabulary and their ability to articulate their ideas and questions. Sometimes a programme is carefully structured to allow the pupils to be the only group to know all the facts about a character or a particular problem. During the course of the programme it becomes necessary for the pupils to explain what they know in order for the action to proceed.

(i) New teaching methods:

It is quite usual for TIE teams to introduce new teaching methods into schools long before teachers would feel ready to try them out. Games and simulations have been a fast developing form of teaching over the past few years, but are more popular with commercial companies to train staff than with teachers in schools. War Games have been on the commercial market for years and can teach history and military strategy, but the game format is not commonly used in schools. TIE, however, has made imaginative use of games and simulations since the early 1970s and has really pioneered their use in schools.

Theatrical elements

(a) Theatrical forms:

The majority of TIE programmes use recognizable theatrical forms such as plot, conflict and characterization. The action is often worked out in a series of stages ("what happens next?"), thus giving a firm plot line, but a team may devise several different strands of plot, or alternative endings, to enable the pupils to decide the course of action. Most TIE plots are based upon dramatic conflict. Characters of opposing points of view meet, conflict arises and a solution must be sought. Actor–teachers usually play one or two characters during the course of the programme and continue in character during the discussion period, thus giving the pupils the opportunity to question the actual character about his or her ideas and actions, rather than talking to the actor about the character. In some Infant programmes actor–teachers have used characterization to persuade the pupils that the characters are real people, involved in real events, but this particular technique was subsequently questioned by TIE teams and used less frequently.

(b) Empathy:

TIE teams use empathy as an important part of audience involvement. Pupils identify with particular characters, accepting the point of view the characters put forward, feeling able to discuss events with them, caring what happens to them. This empathy is often used to make the pupils aware of a moral problem, or to surprise them into a shocked response. In "Pow Wow" the pupils are faced with a dual allegiance and a moral dilemma. They first meet Mr. Tex, and believe what he tells them about Red Indians, then they are introduced to Black Elk, and they realize as they get to know the Red Indian, that Mr. Tex may be in the wrong (see Chapter 5, pp. 145–7).

(c) The actor–audience relationship:

The TIE programme often involves its audience physically, as well as mentally. This involvement is intrinsic to the plot and the pupils become an essential part of the action, either as participants, or as critical observers, whose opinions are sought and valued.

(d) Group devising:

This is a popular method of programme preparation, which involves all members of the team, but it does not exclude the possibility of one or two members concentrating upon research or writing. Any TIE programme is the result of the whole company's discussion of subject-matter and form; a method which tends to lead to high commitment amongst actor–teachers.

(e) Social and political subject-matter:

Important social and political issues often form the subject of a TIE programme. They can be presented from an historical perspective, such as Cockpit's "Marches", which told the history of Moseley and brought out the contemporary problems of racism and fascism. Contemporary problems are sometimes examined directly, as in Greenwich TIE's programme "Unemployment". In the preparation and presentation of such programmes TIE teams can use the techniques of documentary and political theatre.

(f) Theatrical aids:

Sets, costumes, make-up, sound effects and lighting are useful aids to the creation of character and environment. As most TIE teams tour, they tend to carry the minimum of set, and rarely use lighting, in fact theatrical aids are not usually the most important aspect of a TIE presentation. Teams tend to rely on stimulating the pupils' imagination rather than offering them a complete picture of the place and time in which the programme is set.

(g) Grant aid:

As a result of their historical development many TIE teams are attached to Repertory Theatres (see Chapter 3) and share facilities. The grant for the TIE team was requested in the first place by the Repertory Theatre, and the TIE team's money forms a part of the Theatre's total allocation from the Arts Council. Most TIE teams also receive aid from their Local Education Authority, and because of this financial support many teams can offer their services free to schools. Very few TIE companies have managed to set up on their own, with no parent theatre, because the cost of premises and back-up staff, such as caretakers and cleaners, is too heavy a burden on the limited income.

A teaching resource

TIE teams spend months researching and preparing a TIE programme. This research often involves the whole team whilst they are still taking another programme round to schools. When the time comes to begin shaping the new programme the research is discussed, analysed, filtered and finally ready for improvisation, or scripting, or both. Much of the material researched has to be left out of the programme, but it is then used in the

Teachers' Notes that are prepared for schools. These can form sizeable volumes bringing together copies of original documents, related subject-matter and themes, suggestions for follow-up work for the teachers in different disciplines and a bibliography. Teachers rarely have the time to do this quantity of research on a subject, neither do they have the opportunity of working with a group of people to try out different methods and new ideas. TIE can therefore provide a major teaching resource.

Many TIE teams would claim that their role in schools is far more wide-ranging, and that they offer the pupils an experience of the world outside the school, or of time past, in a manner that a school would find hard to create.

TIE and the education system

There is no doubt that TIE provides an exciting method of teaching. A TIE programme often seems able to do what the school curriculum and many teachers cannot, that is involve the pupils, interest them in the subject-matter, lead them to see its relevance to the world around them, and motivate them to learn more.

TIE appears to be having some success in motivating pupils to learn at a time when the education system is being criticized for failing to do exactly that. The last two decades have seen mounting criticism of the education system, in America as well as in Britain. The Americans Ivan Illich and Paul Goodman have attacked the fundamental presumptions made about the need to educate in the present form. John Holt has revealed how the education system can actually prevent children learning. In Britain books have pointed out the value of Progressive methods and Progressive schools, or, in the case of the 'Black' papers by Cox and Boyson, questioned the claims made for Comprehensive schooling, and the Department of Education and Science has produced numerous reports on every aspect of education in the last few years.[1]

Theatre in Education teams keep themselves well informed of criticism and changes in education and are continuously questioning and evaluating what they do in schools. They experiment with new educational ideas and techniques, and with different theatre forms, in an effort to discover the most effective way of working. This effectiveness also relies upon their providing a good theatrical experience, and, although TIE is not in the business of pure entertainment, a TIE programme can be gripping, exhilarating, funny or intensely dramatic.

Theatre in Education and Children's Theatre Abroad

Although TIE is, in origin, a British phenomenon, developments in Children's Theatre abroad do reflect the same concerns with social and political issues. A new Children's Theatre in West Germany in the mid-1960s helped to change the traditional plays for children, the diet of folk tales and Christmas fairy stories. The "Theatre for Children" was founded in the Berlin Reichskabarett in 1966, and from the very beginning the company wrote their own plays. When it moved to a small theatre in the round in 1972 the company changed its name to the Grips Theatre, a name which is indicative of its policy. The nearest English equivalent for Grips is the Yorkshire expression "nouse" — grips is understanding with humour, thinking with fun. After a period with no financial help, the theatre is now grant aided, and can charge a minimum amount for its seats. What makes Grips comparable with the work of TIE in Britain is its approach to its audience and the kind of subject-matter it offers them. The company is concerned with the problems of young people in their relationships with adults and the world around them. The theatre sees its task as helping them to develop a sense of their own worth, to get their bearings in the real world and to learn to see that world as changeable, and open to criticism. To accomplish this the company tackle such problems as property and power, the problems of authority, and the difficulties of the handicapped child. Follow-up material is published as accompaniments to the plays. The Grips Theatre has presented guest performances throughout Western Europe and has had a considerable influence upon the policies and programmes of its equivalent West German theatres.

The Rote Grütze Children's Theatre Company of Berlin share Grips Theatre's concern with social and political themes. Their working methods with pupils are a little more flexible, they go out to schools with programmes that are group researched and devised and use participation, methods much closer to British Theatre in Education. The aim of the Rote Grütze company is that the audience "should learn about themselves and how to relate to the everyday world, to understand relationships and find solutions to recognized problems. The audience learn that the world they are living in can be changed."[2]

America, like Germany, has always been well known for its Children's Theatre movement, but TIE has never taken root there. A few "artists in schools" projects are now in existence, supported by special funding. Community Theatres and Regional Resident Theatres include educational programmes in their work, and the occasional TIE project has been set up. In 1972 the Belgrade Coventry TIE team were invited to Rochester, New York State, as guests of the Genessee Valley Arts Authority. The Authority planned to build a new theatre in Rochester which would house several TIE teams alongside a permanent Theatre company. The Coventry team went to demonstrate their work to teachers, universities, school inspectors, directors, drama critics and people to fund the scheme. The trip proved to be a success, and the first TIE scheme was set up in Rochester shortly afterwards.

Australia, Canada and New Zealand lacked a tradition of Children's Theatre, and TIE found a stronger foothold. It was often promoted by lecture tours given by Young People's Theatre pioneers such as Brian Way, or by visitors from these countries observing British TIE teams at work in their own areas. The Australian Council for the Arts began to support TIE projects and the Magpie TIE company was set up in Adelaide in 1977, based at the State Theatre Company of South Australia. The company undertakes long tours into the Outback to try and contact more of the school population. In New Zealand and Canada similar companies have been formed. The La Marmeille Theatre of Quebec is a Canadian research group whose findings are of use to other TIE and Children's Theatre companies. Using sociological and psychological research techniques "they aim to bring young audiences and participants an awareness" of "their creative potential for individual and collective change".[3]

Number of TIE companies in Britain

TIE is beginning to be recognized at home and abroad, but this does not make up for the fact that there are very few TIE companies in existence. In Britain there are approximately twenty teams who concentrate almost exclusively on Theatre in Education work. Bearing in mind that these teams tend to work within their local area in order to establish a close relationship with local schools, the number of square miles covered by these teams is limited. A large proportion of the school population will never experience regular TIE programmes, although they might see a touring Children's Theatre production, or have a brief taste of TIE when Theatre Centre visits their school; this company travels extensively throughout Britain.

Although there are a few TIE companies, there has been an enormous rise in the number of Community Theatre and experimental theatre groups since the late 1960s. A number of these Community groups work with children as well as adults, running drama workshops for summer playgroups, or taking a play round youth clubs, but they usually perform away from the school venue and outside school hours. In schools creative drama teaching and drama workshops after school hours have greatly increased. The result of all this activity is a profusion of titles describing drama and theatre work with children.

Definitions

The various titles can be most confusing, and as some of them will recur during the course of this book, I will attempt definitions of the most relevant ones. Theatre in Education has already been explained.

DRAMA IN EDUCATION. In a school situation it is both a method and a subject. As a subject on the curriculum, it uses various dramatic elements of movement, voice, concentration, improvisation and role-play to aid the personal development of the pupil. As a method it utilizes role-play and acting-out to teach pupils through experience. For example, pupils may learn the facts of an historical event by acting it out. Many Secondary schools now have drama departments, but in Primary schools it is used as a method to teach a number of subjects.

CHILDREN'S THEATRE. Actors performing plays to children in a theatre or a school. The aim is to entertain, and to introduce theatre to children. The theatrical elements are usually prominent, and participation is often confined to the vocal rather than the physical kind. Scripted plays are frequently used, and rehearsed in a formal theatre manner with a director, rather than the use of group devised work. Audience numbers tend to be large. Children's Theatre is more usually associated with the 5–12-year age group.

YOUNG PEOPLE'S THEATRE (YPT). This is used as an overall title for a range of work with children from Children's Theatre to TIE. However, when a company is described as doing Young People's Theatre this may mean that their work is rather more theatre-oriented than TIE, and may be for the Secondary school age rather than Primary. This definition means that they present plays rather than programmes and perform to a greater number of pupils (100–200) than a TIE team.

COMMUNITY THEATRE. Actors working in, and performing to a particular community. The company goes out to meet the community, performing in a number of different venues from pubs to youth clubs or community centres, and to a range of age groups. The work is often performance rather than teaching based, and in many companies quite a high percentage of the work is for children and young people. Material can be devised by the company, or written for them, and the subject-matter is often related to the area.

YOUTH THEATRE. Groups of children, or young people, who do drama work together out of school hours. The work can be anything from improvisation sessions to the rehearsal and performance of a scripted play. The organizations vary in size from small local groups to the National Youth Theatre.

In the present economic climate many of these developments are under threat, for instance the Arts Council recently cut their grant to the National Youth Theatre. When schools are forced to cut staff the arts tend to suffer first, the reduction in music teachers being an obvious example. Drama is in danger too. Theatre in Education companies are also under threat: the Roundabout TIE team at Nottingham has lost its Local Education Authority grant for work in schools.[5] Other teams are very concerned that further Local Authority spending cuts might see them suffer the same fate. This is exactly the time when Theatre in Education should receive attention, and some analysis of the value of its work in schools be attempted.

TIE has begun to spread through the English-speaking world, and it is at last receiving some attention. Two useful books are now available which look at the theory and practice of TIE: *Theatre in Education* by John O'Toole and *Learning Through Theatre* edited by Tony Jackson. A selection of TIE scripts has also been published, and these contain helpful and analytical introductions by Pam Schweitzer.[4] One magazine exists which discusses TIE work fully and that is the *Journal of the Standing Conference of Young People's Theatre*, SCYPT; the membership of SCYPT consists mainly of British Theatre in Education and Young People's Theatre companies. An increasing number of people and organizations are showing an interest in the work: teachers, theatre people, Local Education Authority advisers and Foundations such as the Calouste Gulbenkian. TIE teams, particularly those in London, receive visitors, many of whom come from abroad.

Can Theatre Teach?

This book poses questions about the teaching capacity of TIE, and it also attempts some answers. A number of these appear in the research on the Theatre in Education programme "Race Against Time" summarized in Chapter 6. This is the first full-scale TIE research project to be published, and, as far as I know, the first of its kind. The research and analysis of the programme raise some important points about TIE, and reveal interesting discoveries about the effect of the programme on the pupils and the school. To place this form of research in some context, Chapter 5 outlines educational evaluation methods and suggests a suitable approach for tackling TIE programmes. This evaluation has little meaning unless placed in the wider context of the educational and theatrical background to TIE, and Chapter 1 examines these, explaining some of the sources of TIE's present methods and ideas, sources that are to be found as far apart as America and Germany. Chapter 2 concentrates upon TIE's first emergence at the Belgrade Theatre, Coventry. These early years were vitally important as they laid the foundations of Theatre in Education and set the pattern for its development. Chapter 3 charts this development, concentrating upon the Arts Council's role, and offering detailed examples of the growth of three different kinds of companies. Changes in TIE policy, finance, company structure, relations with theatre and education, and the shape of the movement as a whole, are dealt with in Chapter 4.

This book draws together a range of information from articles, reports and unpublished material produced by the TIE teams. However, a major part of the information comes from my own research, the viewing of TIE programmes, visits to and interviews with TIE teams over the past few years, and from my own experience both from within the Young People's Theatre movement as a practitioner and from without, as an interested observer.

I hope that the book will not only fill some historical gaps in the knowledge of TIE, but will also stimulate readers to learn more about the subject. I also hope that it will provoke more research and more comment on the value of TIE, and will go some way towards answering the question: "Can Theatre Teach?"

Notes

1. In 1967 the DES produced the Education Survey on Drama, the Plowden Report, *Children and their Primary Schools*, and *Primary Education in Wales*; The Newsom Report *Half our Future* had appeared in 1963.

   Paul Goodman's book *Compulsory Miseducation* was first published in the USA in 1962 and in Britain in 1971; John Holt's *How Children Fail* appeared in 1965; Ivan Illich's *Deschooling Society* was published in the USA in 1971; C. B. Cox and Rhodes Boyson (eds.) series of *Black Papers* were published from 1969.

2. Karin Gartzke, "Rote Grütze Theatre of Berlin", *SCYPT Journal*, no. 4, p. 7.

3. "La Marmeille Theatre of Quebec", an interview with the Company by members of Ludus Dance in Education team, translated by Chris Thompson, *SCYPT Journal*, no. 4, 1979, p. 11.

4. John O'Toole, *Theatre in Education*, Hodder & Stoughton, London, 1976.

   Tony Jackson (ed.), *Learning Through Theatre*; Essays and casebooks on Theatre in Education, Manchester University Press, 1980.

   P. Schweitzer (ed.), *Theatre in Education* (3 volumes): Five Infant Programmes, Four Junior Programmes, Four Secondary Programmes, Methuen Young Drama, London, 1980.

5. Nottingham LEA have recently restored Roundabout's grant for work in schools.

Chapter 1

The Origins of Theatre in Education

Although TIE appears to have sprung to life as a totally new phenomenon in 1965, it is in fact the product of a number of old and new ideas in education, theatre and Children's Theatre. An examination of these ideas will help to place Theatre in Education in a wider context, both historically and philosophically. For the sake of clarity this chapter is divided into three sections, which reflect the three main areas from which TIE grew. The first two sections, Education and Theatre, are self-explanatory. They are the two worlds of TIE's title. The third section concerns Children's Theatre — which can be seen as Theatre in Education's direct ancestor, but also its present close relation. It would be misleading to think of Children's Theatre as giving birth to TIE, but the movement certainly provided the essential involvement with schools, an awareness of the problems of how and what to perform to children, and a variety of theories that were to prove essential to TIE's development. Children's Theatre pioneers played a most important role in helping to change attitudes towards theatre work for children and this assisted the eventual acceptance of TIE.

Education

Many of the ideas, which are central to TIE work today, have been part of educational philosophy for many years. The concept of education as child-centred was a vital shift in approach. First proposed by Jean Jacques Rousseau in the eighteenth century, it is fundamental to education today. The child should not be treated as a small adult, but his or her needs must be understood and teaching should, therefore, be centred round the child, and take the child's interests into account.

Just as a young animal learns by playing, so does a child, but this was not fully understood until the nineteenth century. Froebel's work at his Educational Institute in Germany was guided by the principle that education should lead the child to observe and think for himself rather than just being the recipient of knowledge. He saw the child's play as spontaneous objective-expression, which helped moral, physical and mental development, and in his *Education of Man* he noted that:

. . . play at this time is not trivial, it is highly serious and of deep
significance . . .

The plays of childhood are the germinal leaves of all later life; for
the whole man is developed and shown in these tenderest disposi-
tions in his innermost tendencies.[1]

Educationalists realized that this need to play could be used in the child's
education, an idea which is basic to the development of creative drama, and
also to the introduction of new teaching methods. The belief that actually doing
something, rather than just being told it, can be a more effective way to learn
is certainly important to TIE. Known as "learning through experience" the
method is now accepted, if not always used, by schools. It requires the child
to fully participate in, and be committed to, an activity set up by the teacher,
but the child must also be able to make the link between the activity and what
he is learning. John Dewey began experiments with this method in the late
nineteenth century, because he was worried that the traditional schooling had
become too concerned with developing intelligence and conveying information through book learning. He believed that it was dangerous to separate
knowledge from practice, and he wanted the child to learn basic academic
skills and knowledge by means of everyday experiences and occupations. If a
child was to learn by doing, Dewey noted that the quality of the experience
was of prime importance:

The quality of any experience has two aspects — immediate agreeable-
ness or disagreeableness and its influence upon later experiences . . .
Hence the central problem of an education based upon experience is to
select the kind of experience that will live fruitfully and creatively in
subsequent experiences.[2]

Learning by doing is an accepted part of teaching science today, but placing
the student in the position of an original investigator, carrying out his own
experiments was only introduced at the beginning of this century, and
became known as the heuristic method.

Although these various ideas were being discussed in Educational circles at
the outbreak of the First World War, they had not penetrated very deeply
into schools. Teachers were reluctant to use them, and the actuality of life in
schools in Britain was very different from the experimental establishments of
these early pioneers. Edmond Holmes, a retired Chief Inspector of Schools,
makes this very clear in his book, written in 1911:

Why is the teacher so ready to do everything (or nearly everything) for
the children whom he professes to educate? One obvious answer to this
question is that for a third of a century (1862–95) the 'Education
Department' did everything (or nearly everything) for him. For a third
of a century 'My Lords' required their inspectors to examine every

child in every elementary school in England on a syllabus which was binding on all schools alike. In doing this, they put a bit into the mouth of the teacher, and drove him at their pleasure, in this direction and that. And what they did to him they compelled him to do to the children.[3]

It was not until the 1930s that the new ideas began to emerge in official reports, and these ideas were accompanied by a realization of the different role school could play in the life of a child:

A good school, in short, is not a place of compulsory instruction but a community of old and young engaged in learning by co-operative experiment.[4]

The education system had begun to change and from being a place where the original intention was to teach children how to read and write, schools broadened their aims until, by 1931, they could be said to be teaching children how to live. In Primary school education this new attitude required very different working methods. A new approach to the curriculum was needed and the 1931 Report on the Primary School suggested that: "the curriculum is to be thought of in terms of activity and experience rather than knowledge to be acquired and facts to be stored".[5] The rigid timetable with its watertight compartments had to be broken down, but in fact this had begun to occur as teachers realized the natural correlation between different branches of knowledge. The 1931 Report suggested a closer relationship between subjects with the use of the Project method, which involved the child in his own learning. An involvement stimulated by the child solving problems, and learning in action:

The new project method is still compatible with teaching within subject divisions and implies merely that the teaching, instead of consisting in imparting knowledge of a subject in logical order takes the form of raising a succession of problems interesting to the pupils and leading them to reach, in the solution of these problems, the principles which the teacher wishes them to learn.[6]

The Report warned teachers against adopting the method until they really understood it and came to believe in it. However, the method was slowly introduced, and the teacher's role changed from being a purely didactic one, to a consultative, guiding role. The Project method at its best can help children to use reference books, and pursue individual work, which enables them to actively participate in learning.

A variation of the Project method, known as the "Centre of Interest", begins with a topic, or topics, which can provide sufficient interesting material to stimulate class work for up to a term or more. The 1967 Report,

Children and their Primary Schools, suggested that if this method worked properly the child's sense of personal discovery could make his memory of the subject matter much more vivid. The Primary school's curriculum has become more flexible since this method was introduced.

Secondary schools, however, seem less able to free themselves from the "chalk and talk" form of teaching, and the strict subject divisions have remained. TIE's method of work fits less happily in a Secondary school than in the Primary situation. Therefore the development of creative drama, as an emergent subject in the Secondary school, provided TIE with the means to gain acceptance there. TIE teams formed in the late 1960s and early 1970s were prepared to help the development of drama in schools by offering creative drama sessions, both for the pupils and for the teachers. For instance, the aim of the Flying Phoenix company was to present a series of drama workshops, rather than a play, and by this means help "to create an environment in which the child may develop imaginatively and individually through play and experiment".[7] The team visited Junior and Secondary schools on a weekly basis working with the pupils on improvisation around various themes.

The teaching of drama in schools has usually been associated with English, but even the teaching of English as a subject in its own right is a fairly recent development. In the 1900s English was considered to be the "Cinderella of the curriculum". When the Committee for the Board of Education reported on the teaching of English in England in 1921, they found that it had hardly been taught at all in the past, and even in 1921 the subject was entrusted to any member of staff who had some free time. After the Primary and Secondary school age were divided following a report in 1926, English began to gain acceptance as a subject. Until a Report for the Scottish Education Department in 1959 could claim that:

> The study of English, which has been described as 'the instrument and precondition of all intellectual progress entering into education at every point', occupies a prominent place in the curriculum.[8]

The development of English introduced Shakespeare and other dramatists to the school curriculum. Drama was associated with the study of plays, and possibly the production of one at the end of the school year. The value of drama in developing the individual's personality and imagination was recognized by only a few. Yet, as early as 1913 a Mrs. A. T. Craig, the Principal of the New York Ethical and Cultural School, was proposing that drama was of value to all aspects of the curriculum:

> The dramatic art, offers an almost unequalled method for all-round culture, a method for supplying in vivid form much of the intellectual material of the regular subjects, which is now frequently acquired in a

confused jumble and especially a method for doing justice to that most neglected element in our education — the training of the emotions.[9]

Caldwell Cook, a teacher of English at Perse School, Cambridge, was another early pioneer. His ideas on education were based on the belief that a teacher telling the pupils was no substitute for the pupils actually trying things out for themselves. In his teaching of English and Drama, Cook used the child's love of play as a starting-point and a stimulus, believing that it was the natural way for a child to learn. For Caldwell Cook education was to be by practice, by doing, rather than by instruction. In the practical application of this philosophy (which has strong echoes of Dewey and Froebel) he based his work on the acting out of formal plays and playmaking from existing stories. The boys were allowed some creative freedom in the preliminary exercises before the main business of playmaking. Although he was working within a framework of known dramatic and story material, his approach was very innovative.[10] His ideas began to filter through to other teachers, but it was a slow process and did not produce any overnight revolution.

In fact the idea that play could aid education was not just linked to drama, as Percy Nunn pointed out in *Education, Its Data and First Principle*:

> It is hardly extravagant to say that in the understanding of play lies the key to most of the practical problems of education, for play taken in the narrower sense as a phenomenon belonging especially to childhood, shows the creative impulses in their clearest, most vigorous and most typical form. Hence it is that essentially creative activities such as art, and craftsmanship and in smaller measure geographical exploration and scientific discovery are felt to have a peculiar affinity with play and are in fact, continuous with it in the development of individuality.[11]

In spite of these pioneers drama was still seen as "theatre", or considered to be plays that could be studied as literary texts. In fact the reading and acting of plays in schools had been encouraged in the 1921 Report on English, but few teachers knew how to set about doing so. To try and help them the Mary Ward Settlement in London introduced special courses run by a woman with the training and professional experience of a teacher, actress and producer, as well as some experience of social work. (An early and remarkably well-qualified actor–teacher!)

The Report on Drama in Adult Education (1926) suggested that the value of drama, or play study, lay in the fact that it dealt with humanity in all its most common and varied forms, and at the same time it gave scope for unlimited imagination. The Report also pointed out that drama could be an excellent gateway to different subjects, leading students to other forms of literature and stimulating an intellectual curiosity which would lead to the study of subjects in which the students had previously shown little interest.

Thus, drama held great possibilities for the development and stimulation of learning, an attitude essential to the appearance of Theatre in Education. The 1926 Report concluded with a clarion call for drama:

> If drama is the greatest of all arts, because it comprehends all other arts, is it not, under the right conditions, the greatest of all instruments of education, because it comprehends them all?[12]

The shift in ideas of how to use drama with children began to occur in the 1930s. The *Handbook for Teachers* (1937) suggested that for the infant, drama could be "a joyful game in which he is almost unconsciously trained in all virtues of self expression". For Juniors "it is an excellent discipline in speech, poise and self confidence", but for Senior schools the emphasis was still on classroom and school productions and the dramatization of longer stories or ballads.[13]

The passing of the 1944 Education Act brought an acceleration in the introduction of "modern" methods of teaching, and an increasing awareness that education should provide for the whole individual. This was emphasized by the Report on Secondary Schools in 1947 which suggested that the school had a part to play in providing pupils with legitimate outlets for impulses and emotions.

The 1950s proved to be a turning-point in the popularization of drama in education. Peter Slade, a pioneer of creative drama, focused attention on the relationship between drama and the natural play activity of the child in his book *Child Drama*, written in 1954. He saw play as being the child's way of thinking, and when evaluating children's drama work, he suggested that it was wrong to apply the conventions of adult theatre. The consideration of the child through his play activity was the important factor. Peter Slade took this a step further, however, claiming child drama to be an art form: "There does exist a Child drama which is of exquisite beauty and is a high Art Form in its own right. It should be recognised, respected and protected."[14]

Division of opinion over Slade's views, and the theatre versus educational drama debate, continued throughout the 1950s. By the end of the decade a few teachers' training colleges were running educational drama courses, and by the mid-1960s drama courses had sprung up in a number of colleges. The growth of drama in education as a separate subject from Theatre Arts was helped by Brian Way's influential book written in 1967, *Development Through Drama*. The book emphasized the use of drama in the personal development of the child.

In 1967 the Department of Education and Science issued a special report on drama, which made it clear that Drama was recognized as a subject, but not yet firmly established. In the Inner London Education Authority only about 50 of the 300 Secondary schools included drama on the timetable, and the range of drama in schools throughout the country varied from an aspect of English to personal expression in movement.

It was not just the development of drama as a separate subject, which was important for TIE, but the recognition that drama could be integral to the development of a child's personality. Thus the support given to drama by the Newsome report, *Half Our Future* in 1963, proved to be a helpful statement of belief.

> Though drama comes, by school tradition, into the English field, it is a creative art embracing much more than English. Perhaps its central element is, or should be, improvisation . . . By playing-out psychologically significant situations, they (boys and girls) can work out their own personal problems. Here is one way in which they can be helped to reconcile the reality of the world outside their own private worlds. Once this begins education has something on which to build. In short, drama, along with poetry and other arts, is not a 'frill' which the less able can safely omit or relegate to some minor position on some Friday afternoons, Art is not an expensive substitute for reality. It is through creative arts, including the arts of language, that young people can be helped to come to terms with themselves more surely than by any other route.[15]

Since the mid-1970s TIE has moved away from creative drama workshops in schools and TIE programmes have developed into complex structures involving many different educational and theatrical methods. Programmes such as "Race Against Time", pp. 168–76, or "Living Patterns", pp. 120–2, bear witness to this. The educational ideas behind these programmes have often been drawn from study of the works of educational psychologists such as Piaget, J. Bruner and L. Vygotsky. Background reading of this kind is considered important by some of the most thoughtful and innovative TIE teams.

TIE teams make use of educational theories and new teaching methods, which are not necessarily found in the traditional textbooks, or in the classroom. Innovations such as simulations and board games have been incorporated into TIE programmes for over 10 years, but they were developed by the business world to train their employees. In 1965 the National Bank of New York introduced a game called "Citibank", which was designed to familiarize players with the bank's services. War Games have been on the market for many years and can teach history as well as military strategy. Monopoly is a prime example of a well-known board game which can teach the player something about property speculating. Simulations are considered to aid learning in a variety of ways, and to relate well to today's complex and fast changing society. Arthur Hogan defined a simulation as:

. . . putting the student in an environment and making him respond to its demands. By so doing, the student discovers for himself the results of his actions and is led to abstract the fundamental relationship present in the situation. It is this quality that classifies simulation as an heuristic teaching device.[16]

Teachers have been using a form of simulation over the years, looking at case studies of events or getting pupils to act out particular situations. The use of games and simulations is on the increase in schools, and a few have been produced commercially in Britain. It is the TIE teams who have appreciated their value, and have given pupils and teachers the opportunity of experiencing how these methods work in practise.

Theatre

The theatrical origins of TIE are of two distinct kinds. One is the presence of the right physical and social circumstances in Britain provided by the growth of the Repertory movement. The other is rather more nebulous: the development of certain theatrical ideas, forms, genres and techniques in Western Theatre. TIE did not directly copy any of these; rather TIE practitioners inherited a wealth of different approaches, some of which proved to be excellent material for TIE methods.

Brecht has had such a major influence on Western Theatre this century that it is hardly surprising if certain aspects of his ideas can be discovered in TIE work. Perhaps one of the most important links is Brecht's belief that theatre should not be an end in itself but should communicate. To do this it must deal with subjects that are relevant and understandable to ordinary people. As a playwright, director and theoretician Brecht explored these ideas throughout his career.

Brecht's Lehrstücke (Teaching Plays) were written in the late 1920s and early 1930s when he identified himself with the Communist workers' theatre movement in Germany. These plays were structured to lead the audience to discuss and debate the subject-matter. In *The Measures Taken* (1930), for example, the audience is asked to assess throughout the play whether the main characters' actions are correct or not. These characters re-enact the events of their revolutionary activities in China during which their guide and comrade endangers the mission by acting in too individualistic and emotional a manner. The comrades are forced to kill him, but they do so with his consent. They report and re-enact this to a Control Chorus, and the audience is asked to judge what has occurred.

TIE programmes often attempt to set up some form of debate. Sometimes this is totally within the action and characters of opposing viewpoints explain themselves to the pupils, who are often asked to make a decision. In certain

TIE programmes, particularly for the Secondary school age, the debate is much more obvious. For instance, the idea of debating the theme as it progresses, is found in an early TIE programme performed by Coventry TIE in 1970: "The Emergent Africa Game". The theme of an emergent African state was concentrated on a composite state, Lakoto. The programme was performed to fourth, fifth and sixth formers who were asked by the stage manager "Could you govern a country? We invite you to find out". The audience then watched the Prime Minister of Lakoto discuss priority spending with the Cabinet. The Cabinet disagree on how to use the country's financial resources and three suggestions are put forward: To spend the money on recruiting experts from abroad, or on a Welfare service, or on education. The stage manager then turns to the audience and asks them to discuss which course of action they would support if they were Prime Minister. Further issues are raised throughout the programme, and the audience are asked to debate them.[17]

Of Brecht's main theories only elements of them appear in TIE. For instance the alienation effect:

> The alienation effect . . . consists in the reproduction of real-life incidents on the stage in such a way as to underline their causality and bring it to the spectator's attention. This type of art also generates emotions, such performances facilitate the mastery of reality, and this it is that moves the spectator.[18]

Theatre in Education programmes try to create a believable world, which has a basis in reality, to lead the pupils to consider the cause and effect of what they see. In this way the pupils become aware of the problems presented in the programme and can begin to make decisions on how to solve them. To create the alienation effect Brecht wished to channel emotion to produce a real desire for detached enquiry in his audience, but TIE often uses emotion to have quite the opposite effect, which makes any comparison difficult, and possibly misleading. Elements of Brecht's ideas on Epic Theatre can be glimpsed in TIE:

> The epic theatre uses the simplest possible groupings, such as express the event's overall sense. No more 'causal', 'life-like', 'unforced' grouping; the stage no longer reflects the natural disorder of things. The opposite of natural disorder is aimed at: natural order. This order is determined from a socio-historical point of view.[19]

TIE selects the events that make up a programme so that the socio-political subject-matter is carefully examined, and events are often juxtaposed to allow an argument to emerge. However, TIE does not reject plot or "life-like" grouping, but the realism created is often there for a very specific learning process.

Brecht's Lehrstücke used little in the way of set and properties, and in his later plays he worked against the Theatre of Illusion revealing the mechanics of the stage, using non-realistic settings, but placing very real objects on stage, such as Mother Courage's wagon. As TIE companies travel out to schools every day the amount of technical equipment they can carry and set up is limited, but in fact, they do not often wish to create a theatrical world of illusion. There have been occasions where teams have created a total environment of a rather different sort. Coventry TIE used an inflatable in the mid-1970s for one programme, it created the sensation of being adrift on a small boat at sea, the characters and the pupils being inside the inflatable, lights and sound outside creating the illusion of sea and fog. It is more usual for a TIE team to use only essential items, but making these real, for instance Coventry's programme on gypsies placed a brightly painted gypsy caravan in the school grounds, and this was all that was needed. For the productions of "Pow Wow", a Red Indian tepee was set up in the school hall inside a wire cage; nothing else was used.

Brecht's ideas have had a profound influence on the development of theatre over the last 30 years. The directors and writers who emerged from George Devine's English Stage Company at the Royal Court, were strongly influenced by Brecht and the work of the Berliner Ensemble, as William Gaskill explained:

> Brecht was the great formative influence on my work and I think on most of the people who worked with me. It's an approach to the theatre which is hard to define: it's partly a question of economy, of reducing things to their simplest visual state, with the minimum of scenery and props needed to make a theatrical expression, . . . The influence of Brecht was also connected with a certain sense of moral and political direction. One did have a sense of rather stable moral value which if you like came from Marxism. One was glad to relate to something which appeared to have that much seriousness and point in a profession which can often appear frivolous.[20]

Although it was from the Royal Court that the "new wave" of theatre in Britain began in the mid-1950s, it was in another new wave that Brecht's influence was rather more obvious. This new development emerged as the "alternative" theatre movement and in particular, the political theatre groups of the late 1960s and early 1970s, such as 7.84, and Red Ladder. This political theatre movement provides some of the most obvious links with the Theatre in Education, which uses socio-political themes as its subject-matter to make pupils aware of the world around them. Like the British political theatre groups, TIE does not support the *status quo*, but questions society and demands changes. This is not to say that TIE is propagandist, but it is aware of politics. (The question of politics in TIE work is discussed in Chapter 4.)

The simplest form of political theatre is Agit-prop (short for agitation and propaganda) which uses theatre to convey a direct political message. After the revolution, Russian agit-prop confirmed revolutionary values, and communicated news to a largely illiterate population. Agit-prop in the Germany of the 1920s stirred the audience *towards* revolution. This was certainly Piscator's policy when he founded his Proletarisches Theater in 1920, for it was to be an instrument of propaganda and education. The theatre toured workers' halls performing agit-prop plays, which tended to be only about half an hour long, and whose contents were immediately relevant to the audience and easy to understand. The performers were usually amateur, and the staging very makeshift. The plays, therefore, used simple language and action and caricature rather than characterization. "Russia's Day", performed by the Proletarisches in 1920, was a short sketch developed from a script by Lajos Barta. The opening scenes demonstrated the Communist argument against democracy and then introduced the Establishment as caricatures of a diplomat, an officer and a priest, shown as servants of "World-Capital". This figure was represented visually as a paunched money-bag wearing a stockbroker's top hat and addressed as "Your Majesty".

The Proletarisches lasted only one year, but in 1924 Piscator was offered a job as freelance Director in the Volksbühne, one of the leading Berlin theatres. He began to develop his agit-prop techniques and presented two revues, "The Red Revue" in 1924 and "Despite All" in 1925. These revues were so successful that they provided models for many subsequent German agit-prop productions. The revues consisted of several short scenes using music, song, acrobatics, film, dance and acting.

Piscator began to move away from agit-prop towards larger-scale theatre productions, using all the technical facilities of the theatre building. The work of the small, amateur agit-prop groups was stimulated by a visit to Germany from the Moscow Blue Blouse group in 1927. Many new theatre organizations were founded as a result, selecting titles which reflected their political aims, Red Shirts, Left Column or Red Megaphone.

It was this kind of political theatre which influenced British groups, and in some cases even the German names were used, such as Red Megaphone, set up in Salford. It was a similar group, the Rebel Players, in Hackney which formed the Unity Theatre, one of the best known British political theatre groups of the 1930s. It was an entirely amateur organization formed after the Rebel Players had taken plays out to Co-op Guilds, Trade Union, Labour and Communist Party branches. With their very successful production of Odet's *Waiting for Lefty* in 1935, the group gained recognition and support. Realizing there was a need for a theatre of their own, they joined with other groups such as Red Radio, rented a hall in Central London, and formed the new organization in 1936: Unity Theatre. Their aims were:

(a) To foster and further the art of the drama in accordance with the principle that true art, by effectively presenting and truthfully interpreting life as experienced by the majority of people, can move the people to work for the betterment of society (*sic*).

(b) To train and encourage actors, producers and playwrights in accordance with the above ideals.

(c) To devise, import and experiment with new forms of dramatic art.[21]

The theatre staged short plays, sketches, burlesques and agit-prop to all kinds of groups, and presented the first Brecht play to be staged in Britain, the one-actor "Señora Carrar's Rifles". It also produced the first Living Newspaper-style presentation with *Busman* in 1938, which documented the history of the London Transport Board and its contemporary problems. In spite of these presentations Unity made few artistic innovations; it was more important as a political organization. By 1938 about 130 similar groups had been formed, of which Glasgow and Merseyside were the most successful.

The formation of Unity coincided with the end of the vigorous Workers' Theatre Movement (1928–36). An amateur, Communist-orientated organization, it was concerned with agitation rather than entertainment and used agit-prop style presentation, which were often performed on the street. Amongst all this political and theatrical activity a group called Theatre of Action was formed in Manchester. The founders were Joan Littlewood and Ewan McColl. Their theatre was political and aimed at working-class audiences, and they began to search for the right kind of theatrical form to express their ideas.

The 1930s in America also saw an upsurge in theatrical activity. The link with Theatre in Education can be found in the Federal Theatre Project in America and its Living Newspaper scheme. The Project formed part of Roosevelt's New Deal of the 1930s, to provide work for some of the many thousands of unemployed theatre workers. Tours were sent out from New York and soon local groups were formed. Little money was available and wages were low, but the seats were very cheap, and sometimes even free. Many of the Federal Theatre productions dealt with socio-political themes, and "It Can't Happen Here" by Sinclair Lewis was an anti-fascist play, which opened in 1936 simultaneously in twenty-one theatres throughout the USA. Living Newspaper was set up to help alleviate unemployment amongst the members of the Newspaper Guild of New York, and dramatized newspaper reports in order to educate the audience. The approach to the material was not just journalistic but also editorial, introducing a point of view on the subject. Their production *One Third of a Nation*, for instance, reveals the deplorable conditions in a typical city slum and tries, whilst tracing some of the causes of poor housing, to explore possible solutions. The facts researched for the play were drawn from such sources as the report of the

New York Board of Fire Underwriters, the population figures from "A Century of Population Growth", Government Printing Office papers and newspaper articles. Any TIE programme on a socio-political theme will use this kind of resource material, and some of TIE's present subject-matter bears a striking similarity to the topics selected by Living Newspaper: the natural resources of a country, slum housing, poverty.

The Leeds TIE company prepared a documentary on Housing in 1976, called *A Place to Live*, and asked some of the same questions as had been raised in *One Third of a Nation* in the 1930s. The Leeds programme was about a local housing problem, Quarry Hill Flats; the Living Newspaper play was about a New York slum where there had been a bad fire. To explain the housing problem both productions explored the historical background in the form of brief, episodic flash-backs showing speculating buyers, or landlords and willing tenants. Both plays question what can be done, and although they offer different answers, they place the basic responsibility on the Authorities: the Leeds Council, or the United States Government. Both end with a plea for some kind of action that will help the ordinary man caught up in the problem.

Both these plays have taken as their starting-point the presentation of a problem, and this is the basis of TIE work as well as the basis of the Living Newspaper technique, as Arthur Arent, author of *One Third of a Nation*, explains:

> In any analysis of the technique, the first thing to consider is not style, which is the manner of doing a thing, but content, which is the thing itself. Here we have the primary departure from the March of Time School of playwrighting. For the latter is in essence a dramatization of an event — a news event — while the Living Newspaper is the dramatization of a problem — composed in greater or lesser extent of many news events, all bearing on one subject and interlarded with typical and non-factual representations of the effect of these news events on the people to whom the problem is of great importance.[22]

One of the links between Living Newspaper and the emergence of TIE is the appearance of the documentary in British repertory theatres. The first theatre to develop the local documentary was the Victoria Theatre, Stoke on Trent, under the direction of Peter Cheeseman. The documentaries were first presented in the 1960s and cover a range of subjects from the English Civil War to the story of the local steelworks and a plea for its survival. Although a writer is often used to structure the documentary, everyone in the Stoke company is involved in research and group devising:

> If we had no writer amongst us, we must assume the function collectively, as a group, shape our own material out of documentary

research into the history of this community. The process should be one in which we, the actual practitioners, dominated the presentation of the material. The aim should be to use all our performing experience to create a lively and popular show and a loose format for future development.[23]

In this kind of documentary the subject-matter is usually local, the structure episodic, and the facts conveyed by the use of many different theatrical techniques. Use is made of song, voice over, projection and a narrator, and as a large number of characters must be presented, often by few actors, there tends to be little deep characterization. TIE certainly makes use of the documentary, although not always in the precise style developed by Peter Cheeseman. TIE programmes often centre on historical themes in an attempt to demonstrate the effect of the events in history on the ordinary working man or woman. The pupils are often involved in the action: as navvies in Coventry TIE's programme about the railways, or as factory workers in Tynewear TIE's "Labour for the Lord" (1980):

> The theme of this programme was change and the effects of change in the cause of progress and prosperity. The children were given the experience of being Victorian children working in 1842 in a chemical factory. They discover the reasons for child employment and the effects of the Child Commissioner's Report of 1842, which prevented the employment of children under 13.
>
> The second part of the programme moved forward to the 1850s which saw the huge growth of industrial development in the north east. In an age of great prosperity for the few, many children were unemployed or redeployed in the light of mechanical innovation.[24]

One of Peter Cheeseman's main policies is a commitment to his local area, and the documentaries are an expression of this. Commitment to its local area is an important aspect of TIE teams' policy, but as an idea it is by no means new, or indeed unique to Britain.

In France the concept of decentralized theatre was put into operation by Jeanne Laurent in the 1940s. Finding herself in charge of entertainments in the Department of Arts, she encouraged local organizations to set up their own groups and then request State help. By the 1950s five centres for the arts had been founded.

When Roger Planchon became Director of his local theatre in Villeurbanne in 1957, he went out to find an audience. He and his actors began to eat out several times a week in the canteens of the Villeurbanne factories. In his first leaflet he wrote:

> The Théatre de la Cité is born. It will not be a popular theatre without your help. The experiment, unique in France, will not succeed without

the support of the workers. Therefore this questionnaire is addressed to you: trade union officials, cultural representatives, apprentices. In order that a popular theatre may live, its animators must know what you want.[25]

After the workers had been to see plays at the theatre Planchon would discuss the production with them by going out to the factory, climbing on to a table in the canteen, and begin by joking with the workers.

In England Joan Littlewood's Theatre Workshop, founded in 1945, went out to find its audience, but further afield. The company toured Yorkshire, Lancashire, Scotland and South Wales often organizing the work in conjunction with the trade unions and performing in factories, at mines, and in schools. The Theatre Workshop adopted a left wing viewpoint, and built on Joan Littlewood's earlier work with Theatre of Action in the 1930s. In 1953 the company settled at Stratford East in the Theatre Royal, and tried to develop a local audience, but her work, based on the performance of classics with her own very particular approach to the acting and style of presentation, soon became popular with critics and regular theatregoers, and the commercial theatre began to intrude. Joan Littlewood closed the company down in 1961, returning in 1963 to the new company set up without her, to direct "Oh What a Lovely War".

The concept of working with the trade unions was continued by Arnold Wesker in his Centre 42 Project. He tried to organize a national network of people's theatre through the Labour movement, involving the TUC in a series of arts festivals, and finally finding a home at the Roundhouse in London in 1968. Although the building began to be treated as an arts centre by the Chalk Farm residents, the project eventually failed due to lack of funds.

Despite its failure, Centre 42 embodied many of the ideas of the alternative theatre movement which developed in the late 1960s and early 1970s. TIE is, essentially, part of this development sharing some of the same political and policy aims. The movement was set in motion by two American companies, Open Theatre and Café La Mama visited Britain in the summer of 1967, offering a real alternative to the conventional theatre scene. Open Theatre's production of "America Hurrah!", for instance, used mime, movement and a succession of short scenes to examine some of the physical and psychological problems of living in a city. Theatre practitioners were influenced by what they saw: Max Stafford Clark at the Traverse, Edinburgh, decided to change his method of work, forming an independent workshop on the New York group's pattern. The creation of the London Arts Lab in 1968 helped initiate the movement. Set up by an American, Jim Haynes, the Lab established a deliberately relaxed environment for the multi-media experiments, and several new companies began to work there including Portable Theatre,

Freehold and the People Show. In the same year two other Americans set up their alternative theatre: Charles Marowitz created the Open Space out of a Tottenham Court Road cellar and Ed Berman began to take his Interaction shows out to community environments. The work of Interaction introduced new concepts of what a "theatre" company could offer a community, presenting a range of multi-media work and helping to improve the area of North London by starting a farm on a disused site, to which the children of the area could come.

The fact that 1968 proved to be such a watershed in the development of alternative theatre was also due to the political atmosphere. It was the year of the Paris student riots, the student revolts during the Democratic Convention in Chicago, the brief summer of liberation in Prague, and a whole range of revolts, assassinations and student riots; events which made people question the world around them. The theatre in Britain reflected this, and from 1968 to 1973 the number of small experimental and political theatre groups grew rapidly. Although many were totally unsubsidized, the Arts Council did begin to offer some financial aid and the list of grants to alternative theatre companies grew longer and longer.

It was the Arts Council which helped the growth of the Repertory Theatre in Britain. The reasons for which the Arts Council was established in 1946 are quoted in its Annual Reports:

1. To develop and improve the knowledge, understanding and practice of the arts;
2. To increase the accessibility of the arts to the public throughout Great Britain; and
3. To co-operate with government departments, local authorities and other bodies to achieve these objects.

Although the Repertory system in Britain emerged at the beginning of this century on a commercial basis, by 1958–9 the Arts Council was subsidizing twenty-two theatre companies outside London to a total of £44,500. Both subsidy and number of repertory theatres increased, and by 1971–2, the Council was helping nearly seventy reps., paying out nearly £1,500,000.

The Belgrade Theatre in Coventry opened in 1958. It was the first repertory theatre to be built after the Second World War, and was a civic theatre owned by the local corporation. No more reps. were built until Nottingham Playhouse and the Phoenix, Leicester, were completed in 1963. When the Arts Council started to contribute to the cost of new buildings in 1965 a whole new phase began, and by 1971 the Arts Council had paid out £1,575,500 for new buildings or the restoring of old ones.

With the increasing number of new repertory theatres and the fact that many of them had civic status came the need to contact the community and build up a local audience. Bryan Bailey, the first director of the Belgrade, Coventry, wrote:

> The theatre is a living building much of the day, bringing into its orbit increasing numbers of people. The part played by the new building itself in all this, is, of course, paramount. It is also the foundation of the other most exciting development — the early and whole hearted winning of a young theatre audience.[26]

Coventry adopted a definite policy to attract young people and other theatres began to do the same. Many started Young People's Theatre societies as off-shoots of their adult Theatre Supporters' clubs. These Young People's Societies provided cheaper seats, information and often lectures and practical work. The actual facilities provided for young people varied from a coffee bar and record player at Cheltenham, to Red Lion Yard at Watford which offered several evenings of practical workshops for young people.

Co-operation between the theatre and the Local Education Authority began to grow. In Coventry the LEA bought matinée performances for schools. In Watford a drama teacher was appointed to liaise between the theatre and the schools. Some repertory theatres felt that there was a need to offer special performances for children and employed groups like Caryl Jenner's Unicorn Theatre company to present matinées of special children's plays. Other theatres consulted an advisory committee of teachers and presented plays felt suitable for schools as part of their main programme. After such consultation, Colchester offered "The Glass Menagerie", "The Taming of the Shrew", "You Never Can Tell", "Wuthering Heights", "Great Expectations" and "An Inspector Calls" as part of their season in 1966–7. To improve their policy of making contact with young people, some repertory theatres sent out short schools' tours using company members. In November 1966 six of the Marlowe Theatre, Canterbury company toured Primary schools using known and tried scripts: "There is an Island Far Away" by Caryl Jenner and "The Circus Adventure" by James Ambrose Brown.

Many repertory companies had some kind of contact with schools before the emergence of TIE. One of the theatre staff, such as the Publicity Officer or the Assistant Director, would have begun to liaise with the local schools. This liaison was to draw young people into the theatre, but artistic directors began to be aware that the theatre could go out to schools and that they needed a coherent policy towards young people. When Giles Havergal took over Watford, it had just been made a civic theatre, and he set up a youth theatre project at the nearby Red Lion Yard. The policy of the Bristol Old Vic, in 1968, is an example of the aims of many repertories at that time: "We are making a definite effort to infiltrate schools informally . . . so that we are in personal touch with the teachers most concerned and can find out what the

children are feeling."[27] The mid-1960s saw an increasing activity on the part
of nearly all the repertory theatres to make some contact with schools. When
the Arts Council investigated these various activities in 1966 they concluded
that:

> Lack of time, space and money appear to be the main factors holding
> back the development of young people's theatre by the adult company.
> To a large extent the first two factors can be overcome by adequate
> provision of the third.[28]

The Arts Council Report also noted that where a person in the theatre was
working full time on schools liaison the repertory was able to offer an
impressive list of activities for young people. The Council felt that this would
be a useful area to extend, believing that money to appoint such a person in
other theatres could only be of benefit. By approving the allocation of money
for the employment of someone to liaise with schools, and for the
development of work with young people, the Arts Council stimulated the
repertory theatres into offering a wide range of activities for young people. As
the work of the first TIE team set up at the Belgrade Theatre, Coventry, in
1965, with local funding, became known, other repertories realized the
potential of concentrating their youth activities in and around a TIE team.

Children's Theatre

One of the important elements in the eventual appearance of Theatre in
Education is the growth and development of Children's Theatre in Britain
this century. It has taken many forms over the past 80 years. Until recently
Children's Theatre, in this country, has never been properly funded. Some
foreign countries, however, have had grant-aided Children's Theatre for
years. The Moscow Theatre for Children, for instance, was founded as early
as 1918. In Hungary the first State Children's Theatre was founded in 1948
and now works in two buildings with a company of 170. That country also
has touring groups playing to the children in those provinces where the State
Theatre is not active, and the provincial theatres all perform regularly to
children. The Hungarian State goes a long way towards supporting the cost
of Children's Theatre and Young People's performances.

Children's Theatre in America flourished, in the twentieth century, under
the guidance of pioneers such as Alice Minnie Herts, who directed the
Children's Educational Theatre in New York at the beginning of the century,
and Winifred Ward, who from the 1920s to the 1950s offered a training in
Children's Theatre at the North Western University. The Federal Theatre
Movement of the 1930s established many forms of live entertainment for
children throughout the forty-eight states. By the 1950s an organization
called the Children's Theatre Committee had representatives from over 500

Children's Theatre companies attending its meetings.

In Britain there has been a great deal of activity in Children's Theatre but it has mostly consisted of small companies whose work varied in style and intent, but whose life spans were, on average, fairly short. Frank Benson and his company first took Shakespeare productions into schools at the end of the nineteenth century. The plays were sometimes modified to suit the juvenile audiences, but the company visited only the public schools, such as Cheltenham Ladies College. It was not until Sir Philip Ben Greet began performing Shakespeare for school children at the turn of the century that the elementary and evening school pupils had a chance to experience theatre. The visits were to have some educational value too:

> We not only gave performances at very popular prices in all parts of London, but we held examinations at the County Hall, near the Temple of the work done by the pupils themselves. Only a few schools competed at first but in a year or two the plan expanded so fast that in Spring of 1902, when I left for America we had over a hundred scenes acted by pupils from over a hundred schools. Essays were written by the thousand and prizes awarded . . . I fear that in the re-shuffle at the Education Offices Shakespeare went by the board — then came the war period.[29]

Sir Ben Greet's work was helped by the 1902 Act which established County Borough Councils and Local Education Authorities. In 1915 a member of the Education Board of the London County Council suggested to the London Education Officer that school children be allowed to attend special Wednesday matinées of Shakespearian productions at the Old Vic. Permission was given, but the children had to pay for their seats. A provisional grant by the LCC to the London Central Shakespeare Committee of Teachers, and to the Old Vic, allowed the seats to be offered free to the children, and the Shakespeare matinées were included in the school curriculum as educational visits.

This venture established an interesting precedent, for it recognized that the theatre visit was part of the pupils' education and should be free. There is no doubt that its value was recognized, for when the grant was discontinued in 1921 the Board of Education Committee put in a plea for the continuance of this precedent in their Report on *The Teaching of English in England*:

> We learn with regret that the District Auditor has surcharged the London County Council with the amount of the grant to cover the fees for the attendance of school children at Shakespearian performances. The matter is at present 'sub judice'. We are strongly of the opinion that means should be found of continuing this genuinely educational

work, and that if necessary, additional powers should be given to the Local Authorities for this purpose.[30]

The matter was eventually settled in 1924. Under the revised Elementary Education Code, the Board of Education recognized the attendance of children at dramatic performances during school hours, and paid a grant upon approved expenditure for the purpose.

It was not until 1937 that an Education Authority gave money for productions in schools of anything other than Shakespeare. The grant was to the Scottish Children's Theatre, which was formed by Bertha Waddell in 1927. Her aim was to give performances of theatre that children could appreciate and enjoy. To do this she presented programmes of "combined arts", consisting of dramatized folk songs, nursery rhymes and small plays, placing an emphasis on music and movement and visual presentation. In some Local Education Authorities the company were allowed to play to children during school hours, but the children had to pay. In 1937 the Director of Education for Glasgow approved a scheme that allowed Junior school children to attend free performances. This achievement took a great deal of persuasion and effort, as Bertha Waddell recalled:

> I had approached the Director of Education in Glasgow and he had come to see our work, but he said we must prove ourselves over a period before we could be considered seriously. He attended several performances, and two years later gave his approval to a scheme whereby Glasgow Junior school children would see a series of performances by my company during school hours free of charge as part of the school curriculum.
>
> Before giving their agreement to this scheme, I had to give a performance to the Education Committee with several hundred school children present. Thus began what I think were the first performances to be given in Britain to Junior school children of theatre as part of the normal school curriculum.[31]

This was a major step forward in the recognition of Children's Theatre and its place in education.

Peter Slade, a pioneer of Drama in Education, and author of *Child Drama*, founded two companies in the 1930s to perform in schools and other venues: one company in East Anglia from 1930 to 1931, and then the Parable Players in 1935 to tour London and the Home Counties. The latter company consisted of amateurs, professionals and students and received no financial support. Peter Slade admits that, although these early presentations were rather formal, he was trying to bring together "unconscious drama" and "the great civilized art of theatre". However, he found that there were few companies to provide any examples:

Of course, I was almost entirely alone in those days of early 1930–1. I did not know anyone really trying to do theatre for children, so there were no patterns to go on and I suppose, like many others after me, I was influenced by what schools and others expected or demanded.[32]

It was not until the 1940s that companies performing to children began to experiment in order to discover what was the most suitable form of presentation, in terms of actor–audience relationship, playing space and subject-matter. In trying to find answers to these problems a split began to occur in the nature of the work; a division which was to develop eventually into Children's Theatre and Theatre in Education. Peter Slade formed another company in 1945 called the Pear Tree Players. In summing up what was so special about this particular company he notes several factors, which proved to be important for TIE later:

> They worked so hard and so imaginatively, they could do script or improvisation in any place of any shape to or with an audience. Not only were they good as a team, but they also taught. Not only were they the first professional group entirely devoted to education — that is not just playing theatre but concocting feature programmes and other entertainments — but they also taught in schools and clubs . . . They far surpassed anything I have seen in recent years. They were actor–teachers. I am sure that one day actor–teachers or teacher–actors will be a normal if new profession in our future social set up.[33]

Writing this in 1969 Peter Slade had the advantage of hindsight. However, he had proposed the idea of the actor–teacher in his book *Child Drama* in 1954. His emphasis on the company's ability to improvise, work as a team, to devise programmes and to teach are all essential to TIE today. The realization of the importance of these abilities for presentation and drama work in schools was a major step in the shift away from straight performance to children.

In the 1940s Peter Slade was no longer the only person searching for new ways of performing to and working with children. Brian Way, another pioneer whose work in Theatre for Young People was to be so influential began to work with the Old Vic Company. He joined them as an Acting-Assistant Stage Manager during the war. Whilst touring a Shakespeare production the company would do a matinée for children every week, and it was through this experience that Brian Way began to form his ideas on theatre for children:

> I became fascinated by children; fascinated by what we were trying to do; absolutely convinced of three things:
> (1) That the material we were doing was wrong and couldn't cover the kids of 7–14 we were playing to.

(2) That the shape we were working in was wrong and as soon as a youngster was 7 or 8 rows back he lost touch.

(3) When I sat amongst them I found there was what was called 'boisterous behaviour'.[34]

When on a subsequent Old Vic Tour in the autumn of 1943, he formed a unit with two other members of the company to go into schools. To try and put some of his ideas into practice they took in different programmes for Infant, Junior and Secondary, and attempted to introduce new elements into the performances: trying to perform on the floor near the children, using material which was more suitable to the age group and encouraging some form of participation.

When Brian Way's contract with the Old Vic ran out in 1944, he helped to form the West of England Children's Theatre Company. The company brought drama into the school without a platform, or stage effects and the minimum of costume. Their main purpose was to stimulate spontaneous dramatic work in schools and to allow children to join in the action with occasional scenes for them to watch. Brian Way maintains that they were not doing drama in education, which was little known then, but theatre. They presented short scenes, poems, song, dance and bits of participation, but their major achievement was the break-through in shape, the limit of age group and the limit of audience numbers. What was considered as the value of drama for children at that time was made clear in a report on the company's performance in the *Times Educational Supplement* (26th January 1951). Children who came into contact with the actors were unconsciously "taught how to speak good English, how to walk about, sit or dance suitably and were made familiar with great literature and learned to act as a group". The work still had a long way to go, both in terms of its own development and its effect and use in schools. In 1943 a major innovation was introduced by Catherine Hollingsworth in Aberdeen. As Superintendent of Speech and Drama she wanted to develop the drama and theatre work in the city. To do so, she formed the Motley Players from teachers working in Aberdeen. At first the company went out to schools on Wednesday afternoon, but as the work developed this became a whole day. Now, there are two teams of teachers from the city schools, one performing in Secondary and one in Primary schools on one day a week.

Maisie Cobby, the Essex Drama Advisor, began a similar scheme, but hers was rather grander in scale, consisting of four companies, all full-time teachers in schools. They toured the county outside school hours to take live theatre to children. Miss Cobby's aim was to bring to school children an experience of live theatre which would prove a stimulus to classroom drama activity and lead to an understanding of the art of the theatre.

The development of children's theatre companies in the 1940s was probably helped by a 1944 Act, which gave power to the Local Education Authorities to subsidize extra-curricular activities such as visits to the theatre. Certainly, companies that had entertainment or experience of theatre as their main criteria also appeared at this time. Tom Clarke's aim in starting his Children's Playtime at the Argyle Theatre, Birkenhead, in 1944 was to combat the influence of cinema and to encourage a love of the theatre. He wanted to introduce children to the living theatre by an entertainment which was first and foremost good fun. Like Tom Clarke, Caryl Jenner's company also placed an emphasis on the importance of the theatre experience. Caryl Jenner began the Amersham Mobile Theatre in 1948 to take theatre into schools. Like a lot of companies that were formed later in the sixties, it began as an extension of the work at the repertory theatre — Amersham Playhouse. The theatre, however, closed in 1949, but the children's work continued as the English Children's Theatre. In 1967 it found a base at the Arts Theatre in London. Gerald Tyler, writing of Caryl Jenner after her death in 1972, saw her as "one of the most devoted pioneers and untiring servants of professional children's theatre". Her belief in, and enthusiasm for, Children's Theatre were essential to her long campaign for official grant aiding and professional recognition. "Her own approach was always through the theatre and the well made play."[35] This policy was based on research started at the Amersham Playhouse, and continued when the company were visiting schools. Discussion was encouraged between the actors, children and teachers, and schools were asked to comment on the influence the company's visit had upon classroom work. The teachers' comments resemble some of the contemporary replies to TIE questionnaires, indicating that the company provided a stimulation for written work in English; a greater desire to perform, creation of a lively interest in plays in general and the realization that elaborate scenery was not necessary for good productions. Most teachers agreed that the company's visit provided a valuable experience for the children if they were repeated regularly. This was one of the major problems of the touring Children's Theatre companies. As they were forced to tour all over the country to gain an income, visiting schools on any regular basis was a practical impossibility.

The Compass Players, formed in 1944, also toured all over the country. Like many Community and Fringe companies now, it worked as a co-operative. It was formed with the object of taking good theatre to towns and villages which had little or no opportunity of seeing the work of good professional companies. The company began to take performances to schools and this became an important part of their policy. They presented a wide range of plays from Marlow, Shaw, Synge and Molière to programmes specially written for them. They adopted a definite policy for this work:

In devising these special programmes for schools the educational value and suitability of material were not the only considerations for it was generally felt that if the theatre is to achieve its true function in the educational field it must, above all, be entertaining and *imaginative*, embodying all the exciting elements of colour, movement and atmosphere which are a vital part of any theatrical performance.[36]

This approach was welcomed by schools and Education Authorities who recognized the value of bringing to life pages of dramatic literature which might otherwise have remained purely academic experiences for the school children.

Like many groups of this kind, the company did everything from lighting and stage management to acting. They also undertook the running of courses for amateur societies under the auspices of the Drama Adviser for County Durham. Although the presentation of plays was the main policy, the company were still aware of their role and the use of their work in the schools. They invited comments from staff and pupils and used criticism positively to improve productions. They were also aware of their role in stimulating the audience, but doing so in an entertaining way. They felt that

FIG. 1. The Compass Players, "The Man of Destiny", 1948.

it was important to combat the "spoon-feeding" effect of the cinema and help in creating lively and intelligent citizens of the future.

Two other companies with a similar theatre bias also began in the 1940s: The Glyndebourne Children's Theatre and the Young Vic. The former was founded in 1945 to present scripted plays in a proscenium setting. John Allen, who was the company's director, later became Her Majesty's Inspector with special responsibility for Drama, and was involved in preparing the important 1967 Report on Drama.

Initially, the Young Vic worked as an integral part of the Old Vic, but in 1949 it became a self-contained mobile touring company of ten actors playing to the 9- to 16-year-old age group. George Devine, as Director, wanted to put shows of a good professional standard within easy reach of young audiences. Due to the technical difficulties of touring he recognized that simplicity in a production was essential and that meant the Director "must have a clear, clean conception of the play". This approach also applied to the performance of the actor: "In technique he should be an expert, by disposition he should be simple and direct. The children's audience will not accept laziness or incompetence on the stage."[37] George Devine also noted the real difficulty in

FIG. 2. The Compass Players, "Le Misanthrope", 1950–1.

finding good original plays for performing to children. Of the hundred scripts submitted to the Young Vic there were only four or five which could have been produced and even those would have required treatment.

Thus, the 1940s produced a great deal of work and thought on the whole area of performing to children. It revealed the beginnings of the different approaches to the work which would eventually lead to the formation of Theatre in Education. The advocates of Children's Theatre like Caryl Jenner and George Devine were sure that the experience was best inside a theatre building. To pioneers like Peter Slade and Brian Way there was something else a company could offer by going into schools — the use of theatre techniques to stimulate drama and other class work related to the presentation.

This promising growth in Children's Theatre came to a halt in the 1950s. A number of companies were forced to disband because of the economy cuts in educational expenditure which meant that Local Education Authorities could no longer afford to offer them performances in schools. The West of England Children's Theatre stopped work in 1951 for this reason. Both the Glyndebourne Children's Theatre and the Young Vic ceased work, although it would only have needed a grant of £9000 to keep them both running. The Compass Theatre stopped work in 1952. Those that did survive had a difficult time doing so. Caryl Jenner's company was saved in 1950 by guarantees against loss of £75 each from a housewife, a playwright and Miss Jenner's mother!

If the actual work did not grow in the 1950s the discussion and theory did. Such questions as the value and form of audience participation and the need for the actor–teacher began to be discussed. The debate was opened up by Peter Slade in his book on *Child Drama* in 1954 and continued by workers in the field like Brian Way and Maisie Cobby.

It was a time also of the growth of Drama in Education, and the development of this and of Children's Theatre was recognized by the First Conference on Youth and the Theatre held at the Unesco House in Paris in April 1952. International, qualified authorities on both education and dramatic art assembled for the first time round the same table. Fifteen nations took part and fifty-three delegates and observers attended. The Conference affirmed that creative dramatics (or Drama in Education) constituted an important element in the education of children and young people, but they noted the distinction between the techniques of creative dramatics and formal dramatics (or the production and performance of plays before an audience). In terms of education they recommended the development of creative dramatics in schools and youth groups, and that teachers and youth leaders should be properly trained in the necessary techniques. The exchange of information, play lists, critical works and performing companies was advocated. The recommendation on theatrical presentation gave a clear battle cry:

> That educational authorities at all levels facilitate theatrical presentations and experiments having a real cultural and artistic value, it being understood that dramatic art gives teachers a powerful means of education.[38]

John Allen attended the Conference acting as chairman of a sub-committee. He realized that what emerged very clearly from the Conference was the similarity of the problems that confronted both educational drama and the adult theatre, and the quite astonishing fact that educationalists throughout the world were beginning to use techniques that lay at the heart of the theatrical art. What distressed him was the suspicion with which educationalists and professional theatre people viewed each other. Although the two areas were coming closer together, it was to take a long time for this suspicion to disappear. If, in fact, it has ever really done so.

The recognition of common ground between Drama in Education and Children's Theatre brought the formation, in 1959, of the British Children's Theatre Association (BCTA). The purpose of the organization was stated in the Constitution: "To further education for children through drama and the arts of the theatre and to encourage the appreciation of dramatic art by and for children."[39] To develop this policy the membership of BCTA was open to both professional and amateur groups whose main activity was Children's Theatre, and to interested individuals and institutions. It was this very policy of broadly-based membership which caused a rift in the BCTA ranks. The professional companies like the Unicorn and Theatre Centre left to join the Young People's section of CORT (Council of Repertory Theatres) where they felt their interests would be better represented.

The need for a body to co-ordinate all these various movements in the professional, amateur and the educational world concerned with drama led to the formation of the National Council of Theatre for Young People. The Arts Council recommended that the NCTYP be given funds to set up and a party was held at Downing Street to raise money. The organization was formed in 1966 and its primary object was to concern itself with the "co-ordination, and development of all aspects of Theatre for Young People". Since its foundation, however, it has suffered from financial problems and difficulty in fulfilling its objectives. The fact that it was formed at all, as with the BCTA, is indicative of the need of various organizations working in the drama area to draw together, and their recognition that there were aims and difficulties in common which it was of value to share.

Jennie Lee, as Minister for the Arts, produced a Government White Paper, *A Policy for the Arts* in 1965, which pointed out the educational and cultural value of the arts:

Almost all the activities described in this White Paper are linked directly or indirectly with education. If children at an early age become accustomed to the idea of the arts as part of everyday life, they are more likely in maturity first to accept and then to demand them.[40]

The Paper also recognized that schools needed the support of their local communities, and of the expert practitioners in the various arts. Some schools were fortunate enough to be near a repertory theatre, but for the majority of schools there was very little theatre available that could fulfil the hopes of the White Paper. The possibility of a visit from a professional Children's Theatre company was very limited, for there were only eight groups operating, and all were beset with financial difficulties.

The situation did not improve until the Arts Council initiated an investigation of Young People's Theatre and issued its report in 1966. The report drew together the various areas of development:

> The Committee understands that in the world of Education there are new ideas and experiments in relation to Drama. As the Report shows, this can be matched by a wealth of recent activity in the world of theatre and particularly among the outstanding of the provincial companies which have become increasingly aware of the need to establish contact with the young people in their communities. The London companies are engaged in similar developments. All this has grown up spontaneously and spasmodically and with limited resources. There is a clear need for a pooling of effort in these matters: for the theatre to contribute its professional skill and practice and for those concerned with Education to add their experience of the needs of young people.[41]

The threads were coming together and with the Arts Council's decision in 1966 to fund young people's theatre, a real development could begin.

The Report committee noted the "unique" experiment at Coventry, but felt that perhaps it was a rather separate area from their study belonging more to the world of Drama in Education. As it happened it was Coventry that provided the model for the growth of the TIE companies and proved to be an influence on nearly all the other companies concerned with children, whatever the nature of their work.

Notes

1. Froebel, *Education of Man*, translated by W. N. Holmann, D. Appleton & Co., New York and London, 1887, p. 55.
2. J. Dewey, *Experience and Education* (1963 edition), Macmillan, New York, 1938, p. 25.
3. E. Holmes, *What is and What Might be*, Constable, London, 1911, p. 8.
4. *Report of the Consultative Committee on the Primary School*, Chairman: Sir W. H. Hadow, HMSO, 1931, p. xvii.

5. *Op. cit.*, p. 93.
6. *Op. cit.*, p. 102.
7. Flying Phoenix Information Sheet, 1969.
8. Scottish Education Department, *English in Secondary Schools*, HMSO, 1959, p. 4.
9. A. T. Craig, *The Dramatic Festival*, Pitman, London, 1913, p. ii.
10. See Caldwell Cook's *The Play Way*, Heinemann, London, 1914.
11. P. Nunn, *Education, its Data and First Principle*, Edward Arnold, London, 1920, p. 101.
12. Adult Education Committee, *The Drama in Adult Education*, HMSO, 1926, p. 198.
13. Board of Education, *Handbook for Teachers*, HMSO, 1937, pp. 361, 373, 392–3.
14. P. Slade, *Child Drama*, University of London, 1954, p. 7.
15. Central Advisory Council for Education (England), *Half Our Future*, Chairman: J. Newsom, HMSO, 1963, p. 157.
16. A. J. Hogan, "Simulation: An annotated bibliography", *Social Education*, March 1968, p. 242.
17. Belgrade Coventry TIE, Annual Report, 1969–70, pp. 25–7.
18. B. Brecht, *The Messingkauf Dialogues*, translated by J. Willett, Eyre Methuen, London, 1965, p. 102.
19. B. Brecht, in *Brecht on Theatre*, edited and translated by J. Willett, Eyre Methuen, London (first published 1964), 1977, p. 58.
20. W. Gaskill, Interview with Peter Ansorge, *Plays and Players*, May 1971.
21. M. Page, "The early years of unity", *Theatre Quarterly*, Vol. 1, No. 4, Oct.–Dec. 1971, p. 60.
22. A. Arent, "The techniques of living newspaper", *Theatre Quarterly*, Vol. 1, No. 4, Oct.–Dec. 1971, p. 57.
23. P. Cheeseman, *The Knotty*, Methuen, London, 1970, p. xi.
24. Tynewear Theatre Company TIE, Information Sheet, Jan. 1981.
25. R. Planchon, a Questionnaire quoted by M. Kustow in "Life and work of an illuminated man", *Theatre Quarterly*, Vol. 2, No. 5, 1971–2, p. 43.
26. B. Bailey, "Coventry makes history", *Plays and Players*, October 1959, p. 8.
27. YPTS CORT Bulletin, no. 72, p. 1 (mimeograph).
28. Arts Council of Great Britain, Report on *The Provision of Theatre for Young People in Great Britain*, Arts Council, 1966, p. 22.
29. *Drama*, Vol. 5, No. 8, 1927, p. 114.
30. Board of Education, *The Teaching of English in England*, Chairman: Sir H. Newbolt, HMSO, 1921, p. 317.
31. B. Waddell, "Self portrait", *Outlook*, Vol. 1, 1969, BCTA, p. 17.
32. P. Slade, "Forty years of theatre with the BCTA", *Outlook*, Vol. I, BCTA, p. 7.
33. *Op. cit.*, p. 8.
34. B. Way, personal interview, 7th May 1976, at the Theatre Centre Offices, London.
35. G. Tyler, "Caryl Jenner", *Outlook*, Vol. V, 1973, p. 8.
36. Publicity pamphlet, The Compass Players, 1950–51.
37. G. Devine, "Theatre for children: Art that is different", *World Theatre*, Vol. II, no. 3, 1952, p. 15.
38. "Youth and the Theatre", *World Theatre*, Vol. II, No. 3, 1952, p. 6.
39. BCTA Constitution, Aims — Rule 6b (in *Outlook* magazines).
40. *A Policy for the Arts*, HMSO, 1965, p. 14.
41. Arts Council of Great Britain, *The Provision of Theatre for Young People in Britain*, Arts Council, London, p. 22.

Chapter 2

Theatre in Education at Coventry, 1965–72

Why did Theatre in Education begin in Coventry? Many factors contributed to its initiation, but perhaps one of the main ones was the nature of the City of Coventry itself. Gordon Vallins, who started the TIE scheme there, said of the City:

> I have an enormous respect for Coventry. I think somehow because they suffered enormously in the war, they wanted to be first and better. They put themselves up to be shot at. I can't imagine, quite honestly, anywhere else in the country where TIE could have started, except possibly London.[1]

It was certainly a city which was willing to experiment. It was one of the first Education Authorities to introduce Comprehensive Education. During the war Coventry had been very badly bombed and the centre of the city had been destroyed. After 1945 the rebuilding of the city began with a new Cathedral; a new city centre; the first shopping precinct free of traffic in Britain, and the first civic theatre to be built since the war.

Mr. Charles Barrett, Coventry's Town Clerk, was proud of his City's achievement:

> One of the tragedies of British local government is that it has concerned itself primarily with emptying the garbage and seeing that the drains work. A theatre, run properly, and especially in a re-born city like ours, should also be our responsibility.[2]

When the Belgrade Theatre was founded in 1957 it was charged to provide a drama experience for the school children of Coventry. A resolution to that effect appeared in the City Council's Municipal Handbook of 1957/8:

> The Company shall in the conduct of its affairs have regard of the desirability of assisting the Council in its capacity as the local education authority in the development of an appreciation of drama in the schools in the city.[3]

Bryan Bailey was appointed Artistic Director and the theatre opened on 27th March 1958 with a production of "Half in Earnest". Bailey adopted a definite policy for young people. Shortly after the theatre opened Derek Newton was appointed to develop contacts with young people. He introduced practical drama sessions during the school holidays and weekends showing how the theatre worked and offering improvisation and playwrighting workshops.

When David Forder took over from Derek Newton in 1960 he continued the work and added some ideas of his own. With a group of actors from the theatre company he devised a programme called "Theatre as Entertainment" and toured schools. In addition Forder organized a "Young Stagers" Club so that those in full-time education could buy cheap seats at the theatre and take part in a growing number of other activities such as demonstrations and workshops. When David Forder resigned it was some time before his successor could be appointed and interest began to fall away. It was the appointment of Anthony Richardson as Director of the Belgrade in 1962 that began things moving again.

Richardson was well aware of the civic theatre's responsibility to its city. He was a man with a social conscience and he wanted to involve all elements of the community, civic, industrial, artistic and educational in the theatre. After a considerable search he appointed Gordon Vallins as Liaison Officer. Vallins was a trained teacher, but his job was really Public Relations with the press and the community. He would talk to Women's Institutes, take backstage visits and so on. His job was to sell the theatre, but Gordon Vallins found this rather a sterile occupation.

He began to develop the possibilities of the job, making a stronger contact with schools by going in to take improvisation sessions. Vallins began to take Paul Harman with him, an actor from the main company (later to run the Liverpool Everyman Priority Community Theatre Project). From the improvisation work that they did in schools was born the Belgrade Youth Theatre, a workshop for young people. On taking up the job Gordon Vallins had drawn up a list of recommendations: a Youth Theatre was one of them, another was the establishment of a permanent Children's Theatre company at the Belgrade. At that point, however, there was no money for such a scheme, but the idea was not forgotten.

When Anthony Richardson and Gordon Vallins were travelling on a train to a CORT Conference they began to talk about the possibilities of taking the theatre into the community, of taking actors and designers into schools. The idea would not be to sell the theatre but it would be setting up an experience for the pupils. From this talk grew a scheme including the art gallery, factories, offices and schools with the theatre as a catalyst bringing all of them together. It was to be "a two way process whereby we could contribute to the city by presenting problems in a creative way". The aim was to use theatre to "tell everyone else about each others problems",[4] Gordon Vallins drew this out diagrammatically (see below). He saw the theatre as part of, and contributing to, the whole community.

These ideas were developed and eventually written down in a paper which Gordon Vallins called "Theatre in Education". One of the purposes of the paper was to suggest how to make theatre an integral part of education, and by this means to make the pupils more aware of the world around them.

The next step was a meeting between Richardson, Vallins, Alderman Waugh of the Belgrade Trust, Councillor Thomas Locksley of the Education Committee and David Turner, the Belgrade's playwright in residence. Inspired by the proposals they felt that Coventry, the first city to introduce so many things, should be the first to have a Theatre in Education company. They reckoned that a penny on the rates would produce £50,000. After this meeting the Director of Education, W. L. Chinn, sent a letter to all the head

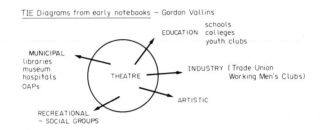

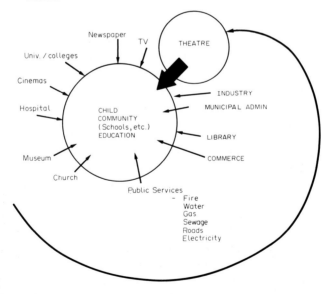

FIG. 3a. Theatre — one of many agents contributing to community. All agents contribute/use theatre as a possible filter.

teachers of the Coventry schools inviting them to a meeting with the Belgrade Trust. The purpose of the meeting was to consider how the theatre could assist in the schools in the development of drama and theatre in a more definite and positive way than contemplated before.

The head teachers liked the idea, but felt the whole scheme was too unwieldy and impractical, so they set up a sub-body from their own ranks to devise a more suitable scheme. Based on the initial ideas they suggested an educational drama service which would be an inspirational teaching service, would operate a permanent Children's Theatre company, and would staff a Theatre centre which would provide aid and guidance to the schools.

The panel suggested a divided staff to do this, teachers to teach, actors to act. Vallins rejected this proposal because it eradicated the major break-through in the initial idea: the combination of both teaching and acting skills into one unit. Conflict and delays ensued, but suddenly the proposals were leaked to the press and in January 1965 headlines such as "£50,000 for Drama Teaching" appeared in the national press. The City Council Treasurer, who had never been consulted on the project, telephoned the Belgrade and demanded an explanation. However, the publicity had committed the Council to some sort of financial support, but the Treasurer felt that a penny on the rates was impossible.

Eventually, after the policy committee had completed and submitted their proposals, and another sub-committee of education and theatre personnel had been formed to discuss finance, the sum to be granted was fixed at £15,000. In March 1965, by order of the City Council, TIE came into being as an experiment for 12 months.

It is interesting that once the initial idea had been formed and suggested by Gordon Vallins and Anthony Richardson, how quickly the Education Authorities took it up. Not accepting it in full, but changing and developing it. Thus the eventual combination of the right idea at the right time, critical assessment and development of the scheme, and a political move to clinch the finance produced the first Theatre in Education scheme in the country. It was a combination of the ideas of those in the theatre and those in education.

At the beginning of the scheme certain provisions were made that proved extremely important. TIE was established as a separate body, responsible directly through the Belgrade Trust to the City Council, but as its budget came under the regular Education allotment it was kept separate from the theatre's budget. Thus the scheme was set up as a joint venture between the theatre and the education authorities and as such it did not have to duplicate the work of the main theatre or the work of the teacher in the school. It was to be a free service to the schools and was given the scope to experiment and develop.

The scheme was to begin in the autumn term of 1965 and meanwhile Gordon Vallins went round the schools, talking to head teachers discussing suitable material, viewing the equipment in the schools, meeting teachers and generally doing an enormous amount of public relations work. By July 1965 Gordon Vallins was able to issue a general information sheet about the project, which contained the essence of the work for the next year. Points 3 to 5 clarified policy:

> 3. The team will concentrate on the Northern Area of the city and will be able to visit most schools in that area twice in the Autumn Term. The team will enter another area the following term.
> 4. The team will spend a day in the school:
>   (i)   dividing into two teams and teaching two classes simultaneously in the morning some form of creative drama which is related to
>   (ii) the performance by the team in the afternoon and
>   (iii) afterwards, discussing with the school's staff what has been achieved, methods, sources, and possible follow-up material. Prepared lesson notes and suggestions will be distributed to the staff which they can make use of if they wish.
> 5. The team, in short, is an animated visual aid to both teachers and children acting as a stimulus to the creative work in the school.[5]

These points reveal a very definite attitude, the concentrating of resources, visiting only the northern part of a small city with a school population of roughly 65,000. It was placing an emphasis on creative drama leading into performance, a policy pursued by the team for several years. Whilst Drama was hardly an established subject in schools and there were no Drama teachers in Coventry, the team were providing both a stimulus for, and an example of, creative drama, not only as a subject in itself but also as a method to teach other subjects. The team took on the task of being an "animated visual aid" at a time when little else was available to schools except the BBC Music and Movement programmes.

To implement this policy Gordon Vallins advertised for three people with both acting and teaching experience. This was an unusual and, as it turned out, a vital step in the development of TIE. He wanted people with both qualifications:

> Basically because they are not primarily egocentric. What I wanted is people who were primarily interested in teaching, to try and make the teaching experience an exciting one and turn the two dimensional experience into a three dimensional one.[6]

When the team began work in September 1965 they established an attitude and way of work that is basic to TIE today:

> The team is always open to constructive criticism. We ourselves, all the time we have been working together, have equally contributed ideas

suggestions and modifications; we ourselves are highly critical and enthusiastic about each others' work as individuals and of the team as a whole. We are learning from our mistakes and continue to improve our skill.[7]

They developed a method of group devising to which they applied a self-critical attitude. They planned to use creative drama and theatre, and the value of theatre in this context Gordon Vallins saw as:

its ability to exercise us as people. Properly used it can encourage us to think in greater depth, and give us a greater realisation of the world about us, perhaps more so than any other subject because it deals with the interaction of personalities in three dimensions . . . One of the nice things about theatre is that it has this aspect of danger — it's here, it's now.[8]

With these ideas and ideals the company of four faced the problem of material, and structure of their work. Unlike Children's Theatre companies the team were planning to work much more closely with the pupils. Unlike drama teachers they planned to include an element of performance. There were no models to use, no plays to take off the shelf and there were a number of vital decisions to be made. Too much free improvisation would limit the amount of teaching, and too much planned performance would not relate to the skills and interests of the children. Yet, how should the material be planned in the first place, should the drama or performance session be planned first and how would the two relate? In general approach to the work Gordon Vallins acknowledges a debt to Brian Way, whose work invited the children to grasp a situation imaginatively, not just by thinking about it but by participating in it. However, the company did not use Brian Way's plays, but determined to devise their own.

In an interview Gordon Vallins explained that the general theme behind the work in the first months was "about the taking of responsibility. What can you do to help somebody else." To put this aim into some kind of format the company tried to give the children "the dual experience of doing and watching" and through this experience they hoped that the children would gain "a measure of learning and a measure of understanding".[9]

These ideas can be seen in the first infant programme created by the team. It was called "The Balloon Man and the Runaway Balloons". It utilized story and fantasy elements and was structured in two parts. The first being a 20-minute lesson, when two classes were taught simultaneously in separate classrooms and the second part being a 30-minute 'happening' when the two classes came together in the hall.

PART ONE: This included the telling of the story, and the children themselves contributing to the telling of the story by making up all the

sound effects, and while sitting down, making movements with their
hands and arms: a railway train, a fairground roundabout, the sea, feet
upon the sand, rain, wind, sea and storm, the blowing up of balloons
and learning the balloon man's song.
PART TWO: This included the acting of the story: being carriages on
the train, horses on the roundabout, children at the seaside building
sand castles, having a picnic, eating toffee apples and being the balloon
man's balloons: round ones, long ones and twisty ones who escape from
the balloon man while he is asleep and float out into the sea. The
balloon man tries to catch them but a storm breaks and capsizes the
balloon man's boat. The balloons rescue him.[10]

It was at the point where the balloon man was drowning that the children, as
the balloons, had to work out how to help him. The programme was basically
a children's story and it was not aiming to teach facts but rather to involve the
children in an imaginative situation. By telling the story first the team were
adopting the same role as an Infant teacher. Taking it one step further, with
the addition of the children's sound effects, moved the reading into the
beginnings of drama. The second half moved into creative drama, with a
mixture of occupational mime "building sand castles" and animating the
inanimate: "being carriages on the train". The company took on roles to lead
the acting out of the story, such as the balloon man or the lady working the
roundabout. They actually created a team-teaching situation with the
addition of visual aids such as costumes, but being performers they could do
more than lead a drama session that brought the story and the characters to
life.

    When the team came to re-think the programme for the second half of the
term they changed the structure. They explained their reasons in their report
of the second tour. Instead of bringing the two classes together in the hall,
they divided the day so that each class went from part one to part two with
only a short break. They took a whole morning or afternoon with just one
class, the team felt this to be necessary "because eighty children minimised
the value of the work". Although they had retained this particular
programme the team did feel that the work was "too young for the older
infants, and that they really needed a story with more depth and bite". In
spite of this criticism the programme did have a definite impact. When a
team member visited an Infant school in the spring of 1966 a teacher spoke
"of the deep effect which the Balloon Man story had had on her class and how
much they were able to remember since well before Christmas".[11]

    The Junior programme, "Secret of the Stone", was devised by the
company and was a story with a mythical element. It used the same structure
as "The Balloon Man". The Secondary programme, however, was a straight
piece of didactic theatre, but, as in the other two shows, it also had the theme

of responsibility. The play used was "High Girders", adapted from a radio script about the building of the first Tay bridge and its destruction in 1879. It was presented as a documentary with sound effects, folk songs, projected pictures, a giant map and innumerable properties, in the style of a "living Newspaper" production. This deliberate presentation of theatre was followed up in the classroom with two drama lessons taken by the team in pairs, in which the class were encouraged to act out a situation where an accident occurred through someone's carelessness. For this, the company set one lesson in the docks and one in the precincts of Coventry. Although the two parts were different in form they were essentially linked to the theatre piece providing information, and stimulating thought.

At the end of the first tour Gordon Vallins wrote a report, the beginnings of a policy that has made Coventry the best documented team in the country. Although the first half of the term had been very hectic the team did feel that the response from the children involved had been most encouraging. The company's concern was that the work should be used and followed up by the schools. To help this process the team provided follow-up notes to suggest ways of developing the themes and methods in the programmes.

In his first report Gordon Vallins listed areas for immediate development. Apart from the practical needs for a van and premises he emphasized the educational development of the work and the need for continuity of contact:

1. That Headteachers, especially if they believe that the work we are doing has real educational value, make sure that some follow-up work is done.
2. More intensive work with teachers who are:
   (a) keen and have already used dramatic methods (or music and movement) and would like to extend the work that they themselves have already started and
   (b) those teachers who are not sure how to start but would like very much to "have a go".
3. The continuance of the work in the Northern Area in the first instance and working with the same children until the end of the 1965/66 academic year.
Reasons: (i) There can be a greater assessment of the value of the experiment.
   (ii) There can be a greater assurance that work is developed, therefore a greater insistence on standards.
   (iii) Opportunity to assess how the child's interests and needs change and develop in the school year.
(We are concerned about progress and not remaining in "Square One.")[12]

These recommendations show the team's concern with the use and understanding of the work, and the realization that for it to have any real effect there must be contact with the same group of children over a period of time.

For the second tour in the first term the company re-worked "The Balloon Man", but introduced new Junior and Secondary programmes. The Junior one was based on a Viking legend. The idea of using myths and legends had come from Gordon Vallins' previous teaching experience, when he used the BBC "Living Language" programmes. These relied heavily upon myths and legends.

Junior programme two:

Baldur the God of Light, or how the mistletoe came to grow on trees

The story was adapted from the version in "The Larousse Encyclopae-dia of Mythology". It tells how Baldur, the God of Light and son of Queen Frigga, was troubled by a strange and terrifying dream which left a shadow over his heart. To allay his fears the Queen calls before her everything and every being, to ask them to promise never to harm Baldur. This they do, but she didn't call the mistletoe who she thought too young to make a promise. Loki, the God of Evil, discovers the flaw in the protection and gets Hodur, Baldur's blind brother, to throw a branch of mistletoe which pierces the hero's heart during a game on the Plain of Peace. This leads to the building of a Viking longship to send Baldur to the land of dead heroes and finally, the placing of the mistletoe high on a tree so that it can never do harm again.

The basic pattern of working was the same as the first programme: it was done in two parts with the team of four dividing into pairs to teach two classes simultaneously and after break, bringing the classes together in the hall to enact the story.

In this story we also make available opportunities for more dialogue to be made up by the children, and also opportunities for making sounds and painting: the sound to accompany the action and paintings to form a backcloth for the story. We took with us into the schools brushes and palettes, and a collection of percussion instruments which the team had specially made. The sound effects developed and as we went from school to school, we learnt how, in a short space of time, this could be worked to the greatest effect. Sometimes our instruments were augmented by instruments from the school's own collection and on one occasion we had a specially composed funeral march which was played on recorders. The painting was not so successful and after the first four Junior schools, we abandoned the idea because we felt that the results achieved could be done much better by the class teacher after our visit.

We had hoped that we could have found a way of making acting and painting a continuous experience but, within the hour available, we found this unsatisfactory but we have not entirely abandoned the idea and will one day work on a project which will more easily provide this opportunity.

In the classroom the lessons concerned themselves with the teaching of the elements: class one learnt about mountains and water and class two about wind and fire and the interaction of one element upon another, both classes were also taught some Viking history and how legends evolved and also listened to the story. (Many of the classes knew quite a lot about Vikings and their collective knowledge was often astounding. Later we learnt they had seen a film called "The Vikings" on TV.)

In the hall seven areas were chalked on the floor: Asgard (where the Gods lived), the shape of the Viking ship, areas for wind, sea, fire and mountains and the orchestra. We rehearsed the building of the ship and co-ordinated sound effects with movement. We played "Neptune" from the Planets Suite/Holst to set the atmosphere: the team played the Narrator, Frigga, Loki and Baldur and gave opportunities while acting the story, for the children to talk within the context of the action.

Many teachers preferred this programme to "The Secret of the Stone", they felt it was more exciting as a piece of drama and could see how an existing story could be adapted for the classroom. They liked its factuality and the extension of these facts into a story where we all hope the children gained some knowledge through enjoyment as well as experiencing group creativity.[13]

The format is still the same with the team teaching in the classroom and then acting out the story, but this time with both classes in the hall. However, unlike "The Secret of the Stone" there is a definite learning situation involved with the elements and Viking sections, so that the myth provides a framework for the teaching of facts from different subject areas. Not only this but the areas of art and music are included, so that the whole programme becomes like a Centre of Interest project in a school, many subjects being related to the one theme. Therefore the nature of the work fits into the pattern of the school's activities.

Using the facts taught in the classroom the team incorporated them into the action, so that the first half, although useful on its own, was an essential part of the second part — the acting out. Like the Infant programme the story had been told in advance, the session was therefore an acting out of the known. The pupils, although able to talk within the action, did not, in any way, change the course of the story. Their participation was a sharing in the "performance" of the legend. This can be seen as a drama session, yet it also has all the elements of theatre; the interaction of characters, dramatic conflict, plot, tension, and the bringing together of words and movement, music sound and art.

It is interesting to note that as soon as the team realized that the art work could be done better by the class teacher they dropped it from the programme. Thus, the team were aware of the value of their work in the classroom situation and where they were offering something that the teacher was more able to do with the children.

The programme itself obviously did more than teach, it involved the pupils in group creativity, and not only stimulated the pupils, but the staff as well. In the spring term a school embarked on a production of "Ali Baba and the Forty Thieves" the enthusiasm for which had been engendered by the Company's visits the previous term.

The Junior schools varied enormously in their use and understanding of drama. When the team made a special study and wrote a report of the state of drama in North Coventry schools in the spring of 1966, they discovered that in some schools there was not "time for drama in the timetable", and in others it was only used as an aid to English. At the other end of the scale teachers were "enthusiastic and creative and interested in drama as a teaching medium". In 1966 there were no drama teachers in the city and the TIE programmes could provide a real stimulus for the development of drama within the school.

For the Secondary school programme the company devised an entirely new format.

Secondary programme two:

"Noise, Noise, Noise, or What annoys a noisy oyster most?"

> . . . With our second secondary programme we thought we would show children and the teachers how they themselves could make up their own programme from scraps of sound, comment and improvisation. We chose the subject of noise because it specifically dealt with one of our senses and is a subject which could be readily understood. Everyone has something to say about noise as it is one of the more characteristic annoyances of our society.
>
> We chose to set the documentary inside a television studio, to give the programme another dimension and a greater element of interest. Also certain disciplines have to be observed in a studio which we also imposed in the classroom and in the school hall; this strict observation of silence while broadcasting is in progress, from others in the studio who were not at that moment acting, was a great aid to concentration. (Before embarking on this programme, the team visited a TV studio to

learn jargon and sense the atmosphere; we could then communicate this to the children.)

We evolved a simple story set in a fictitious street called "Caterwaul Crescent" which had "The Beat Bar" café at one end and the public house "The Hammer and Tongs" at the other. There were houses in between; marked out by chairs. One end of the hall became a studio area where we kept recorded sound, live sound (effects made up by some of the class) and a group to read newspaper cuttings, definitions, a piece of poetry, and letters on the subject of noise, while at the other end there was a bingo hall and a cinema. Also, we had two box-type spotlights which represented cameras one and two and these were also operated by two of the class.

We tried to create an authentic television studio atmosphere with its dramatic tension and excitement, using television documentary techniques with an interviewer, a floor manager, a sound supervisor and a producer with the young people creating real life examples of noisy situations to explore the problem of the noise nuisance. This was entirely the children's work based on the provided production plans and using their own skills with the team shaping and channelling their efforts. This experience showed how an entertainment could be formed from separate but linked activities: an animated project in fact.

The organization of this was similar to the junior programme: the team divided into pairs and taught simultaneously, each pair taking the activities of one side of the street. Four lessons were taken in the morning and two "happenings" were organized in the afternoon.

The situations around which the classes were asked to improvise were mostly of a domestic nature and ones they readily understood: noise of games coming home from school, television programmes, noisy motor bikes, using radio and juke box, arguments, carol singing, using power drills, hair driers, sewing machines, etc., and ending up with a protest march upon the Town Hall to complain about the excessive noise in Caterwaul Crescent.

The young people involved in this programme learnt something, we hope, about the enjoyment of group creativity. They have learnt that you don't have to rely upon a play to create satisfying drama and that they also can research into a chosen subject, make up dialogue from improvisation and create dramatic situations from their own imaginations and experience. From this programme they also learnt about various noises and how they are made and have been made conscious that noise can be a social irritant. And if some of the follow-up suggestions are used they will discover something about the causes of deafness, the teaching of deaf children, the sending of messages, the use of vibrations, etc.[14]

Although the structure of this programme is similar to that used for the Junior programme, "Noise" is a very different offering. By taking into Secondary schools an "animated project", the company were making an enormous step in curriculum development. For the programme worked across the curricular, linking different subjects which in most schools were kept strictly separate and taught in 40-minute blocks. Not only this, but the actual subject matter was social and dramatic and not examination material. As this was not a performance but a day of involvement and interaction between the team and the pupils, the entire concept in a Secondary school situation was an extraordinary innovation!

With the use of a television-studio setting for the programme, the company provided the pupils with a known phenomenon but an unfamiliar environment. The setting of the television studio required disciplines of silence and concentration without these having to be imposed by the team. Within this setting the company became team leaders, adopting roles within the studio, but not specific characters. Under their guidance the pupils created dramatized examples of noisy situations, and all were therefore involved in a creative drama session, rather than a piece of theatre.

The programme was aimed at encouraging drama work in the schools, and this it did. In the report on Drama in North Coventry Schools (1966) a team member noted, of one of the Secondary schools, that:

> This school is also taking great advantage of the work we started. They have used dramatic methods in general subject teaching and the standard and interest in drama throughout the school is rising.

As in the Junior schools, drama work in the Secondary schools was not consistent. A lot of teachers felt themselves in the dark about the use of drama and were only too grateful for the company's advice, but many Secondary schools suffered under exam pressure, and the exam syllabus allowed no time for drama. If drama was taught or used as a teaching method it was often because of the interest of an individual English teacher. By wishing to stimulate drama in schools and offering in-service courses to teachers, the company began to develop into a Drama Advisory Service. This development meant that Coventry did not appoint a Drama Adviser. The general feeling was that the company was doing the Adviser's job, but in fact it has never set out to take the place of a Drama Adviser.

By the end of the second tour in the first term it was obvious that the scheme was a success, and funds for the following year were assured. A separate TIE budget was established which the company were to administer, and to solidify the organization the first steps were taken to establish a management committee.

With the success of the scheme the Belgrade advertized for a Head of Department. The job was given to Rosemary Birbeck. She was a trained teacher, and taught drama at the Inner London Comprehensive School. She had developed a Youth Theatre based on the school, which consisted of ex-pupils.

Gordon Vallins had also applied for the job, but as he was not offered it, he felt that the only thing he could do in the circumstances was to resign. Before he left he drew up a series of suggestions for anyone who was to embark on running a Theatre in Education scheme. These proposals are basic to the way TIE functions today and their identification is indicative of the fact that Gordon Vallins had based the Coventry team on well-thought-out principles that were relevant and useful to the school situation. It is much to his credit, that in such a short space of time (only 3 months in fact) he should have worked out both a philosophy and a method of work that were to be essential to the development of TIE as a recognizable and separate movement. As these recommendations are of such importance, they are quoted in full:

An outline of work for anyone responsible for the practical working of 'Theatre in Education'.

1. The integration of the team as an organic unit working to a common objective; each member contributing and exploiting their own special skills as fully as possible. (A strong say in who is appointed to the team and qualities demanded.)

2. The structure and deployment of the team: the maintenance of discipline and standards. (The 1965 Autumn Term included one Producer/ Teacher, three Actor/Teacher Assistants, one driver/ technician and one part-time secretary.)

3. (a) The collection of material, the final choice of material and the manner in which it is used.

   (b) The final choice on necessary equipment, provided the purchase of same comes within the allocated budget.

4. Assessing and getting to know the terrain and the schools in which the team will work, evaluating working space and making contact with the members of staff.

5. The organisation of the timetable for (a) the schools and (b) the team.

6. The preparation of organisation notes for Infant, Junior and Secondary schools, so that schools will clearly understand what is required regarding space and equipment and the timing of the lesson and "performance".

7. The arranging of a meeting with the Headteachers before work actually begins in their schools so that details of methods and material used can be explained in full.

8. To go to the school to teach, perform and lead the discussion in the staffroom on the completion of the day's work.

9. The organisation and writing of follow-up notes, the suggestions for teachers and how they might be able to extend the work already begun by the team.

10. The writing of reports, so that everything done is put on record. This will prove valuable for committees and when other authorities wish to investigate the history and the working of "Theatre in Education".

N.B. The work is unique and highly personal; it's like being gardener with a tree, planting the seed, nurturing it so that it grows strong and in the direction the gardener believes it should grow; another gardener will plant a different tree. [15]

To continue Gordon Vallins' analogy: although he sees the work as highly personal and therefore different with each new planting, there is no doubt that a number of teams were actually grown from the same species of tree as the Coventry one, although their actual size and shape may vary!

By the time Gordon Vallins left, the exact nature of the scheme was clear:

The scheme is a service: an efficient mobile school with a growing storehouse of visual aids for teachers and children. This is the scheme's value: an animated aid to the stimulus of creative work through all the creative processes — yet intensely practical. The team is primarily concerned with the needs of the children and in development at particular age levels and in helping teachers in finding lively ways in the bi-polar process of communication with young people in helping them understand and to use the world around them. We are concerned with letting children learn about life rather than filling empty buckets with information. [16]

This was the scheme that Rosemary Birbeck was to take over in April 1966. Before she did so, the company was made up to four by Gordon Wiseman, and from January to April the company went out into schools to take drama lessons and to perform their two new Junior programmes. One was very similar to the Baldur legend and the other was on the theme of teeth, a subject that did not meet with great enthusiasm, as the team noted in a Report in 1966: "Teeth is not immediately evocative to everyone as a subject for drama, several teachers were not inspired by the theme."

The summer term could only be very exploratory. Of the original team, only Dickon Reed stayed on. Rosemary Birbeck was new and was, therefore, finding her feet. In addition, Warren Jenkins took over as Artistic Director of the Belgrade on 1st June. In September the TIE company expanded from four to nine: all nine had some kind of educational experience or training.

The TIE team under Rosemary Birbeck decided to put their efforts not into recreational drama, but into main stream education, and to carry on along the lines set by Gordon Vallins. The company aimed "to explore the use of drama and theatre in relation to the class-teacher in primary schools and Arts teachers in Secondary schools. To ally the best in theatre techniques of communication with the most progressive movements in education."[17]

Between 1967–70 the work developed rapidly as the team experimented with different techniques and the relationship with the schools and teachers grew stronger. Initially there had been a great deal of suspicion of the team and what it was trying to do. Theatre directors felt actors should act in the conventional manner to an audience, and educationalists felt that it was the teacher's job to work with children in a school situation.

Some of the suspicion from teachers was eliminated by Coventry's system of in-service training. Shortly after the team started work they were given a week's course with thirty teachers. As a result of the course the teachers began to trust the team, and indeed made friends with them. This meant that when the team visited one of those teacher's schools the whole approach was one of working together not of judging outsiders. From this the team realized the importance of liaison, and introduced teachers' work sessions where they invited the teachers to a workshop about 2 weeks through the programme preparation period to explain, and work on, the material, and to make sure that the teachers knew what was happening. Another meeting was held when the programme had finished its tour.

This method of liaison and discussion firmly established that there was a collaboration between the team and the teachers, and in fact the work relied on it, as Stuart Bennett explained during an interview:

> I think I would take that as being the key thing that TIE is: a collaboration, a group of people draw up a system, become specialists in drama and collaborate with teachers to provide something. That is what emerged when we were set up, rather than an individual inspiration.

Stuart Bennett joined the team in January 1967, and was to take over from Rosemary Birbeck when she left in 1970.

Rosemary Birbeck developed a very definite method and approach to the work of Theatre in Education:

> Her policy had been to strike a balance in the composition of the company between those with professional theatre experience and those with teaching experience. Rosemary encouraged constant discussion and evaluation. She was concerned that Theatre in Education did not divide into Theatre (imaginative and exciting) and Education (straight-forward, factual). Education to her concerned the whole child. Drama was a vital force in the learning process and learning was above all enjoyable. She saw our work as a dynamic force in the school not a cultural frill.[18]

Stuart Bennett was to continue this policy.

The actual method of work involved the division of the company into two separate groups each term, each group being allocated an age group and having an autonomy over their material. The company numbered eight plus the director, designer and secretary. The company split into two fours for Junior work, or a three for Infant, and a five for Secondary work. The devising, scripting and rehearsal period lasted 3 weeks and the programme would then tour for 5 weeks. This process was repeated twice a term, the company producing four programmes a term, and twelve in a year. By means of this method of work and the policy developed, Rosemary Birbeck created a company with a deep basic commitment to its work, and the average length of stay was 2½ years. In theatre terms this is a long time for actors to stay with one company. It is quite usual for an actor to be engaged for one play only, and the longest contract is usually a whole season — a period of 8 to 10 months.

To see exactly how the work developed and changed over a period of time it is probably clearer to split the programmes up into the three age groups that Coventry used: The Infant, Junior and Secondary. The company were, however, working on a sequence of Infant, Junior and Secondary work over a school year, and thus the main shifts of thinking in one area of work such as the Infant could actually occur in the intervening Junior and Secondary work. Each age group required a very particular approach and specific material, although the same techniques often appeared in all areas.

Infant Programmes

Very few of the actor–teachers had experience of Infant work, and they turned to the pioneers for a model to base their work on. Both Peter Slade and Brian Way's work were influential. The nature of Brian Way's Infant programmes gave the Coventry team a starting-point. The main features of this kind of approach to Infants were the performing to 100 children or more, at one time. The audience were therefore kept seated, and participation was vocal rather than physical. They participated in the action at significant points, identified with the main character, and experienced direct emotional satisfaction in so doing.

As the Coventry company began to play to smaller numbers of children at a time, there was more possibility of individual involvement for the children in free-moving situations. However, it took a few years for the team to move beyond these early influences, and programmes like "Journey of the Running Deer Tribe", about Red Indians, still relied heavily upon Peter Slade's ideas. By "Kenny's Comic" the team had found their own forms.

The first infant programme in 1966–7 season was along similar lines to "The Balloon Man". It was a fictional story that was acted out by the team and the children, called "The Princess and the Fisherman". The company worked with one class, usually 7-year-olds in the hall of the school for the first 10 minutes in a general drama session using movement and voice, and introducing a series of activities which would be used during the programme. The story was structured so that the children had opportunities of participating in the action. This form could be found in many of Brian Way's presentations in schools.

The next presentation for Infants that year was the Main house production of "Pinocchio", written by Brian Way and Warren Jenkins. All the TIE team were involved in the play, and it proved to be particularly suitable for the Infants and young Juniors.

The idea of working closely with the teacher and helping to introduce drama-teaching methods was still an important aspect of the company's approach. In the summer of 1967 they devised a programme on the theme of Noah and the animals. Its aim was stated in the team's Report of 1966–7: "to explore the value for the infant of a theatre project simple enough to be mounted by the teacher". For this purpose only one actor–teacher took each class, first working on a drama session dealing with the movements and sounds of the different animals, then putting on a simple costume and becoming Noah, whilst the children became the animals. This was not just left as a demonstration, for the company were anxious that the teacher had positive help. So, a team member collaborated with the class teacher on a different project, which the teacher could go on to use.

In that year 1966–7 the TIE company began to use historical and geographical themes for their Junior and Secondary work such as "The Great Fire of London" and "The Frozen Lands". These programmes placed an emphasis on the total involvement of the pupils both mentally and physically. Both the subject-matter and form of presentation used in these programmes began to appear in the Infant work of 1967–8. For by the new school year the company began to ask themselves fundamental questions about the nature of their work in schools. The resulting experiments helped the company to develop their work and gradually move away from their first programmes. In their Infant work the team decided to examine two methods of fully involving infants (6–7-year-olds) in the action and presentation of imaginative stories. The team developed two programmes for the autumn term of 1967 so that the effects could be compared. The two had different structures. One was a theatrical presentation, with a central character with whom the children could identify. He was Person, and he was looking for a name. The children's role was to help Person in his search, and the method used was that of planned participation. A structure much closer to that used by Children's Theatre companies. In contrast, the other programme, "The Journey of the Running Deer Tribe", was much nearer to a creative drama session and to the format of some of the Junior work. It used one class only, the subject was

Red Indians, and was based on fact, but the story of the programme was fictionalized. The children were totally involved in the events: a tribe's journey across a river and mountains to find a new home. The children role-played as Red Indians and the actor–teachers, in costume, worked with them. Although both programmes were so different the company concluded that, actually, both methods were valid, and they would not exclude either the theatrical or the creative drama approach. They continued to develop both aspects.

During the autumn of 1968 the structured Infant work was further explored in "How the Rain Came to Hweng Chow". This programme involved the Infants in an imaginative story heightened by the use of a very theatrical style based on the Chinese Theatrical convention. This form of presentation fired the children's imaginations and teachers found the programme a real stimulus to the class for further creative and research work. The Chinese legend placed the story of the villagers' need for rain to grow their rice into the symbolic context of the Dragon Gods, bringers of rain, withholding it because they are angry with the villagers for taking all the fish from the river. One of the aims of the programme, however, was that the story should introduce elementary facts about people in another environment. Thus, even within a symbolic context, the team's thinking can be seen to be shifting towards the presentation of the real world and its problems. This line of thought, begun with "The Journey of the Running Deer Tribe", was carried further in an Infant programme presented in the spring of 1969, "The Mysterious Wanderers". This programme marks a real shift towards social reality themes. A shift which could be seen throughout the whole range of work. The Secondary programme "If it was not for the Weaver" (autumn 1968), for example, used local history to show the social effects of industrialization.

"The Mysterious Wanderers" was about gypsies. The company's aims for the programme quoted in the team's Annual Report of 1968–9 illustrate the link between it and the programmes on Red Indians and Chinese legend.

The Mysterious Wanderers

Aims: 1. To interest the children in a community with a different way of life from their own by involving them in the imaginative experience of going on a journey as a group of gypsies.
2. To provide a stimulus for further research work into gypsy life and folklore.
3. To incorporate preparatory work by the teacher into the programme.

In the summer term of 1969 the programme was presented again, but this time it was called "The Gypsies", and it had been developed further.

The children are in their classroom. A visitor gives a talk on gypsies. She shows pictures of their encampments and explains with a model how they harness horses to their caravans. They have a secret language and call anyone who is not a gypsy, a "gajo". She turns to write the word on the blackboard. The door opens and a gypsy woman peers round with her finger to her lips. "My name is Rosie . . . I can show you what gypsies are really like. Come with me on a gypsy journey." The children tiptoe out, unseen by their lecturer.

In the corridor they meet Jim. He plays his hurdy-gurdy and leads them to the hall. "You don't live in houses now. You live in caravans. Harness your horses. Take the reins and we'll begin our journey."

They journey in their imaginary caravans round the hall and then make a camp. Jim teaches them how to make secret signs out of twigs and pebbles. The farmer's wife discovers them on her land. What do they think they are doing? Children answer her themselves. "There are too many of you. Half will have to go", she says. Rosie gathers half the children to her. "We'll see you at the Horse Fair." They climb into their caravans and journey out of the hall.

Jim and his family groom their horses. Then he teaches them how to tickle trout. The children lie down on the river bank and plunge their hands into the water. The farmer's wife arrives again. This is too much — poaching, they must all go. Her husband is away on business. She must look after the farm in his absence. Jim and his family harness their horses, but before they go they leave a sign with real stones and twigs to show other gypsies that this farm is unfriendly, and also a shoe which means the farmer is away. Jim and his family leave the hall and journey into the playground, where they practise gypsy music.

Rosie and her family had journeyed to the classroom, picked fruit and learned how to read fortunes. On their return journey they find the secret sign and interpret it. The farmer's wife comes to evict them. They make friends by telling her fortune. Her husband is away on business and will come home rich! She is pleased by this (How could they have known!). She offers them work in her orchards. Jim and his family arrive and are given the job of grooming her horses.

They are paid and are able to go to the Horse Fair where they dance and listen to a gypsy story about Jim's hurdy gurdy which plays a lucky tune.

The story is told by the teacher who is now the head of the gypsy tribe and can take them on further journeys using themes prepared at the Day Course.[19]

Comparison with "The Balloon Man" programme shows how the work for

Infants has developed. The imaginative movement has become occupational mime. The question and answer between the actor–teacher in character, and the children, has become a dramatic conflict situation. The children are in a role — as gypsies, but they are not asked to become different ages, they are asked to understand what it is like to be a child and a gypsy. The characters they meet have a place in reality, they have prejudices that can be argued with, ideas that can be challenged. The story happens *to* the children not *in spite* of them. The ending is indicative of the very much closer liaison with the teacher. Here, the teacher is an imaginative part of the story and as Head of the Gypsy Tribe can continue the theme without feeling the loss of the TIE team. Therefore the gap between the presentation and the follow up in the classroom is bridged, and the teacher, having attended the Day Course, has information and ideas enough to build on the situation. When such characters as Rosie and Jim befriend the children, they give them a sense of security. A child can turn to the character at any point to ask a question, or to be reassured. Also the characters have the freedom within this structure to use or adjust to any unusual situation that may occur. Thus, the journey format and the episodic structure can allow for the child's contribution at any stage. The new school year, 1969–70, produced a further shift in the Infant work. The programme structure of a journey, and the theme of people in different environments was tried again in "The Cocoa Tree" (autumn 1969), a programme which involved the children in a journey to an African village.

During the same term the company presented "Rama and Sita", a programme which explored the relative emotional depth children can absorb in playing out a story they already know. The Indian legend was chosen as a story of symbolic good and evil, and repeated in several different ways to the class, by story-telling, models, acting out. These various methods were to give the teacher ideas on different ways of playing out a story.

During 1969–70, the Junior work concentrated upon history themes whilst the Secondary work took a major step in utilizing simulation, and decision-making within their programme, "People Matter More than Plans, Councillor Kean" (summer 1969). This kind of development fed into the Infant work. The Infant programmes which the company devised for the summer term of 1970 were a response to the introduction of vertical, family grouping in Coventry Primary schools. To make sure that the work was suitable for all the children in one class, the programme had to be more open-ended allowing for different ages and experience within the same group. To experiment in this area, the company developed two new programmes, the aim of which was "to discover ways of organizing the children's own ideas to create an instant play in which children and actors could be involved".[20] In one programme the company, after a brief warm-up session, introduced a character such as a tiger and asked the children for ideas. The stories developed according to the children's imaginative flow and concentration span with the children joining in as the characters they had suggested. The other programme, "Kenny's Comic", consisted of three visits to the school, and the children were confronted with a real car, characters and a situation, but how the situation was to be solved was up to them. They had certain facts to work from. This programme revealed just how easily children could mix up fantasy and reality:

> Kenny arrived in a real car with real comics. Was everything else real? The children did not appear to distinguish between the real car and their own imaginary telephone. It was all part of an exciting game, and stimulated a great deal of story invention.[21]

The Infant work had developed and changed as the team applied the lessons they learnt in working with all the age groups. The most obvious development was away from fantasy and towards reality. A reality which was unknown, for instead of acting out a known series of events from a story already told, the children were involved in an experience where they met characters in situations that were recognizably of the world today. Instead of being balloons they became gypsies, and with that change of approach came a whole wealth of educational and imaginative stimulus. The children's involvement becomes absolutely integral to the programme and their views and thoughts asked for and responded to. The teacher's role developed too, and the use of real collaboration between the TIE team and the teachers meant that the programmes could become an important part of the work of the classes involved, and not just an afternoon's entertainment.

Another obvious shift over the 5 years was from the use of very structured work to the introduction of a number of unstructured programmes. The value of a structure was recognized by the team, for it enabled the children to extend their experience in situations outside their own environment. This form appeared more suitable for the older Infants who could understand and develop an idea as a group. The unstructured work allowed the children to develop their imaginations and find their own contributions.

The team also shifted from programmes which used emotional involvement, such as the exploration of fear in the Red Indian programme to a more subtle use of the children's emotional involvement in the social relationship themes of the programmes of the late sixties. Although it was not possible to offer Infants difficult intellectual problems to solve, or complicated arguments, the company attempted to stretch the pupils within an imaginative experience and to encourage questions and discussion.

Junior Programmes

The programmes developed by the company from 1966 fitted very easily into a Junior school situation as Stuart Bennett explained in interview:

For Primary teachers if you brought in a lively project-based session in which there were drama activities you were really picking up the kind of work they were doing, giving them the research which made it more accurate giving them the impetus which got the kids involved. Providing the kids with an opportunity to express how they would experience a situation and subsequently giving them an experience which they could use to articulate concepts.

The Infant work of summer 1966 had consisted of a structured fantasy programme, "The Princess and the Fisherman", but the Junior work that term moved away from mythology and legend, used by Gordon Vallin's team, to history. The programme, "The Siege of Kenilworth", used an approach which enabled pupils to see history as a set of real situations with real people. The teacher's reactions were recorded in The 1966–67 Annual TIE Report. They felt that: "the experience of participating in this performance with the actors had stimulated great interest and enthusiasm among the pupils as well as giving a reality to the historical figures of the text book". It is here that TIE can be seen to be working in an obvious educational sense. It can be a real stimulus to the child to wish to learn more; it can motivate learning.

This motivation was achieved by a basic structure similar to the programme on the Baldur legend (1965), with a teaching session first and then the two classes coming to the hall. However, the two classes were placed in conflict, an immediate dramatic device, one class was Prince Edward's army, who were to attack the castle, and the other class were the defenders of that castle. With basic information and a few skills learned in the earlier drama session the pupils were asked to role-play in this situation. Within the structure of basic historical accuracy, situations were improvised freely with the pupils. To help create the atmosphere, certain devices were used that were basically theatrical. The four actor–teachers wore correct period costumes, a tape was used with narration, sound effects and music. Slides were shown during the action picturing the castle, the main characters, and weapons as reminders of the realistic details. The actual castle which the pupils were to besiege was built of climbing apparatus, benches and mats. Thus the whole setting became a combination of the real and the accurate and the atmospheric and symbolic. The castle is a symbol easily understood by the pupils, enhanced and made real by the actual castle on the screen. The music helps to create atmosphere, and effects the mood. Thus, the children play at besieging the castle with real live characters (who are also playing!) but this activity is channelled into situations where they must articulate, must ask questions, must answer, must understand, or the play cannot continue.

For their Secondary school programme, in the spring of 1967, the team also used historical material: the Fire of London. In the same term, however, the company introduced a drama teaching programme for Juniors on the theme of "The Frozen Lands", which entailed three visits to each school, working with two separate classes.

This kind of project work had been initiated by the early programme on "Teeth" (1966). In "The Frozen Lands" the three sessions explored such topics as Eskimo life, the effect of cold, and adventures on Shackleton's ship voyaging to Elephant Island. However, teachers felt that in this series the team were attempting a subject beyond their experience and that it might have been better taught by the class teacher. Also, they felt that the three visits by team members were too far apart. Later historical projects drew the team and the teachers into a much closer collaboration.

The social history programmes for Juniors were continued in the next year, 1967–8, with "The Conflict in Coventry" set in a market place in Medieval Coventry. This programme used the same kind of formula as "The Siege of Kenilworth". The Secondary work for that year was also historical: "If it was not for the Weaver", and had been devised because the success of "The Conflict in Coventry" had shown the value of using local history as material for TIE programmes.

The Junior work of the following year, 1968–9, concentrated mainly on the gathering of material for a Children's play to be presented in the Belgrade Theatre in spring 1969. The team went out into schools to work with pupils in creating characters and stories. The experience gained from this work seems to relate directly to the unstructured Infant work of the summer of 1970.

"The Lunt Fort at Baginton" was presented in schools in three terms (autumn 1968, spring 1969, and autumn 1969). This Junior programme combined elements of the drama teaching session of "The Frozen Lands" and the historical themes developed in the Junior programmes over the previous 2 years. The aims for this programme clearly show the coming together of the several strands of the team's work:

Aims: 1. To make vivid an incident in local history — the coming of the Romans to the Coventry area.
2. To concern pupils with problems of human relationships by highlighting a conflict between two different cultures.
3. To devise a team teaching project involving two members of the Theatre in Education Company and two class teachers.[22]

By 1968–9 the team had built up a much closer contact with schools and the introduction of the teacher's workshop allowed for the collaboration between the team and the teachers to be properly planned and executed:

FIG. 3b. Coventry TIE, "Lunt Fort at Baginton", 1978, 1979.
Preparation for battle.

FIG. 4. The Romans.

Preparatory work

One class of pupils are the Celtic farmers of the Dobunni tribe; the other class are auxilliaries in the Roman army. General background work on Romans and Celts is done by the teachers with their classes before the Theatre in Education visit to the school. The details of the preparatory work are introduced and worked through practically by the teachers at two workshop sessions.

Drama session (half-day visit to the school)

One member of the Theatre in Education Company and one teacher are in charge of each class.

After an introductory movement session with both classes, the Romans march off to their training ground in the classroom, while the Celts establish their farms in the hall.

The Romans drill, learn how to construct a temporary camp and how to assess the natives for taxation. The Celts rehearse a funeral for one of their war leaders who has been killed fighting the Brigantes. As the ceremony is about to begin, the Roman soldiers march in.

The Romans watch the ceremony, then build their camp at one end of the hall, watched by the Celts from their farms. The soldiers are sent out to each farm to assess the family for taxes. The Celts feel unjustly treated and send a delegation to the camp Commander. Roman section leaders meet the delegation at the gate and answer the complaints.

Each member of the teaching team now takes two groups of Romans and Celts. He gives each a situation involving a meeting and asks them to prepare a scene to show to the other group. After the demonstration, he questions the Romans and Celts on their actions in the scenes in order to encourage an individual response. The groups can develop the scenes as they like but the Romans are likely to emerge in a strong position in one situation, the Celts in the other.

Both the Romans and Celts learn of the Boudicca uprising in the South. The Celts decide to attack the Roman camp. This attack is rehearsed and then run as a continuous sequence, controlled by cymbal (Celts) and drum (Romans).

The Celts cannot break through the Roman defences and are forced to withdraw. News is brought to both sides that Boudicca has been defeated and she has taken poison. The Romans discuss in their camp how they should treat the rebels. The Celts argue as to whether they should flee or return to their farms.

Both classes meet finally in the hall and one or two spokesmen from each side report on the discussions each group has just had. We end by explaining that we have tried to reconstruct what happened in A.D. 60 from the evidence that the present-day excavations of the fort at Baginton have revealed.[23]

The company wanted the pupils to try and understand what it was like to be an ordinary person, Celt or Roman, and what their everyday lives were like. For this purpose they used a lot of occupational mime. Through this, and with the historical facts they introduced, the company worked at the pupils' personal identity with these peoples and at an understanding of the interaction of the two sides and different cultures. By the fact that the situations in history were suddenly made contemporary — they were happening there in the hall or classroom — the pupils were asked to experience and evaluate these relationships.

By giving the pupils sufficient knowledge and some highly controlled movements such as the drilling of the Roman troops, or the rehearsal of the battle, the company felt that the pupils could improvise freely and with greater imagination.

What the company had produced was a well-thought-out drama lesson using good original historical research. They were aware of this, and the fact that the teacher could undertake such a programme. Due to its drama session form the programme lacked a strong theatrical element, although there were moments of dramatic tension, as on the first meeting of the Romans and Celts. The company considered it as a team-teaching project and felt that the result was valuable for both themselves and the teachers. To try and make sure that the stimulus could help teachers produce further work on the same lines, the team prepared background notes and suggested ways in which a teaching team of staff in the school could organize a similar project on a Civil War Theme.

As the programme placed such emphasis on the drama session and not on theatre performance the actor–teachers often found their roles inconsistent. At times they had to enter into the scenes as Celts or Romans to give orders, or possibly feed in information to sustain an improvisation, and then they would have to step outside a scene in order to set up the next situation or fill in background information. They had to adopt a role, and then slide back into themselves as teachers, without making the process too obvious. The pupils appeared to accept this, and did not even seem to be aware of it. Neither did they mind the organization where it was necessary. As Rosemary Birbeck pointed out in the team's Report for 1968–9: "The game is more fun if everyone knows the rules."

By 1969–70 the Junior work had begun to fall into two distinct kinds, theatrical presentations and team-teaching projects, which used drama. The latter became possible by the growing co-operation between the team and the teachers. By the spring term of 1970 the company and the teachers were able to alternate in work with the pupils to build up a picture of an historical period through drama. The theme was the Industrial Revolution, and first the individual team members visited the schools taking drama sessions on the handloom weavers of Coventry. Then teachers attended a workshop with the team on factories and tried the methods and material from this with their classes. The team visited the school again building up improvised scenes on families, their economy and their fear of the workhouse. Next the teachers came to a workshop on the Great Strike of 1860 and the family discussions to emigrate or stay at home and chance finding work in the bicycle trade. The teachers took this back to their pupils, and finally the pupils themselves put together their own saga of the Coventry weaver from the cottage industry to the emergence of engineering.

The 1969–70 drama historical projects were linked to the BBC Schools programme "Out of the Past", and covered Romans and Celts, The Industrial Revolution and Slavery. The company deliberately selected each topic and its particular term for presentation to fit in with the BBC series, and therefore give the schools a chance to utilize the different media available on the same topic. The company offered "The Lunt Fort at Baginton" for the first term; the "Industrial Revolution" programme, just described for the spring term; and in the third term two teachers' workshops on slavery to offer ideas to teachers, who could then continue the work on their own. The three programmes were a definite progression which placed more and more emphasis on the teacher, as the team slowly withdrew. The company were working both as a TIE team and as drama advisers, and had managed, in that particular set of projects to combine the two roles very happily.

The other aspect of the Coventry work was the theatrical presentation. The company moved into the area of Children's Theatre, which they regarded as a challenge at a time when there was an increasing interest in Children's Theatre, but controversy over the content and form it should take. For the 1968–69 season they decided to present a children's play in the Belgrade Theatre, but this was planned in stages. In the summer term of 1968 the team began a "Junior Playmaking Project", the aims stated in their 1968–9 Report of which were:

1. To try and find out what characters, situation, plot lines in stories have a particular appeal to the 8–11-year-old child and why.
2. To investigate what is relevant material for Children's Theatre.

Members of the company took drama lessons in which the various stories were tried out from the traditional folk tale to the modern science fiction; and the children were also encouraged to tell their own stories. The team discovered that in fact many of the traditional folk tales and legends still had the greatest impact on children. They also discovered that children's ideas and responses varied little throughout the city in spite of differences in material welfare.

Based on this drama work in schools, the company planned a presentation in the Belgrade Theatre written by two of the team, but they decided to lead up to the performance through a process of familiarizing the Junior pupils, first, with some of the characters and then with the actual format of presentation. They visited schools to work with the pupils, introducing the characters and the idea of pre-industrial village life. Then, on the next visit they acted out a situation with the characters, keeping the pupils seated, but seeking their assistance at every stage. By this method the children became accustomed to the way in which their help was to be sought in the Belgrade Theatre itself. Well over half of the 1000 children who saw the play, "The Secret of the Sun", in the theatre had met and worked with the characters in the play in their own school.

In the summer of 1969, the company re-worked their Infant programme "How Rain Came to Hweng Chow" and presented it as a play for Juniors which used planned vocal, rather than physical, participation to a seated audience in the round. The play was more conventional than their other school's work, but it could be played to a larger audience.

In the autumn of 1970 the company again took up the challenge of participation with a large audience. This time it was to be for performance in the Belgrade Theatre, but unlike "The Secret of the Sun", the team did no preparatory work in schools. The play "Adventure" was improvised by the company and to try and utilize the theatre properly the team began work on the project by looking at the architecture of the Belgrade auditorium. To the team it suggested a cave with tunnels opening off. To build on this idea they decided to use the stalls only (450 seats) and to take the children on an adventure underground. The events of the story happened to everyone in the auditorium, and the whole audience journeyed underground with two of the characters from the play, and once down they overcame the evil King, blew up his castle and freed the cave people, and at last escaped back up to the surface. The play was followed up in the Primary schools during the spring term of 1971.

The Junior work had developed away from an emphasis on legend to a concentration upon social history. History proved to be a major stimulus for interest and follow-up work in the classroom and offered the pupils a world of adventures, storming of castles, and drilling as soldiers, which was close to their own world of play. History became alive as its events took place there and then, and it was no longer a world of Kings and Queens but of ordinary people. The format of beginning in the classroom and coming to the hall worked well, as it provided a contact and preliminary teaching session for facts and skills. However, more work was expected of the teacher in the filling in of historical details. Without these the programmes would have become isolated adventures.

The development of the drama advisory role where help and advice were given in the context of a series of projects was a major step forward. For the teachers could see how material could be used dramatically in the classroom, and at the workshop sessions with the team they experienced the process themselves.

In both the historical and drama project work the company began to involve the pupils in decision-making. In "The Lunt Fort at Baginton" the pupils, as either Romans or Celts, must decide how to respond to the news of Boudicca's defeat and her consequent suicide. The pupils are asked to help form and change events. They are no longer treated as passengers in the programmes but become active participants with a real purpose. In this, as well as in the use of social history, the Junior work can be seen to be developing with the Secondary work. The one contributing to the other.

The work in Children's Theatre for the Junior age group was a real breakthrough. For the application of the techniques and ideas used in the classroom into a play in a theatre setting gave Children's Theatre a whole new meaning and form of contact with its audience. The work was based on sound research with the audience. Like a programme in a school all the "audience" were part of the action: they were essential to it. Unlike many Children's Theatre plays where the audience were expected to sit and watch as outsiders, here, they were to experience as participants, although physically they remained in their seats. This was a basic, and most important change of approach, and one that was to lead to some very exciting Children's Theatre work by later Coventry teams. Essential to this was the use of the theatre itself: no longer an auditorium, the whole place was transformed (not necessarily physically). In the imaginations of the audience their seats were part of that action on the stage, they were *inside* the environment of the action, not *outside* it.

Secondary Programmes

Rather like the Junior programmes the work for Secondary schools began to develop in two definite areas — creative drama and theatre. For the theatre-orientated work the company began to link their presentations to the work of the Belgrade, and the techniques of the actor.

The Secondary programme of the autumn of 1966 was "The Actor and his Work", and used acting exercises, a performance of Chekhov's "The Bear", and discussion or improvisation with the audience. As a result of this programme going into schools, fourteen Secondary schools brought parties to the Belgrade Theatre to see "Cyrano de Bergerac". When the Theatre were performing the 'O' Level text "Julius Caesar" in the same term the TIE team organized two morning lectures for schools, about the theatre and the play.

This kind of liaison was further developed in autumn 1967 with the TIE team's three-part programme devised in conjunction with the production of Brecht's "Mother Courage" at the Belgrade. The three parts of the TIE programme consisted of an improvisation session first, to explore the way war affected people. The second part was the school's visit to a performance of "Mother Courage" at the theatre and the third part was further improvisations followed by a presentation, by the team, about the experience of the German nation during Brecht's own lifetime using documentary material. This method of approach did certainly help in the pupil's enjoyment and understanding of "Mother Courage":

> The improvisation sessions held before the theatre visit were felt by teachers to have created a receptiveness to the theatre among pupils, many of whom had no previous experience of it. There was an atmosphere of anticipation during the performances which rose because of it.
>
> The follow up presented Brecht as a man deeply concerned about the problems of mankind as he experienced them, and served to counteract the feelings pupils sometimes have that authors write for no particular reason but to perplex them. The work on the Second World War also linked theatre and modern history studies.[24]

Thus, the company took a play that was relevant to the pupils, and used this as a centre of their project. They linked, therefore, the experience of theatre with the ideas that the play had to offer, and clarified these through drama and documentary. They did not attempt to explain the play, or how it should be performed.

When the Belgrade Theatre presented "The Daughter in Law" in 1969 the company used this occasion to take a recital programme to Fifth and Sixth years in schools to stimulate an interest in D. H. Lawrence. Were the company then, working as salesmen for the theatre? This was certainly not stated as one of their aims. The team were aware of the value of theatre for the older Secondary pupils and they realized that their policy of using ideas and drama methods to stimulate thought, and question concepts, could be aided by the use of a suitable play that was being presented in the Belgrade.

The TIE team also used one-act plays to stimulate work in schools. The presentation of Alan Plater's "Excursion" to the Upper Secondary group in summer 1967 was to stimulate an interest in perceptive and skilful script writing. In the 1968–9 season the same format was followed with a presentation of Alan Plater's "The What on the Landing". This was preceded by improvisation with the pupils and the aim of the programme (stated in the 1968–9 Report) was "to encourage a critical awareness among pupils, especially those about to leave school, of the problems of communications in the life and work of an urban society". This was actually the subject of an

International Conference being held in Coventry at the time.

These programmes made use of theatre pieces to stimulate and question. The performance of a play was linked to a discussion or a drama session, or both, so that the ideas in the play could be pin-pointed and explored further. On the creative drama side, the use of historical material developed along the lines of the Junior work. The team presented the story of "The Great Fire of London" (spring 1967) to second and third years in the familiar format of teaching in the classroom first, conveying the historical background and involving the pupils in group improvisations on the life of the times. This teaching session was actually done in pairs as a team-teaching project. During the second hour the classes went to the hall and the story was enacted with the actors in contemporary costume and with the use of sound, lights and slides, but allowing for creative improvisation by the pupils. The programme was aimed at stimulating work in many areas, and did produce considerable follow-up work in English, Drama and history lessons. However, the project did raise some difficulties, that were representative of the difference between the Junior and Secondary school situation. Teachers pointed out that:

> The organisation of a project with a drama bias might present timetable difficulties and it was agreed that it would be valuable to investigate more closely the possibility of future visits, planned in direct collaboration with teachers and developed in conjunction with the school syllabus.[25]

To try and stimulate cross-curricular projects the team presented another historical documentary in the spring of 1968. "If it was not for the Weaver" dealt with local history to bring the effects of industrialization closer to the pupils by providing them with opportunities in that period of history. An aim similar to those for the Junior history programmes. In the Secondary schools the actual teaching programme, which introduced the subject, was divided between the company and the school departments and was extended over several weeks. Through improvised drama the pupils learnt about the life of the silk ribbon weaver in the early part of the nineteenth century and how life changed with the collapse of the trade. The pupils were asked to assume the characters of the weaving community during this time of strife and poverty. The project consisted of a whole day in school and, as in the Junior programmes, the team worked with classes in the morning. This time there were four classes taking different roles, two classes as cottage weavers and two classes as factory workers. In the afternoon the pupils watched a performance of the documentary on the weaver and were included in the crowd scenes. Although the programme was very successful from the point of view of the pupil's interest, involvement and contribution, it was not so effective as an integrated project in the schools. Over fifty teachers attended the introductory workshop sessions, but later, many staff found that

FIG. 5. Coventry TIE, "If it was not for the Weaver", 1969.
Morning session, pupils' improvisation.

timetable difficulties, examination syllabuses and problems of communications between departments in large schools prevented the project being
undertaken in any depth by more than one department.

So, although the company had introduced cross-curricular work into the
Secondary school, the reception and use of the programmes were limited by
the structure of the school timetabling and methods of work. Whereas in
Junior schools this type of history programme proved an excellent vehicle for
stimulus in all areas.

In 1969 the company changed the nature of their Secondary work. The
beginning of this change could be seen in "If it was not for the Weaver", in
the relating of the pupils to the working-out of the theme of the programme,
and in demanding that they make decisions during the course of the events.
This area of decision-making became of increasing importance, and formed
the purpose of the programme rather than being peripheral. The change in
the nature of the Secondary work marks the ability of the team to handle
social and political themes and to devise a format within which the pupils
could be led to some social and political awareness. This format allowed the

FIG. 6. Afternoon session, the play.

pupils to discuss their experiences within the imaginative context created by the programme. It introduced the pupils to an element of role-play, so that they could use these roles to enable them to understand and express different view points on the subject and begin to ask questions. The pupils were not involved in free improvisation, or the kind of creative drama sessions of some of the Junior work. This change of approach moved the company into the area of Games and Simulations, which was a method little used in Secondary schools in Britain at the time. This area of simulation, involving the pupils in decision-making, was part of the increasing awareness of the importance of pupil-centred education developing during this period.

The idea for the first TIE programme of this kind stemmed from the Belgrade's production of John Arden's play "Live Like Pigs". The team decided to do a programme based on this play for the CSE group who were about to leave school. Instead of using the play, and holding a discussion or drama session afterwards, the TIE team decided to research the theme itself: the unsocial behaviour of a family in a council house. The team began their research by asking social workers and council officials for their views on the quality of life on the housing estates in Coventry. They also began to find out how local government operates. They felt that the play "Live Like Pigs" had a lot to say to young people about the degree of conformity society demands, and it certainly had a strong impact on the CSE groups who saw it. From these various factors the team worked out their aims and then their programme.

"People Matter More than Plans, Councillor Kean"   *Summer 1969*

We felt strongly that given the opportunity young people could and should want a voice in the way their community is run. This did not mean a lecture on civic administration but an experience. Our aim became to place them firmly in the midst of a community problem and let them have the opportunity to talk their way out of it if they could.

The Drama session

The four of us . . . worked with sixty CSE pupils for a half-day session. We used the Belgrade small Studio Theatre and three working spaces.

We devised a composite community STOKE HILL WOOD and sixty inhabitants varying in age and social background. This was to be the 'text' which we would ask them to bring to life and explore. The sequence is therefore structured until a crises overtakes the community when the pupils are free to cope with it as they wish.

The first stage is to arouse interest in Stoke Hill Wood and for the pupils to identify their roles within it. As they arrive they are given lapel badges — e.g. Mrs. Baker, Station Close; Mr. Thomas, Lime Lane. The chairs are set out for a meeting.

Stuart Bennett begins as chairman, "Ladies and Gentlemen, you will be pleased to hear that our newly-elected councillor, Councillor Kean, has given up some of his precious time to come and talk to you".

"Thank you, Mr. Chairman. With the aid of photographs I should like to show the people of Stoke Hill Wood some of the splendid things to be found in our locality. I call my talk "Know your own".

Colin White, as Councillor Kean, delivers a short, humorous lantern lecture. We see large council houses on Stoke Grove Road, smaller ones on Stoke Terrace, private property in Lime Lane, and old terraced cottages in Station Close.

The audience is then divided. What kind of people live in these houses? We are about to find out. Judith takes Stoke Grove Road; Rosemary Stoke Terrace; Colin Lime Lane; Stuart Station Close.

Each of us works separately. There are four families in each group and each is given a family card.

When they have identified themselves each family is given the beginning of a domestic situation, e.g. The Baker family are overcrowded — should Gran, who has lived in the house since her marriage, go into a home? Amongst other situations are being put on short time, a young married couple living with in-laws, illness, parental strictness, keeping up with the neighbours, retirement and the generation gap.

The aim at this point is to create an awareness of each character in a family setting. Each family is only expected to improvise a simple moment as this is their first creative work in the session.

The next step is to place the families in their neighbourhood. Something has happened in the street which could affect each family. In Station Close a child is injured playing in the derelict houses opposite . . . What can they do? On the council estate parked cars have been scratched by vandals. Buses are left standing at the terminus with their engines running late at night. Some of the residents of Lime Lane propose that their road is adopted. Each group explores the issue as they decide.

Individuals call on individuals, or groups improvise street discussions.

They begin to use the information established in the family scenes. Age, income, responsibilities, affect reactions to the street problem. Although there may be a general demand for action, not all can or will respond.

At this half-way point, which took 60–70 minutes, the pupils have given some extension to their basic characters and some have organised protests. Simple democratic action has emerged.

In the second part of the session we take Stoke Hill Wood out for the evening. Those taking part regroup. Those under 20 (in their roles) go to a youth club. Those over 60 to the Good Companions Club. The younger married couples to the Football dance. The older couples to the Social Club. We consult the map. Each of these clubs meets in a building in the Recreation Area.

We organise a further improvised session. What kind of activity would people of each age range pursue? Those in the Social Club, for example, might suggest a bar, raffles, darts or dominoes, bingo and gossip. Each group improvises the appropriate activities separately. When they are well established the radio (i.e. the tape recorder) is switched on.

"This is Midlands Focus. A report on redevelopment at Stoke Hill Wood with an interview with Councillor Kean."

Each club learns that the building they are in is to be pulled down and the football pitch built on. Kean will give further details at a public meeting. The council believe in giving the people what they want.

By now they have made the imaginary town their own, and it is natural for indignation to break out.

We return to the auditorium. Colin White resumes the role of the now controversial Councillor Kean. He is greeted with a response varying from a chant of "Hands off the Football Club" to polite applause.

The Chairman asks for the club spokesmen to state their points of view. "I'm Mrs. Jones and I've been going to the Good Companions for nearly ten years. If it's pulled down what are we old folks supposed to do? We meet our friends there. We have whist drives and social evenings. It's the only place for us to go". She is given warm support.

Representatives from the other clubs are given a chance to speak. Then Councillor Kean is asked to explain the plan. He refers to a map with the redevelopment areas coloured.

"As you will know the council intends to develop Stoke Hill Wood. For this we need money which we propose to raise by selling the land now occupied by the football pitch and the huts to private development, as a site for office blocks. This will bring business and employment to the area. The revenue will be sufficient to finance a limited project. The old school and chapel will be demolished. The council have had to decide on their priority and their decision is that the best plan is to invest in Youth. A Youth centre will be erected as soon as the site is clear."

The meeting is now thrown open. It is improvised (that is to say the words are spontaneous and not scripted). It relates to something specific (the development map) and there is an emotional motivation (the pupils in their roles, care about the loss of their amenities). The situation has an internal dynamic which will carry it forward unassisted.

There may be a storm of protest or a respectful concentration. Whoever speaks now expresses what he feels or sees. "You're selling our land" — "You could develop land on the outskirts and leave the recreation area" — "Why haven't we been consulted?"

Kean's defence is that revenue has to be raised. The alternative is to raise the rates. Are they prepared for that? Perhaps Stoke Hill Wood will not let him off the hook though. Questions may be asked about Kean's financial interest.

If they allow him his point about raising the rates they must think again. "Then we don't want to be developed. Leave us alone."

The council's proposal is to use the revenue to finance a Youth Club. What is the meeting's priority, youth, football, social club, old people? Again the people may deny that there should be a choice.

If so, and the community feels it deserves more than this piecemeal effort, someone may propose to organise fund-raising efforts to build a proper Community Centre for Stoke Hill Wood. Or they may insist it is the council's job to provide everything.

The neighbourhood problems had possible solutions but the development issue was concerned with means and priorities. Teachers felt that pupils reflected parental attitudes and the session tested these attitudes. Those who had done drama before readily brought Stoke Hill Wood to life. The reaction of those to whom it was a first experience of drama varied. Some found the badges and cards "silly", others used them as a mask to advance attitudes they were not confident about.

. . . Our first aim was to organise an enjoyable drama session, our second to stimulate an awareness of how the individual relates to society.

We suggested questions — not answers — though possibly we suggested that there may be answers and you, the individual, could have a say in them. The results of our first aim were easy to assess, not so our second.[26]

Unlike the historical programmes the situation was fictional and the pupils were asked to create characters out of everyday life. They had to play inside a situation that could happen to them as part of a community. For the pupils to learn and participate properly it was essential that they gained a sense of personal identity with the characters they created and the imaginary area of Stoke Hill Wood. With an emotional involvement and personal identification the removal of the social facilities and the problems raised created a genuine need in the pupils to protest, argue and generally articulate a point of view. That this attitude was not necessarily theirs, and that they were forced to consider several different solutions to the problem, meant that they were involved in an experience through which they could discover and come to understand various character's attitudes and the difficulty of planning for a community. The pupils have been involved in a simulation:

Because it is a way of learning that excels the traditional and pseudo-modern methods of communication, simulation is a process that involves the participant in decision-making, often under emotional conditons that intensify his motivation.[27]

It is interesting to note that there was some reserve amongst pupils who had never done drama before, indicating that even such immediate subjects may require some basic understanding of role-play before being successful.

The next Secondary programme was also a simulation but this time on African politics rather than local ones. "The Emergent Africa Game" played in schools to fourth, fifth and sixth years, and involved them by means of discussion. The theme of the programme was a new state in Africa, and the decisions that the Prime Minister of this state had to take, such as "What is the new nation's first priority?" Within this structure the pupils did not change the course of the action very much, but it allowed them to fully discuss the questions raised and involved them in some improvisation. In these particular programmes the team had found a remarkably successful form of conveying facts and opening up discussions within the Secondary school situation.

By 1970 it can be seen that the Coventry team's work had developed in a series of stages. The first stage being that of making the scheme known to teachers and to adapt their work to the activity and the syllabus in the schools, and the limitation of the buildings. At this stage the subjects of the programme were still based upon fantasy, legend and myth, or a play being presented in the Belgrade Theatre. Areas that were, to a certain extent, tried and tested by BBC radio schools programmes, by Brian Way and Peter Slade.

The second stage could only begin when the company could "arrive in school knowing we would not meet with any misconceptions". Once this very important stage was established the work could develop:

> The work expands in two ways. We would hold a day course for teachers before we went out and follow-up sessions for them after the visit. This was basic to the concept of the work we had developed. Our aim was to provide a meaningful experience for the children but to leave a teacher stimulated to continue with the work. The projects began in the classroom using the resources of a drama teacher to create a situation in which all the pupils had a role of their own. The sequence then moved to the hall where the resources of the actors extended the situation and provided a vivid experience. The class teacher could continue the activity after our visit using his own methods.[28]

This statement by Stuart Bennett sums up quite clearly the way of working that the company had built up over the years. A way that related strongly to the teacher and the pupil in a school situation, and provided an experience through which the pupils could learn, and be motivated to pursue the subject. For the teachers it was both a resource and a constant source of stimulus on drama methods, and techniques of working with pupils.

This much greater co-operation with teachers produced a change in the work. In the Junior programmes the team introduced history and geography themes, belonging to the "real" world. They loosened the structure of the programmes considerably to involve the pupils both physically and emotionally. This approach was also tried in the Secondary work with the social history themes of "The Great Fire of London", and "If it was not for the Weaver", and in the Infant area with the Noah project and "The Mysterious Wanderers", the programme about gypsies.

The third stage developed when the company were sufficiently established and confident about their work that they could begin to theorize, examine and critically assess the methods developed. Thus, the team were able to ask, after the Stoke Hill Wood Programme, whether drama should have a structure:

> The topic material suggested the shape of the project to us. Perhaps the question is, has the structure become an end in itself or is it a framework inside which creative thought can emerge?[29]

Other methods and techniques came under the same scrutiny: the best method of working with infants; the nature of participation; the way of dealing with family grouping; how to work as both actor and teacher; how to create the pupil's sense of personal identity and so on.

By this stage the team had pushed their work much further and linked it more closely with the developments in education: such developments as the pupil-centred approach; the concentration upon the importance of the pupil's personal discovery in learning, and the pupil's ability to articulate these discoveries.

The programmes became much more adventurous: the unstructured Infant work, the social history projects for Juniors and the use of the simulation game for Secondary pupils. Whilst pushing the work forward in educational terms, the team did not neglect the importance of the use of theatre and began to integrate this within their programmes more thoroughly.

By the time Stuart Bennett left in 1972 the Coventry team had established a very definite approach to the work, which effected the work of many other teams. The Coventry company tried to combine suitable theatre and teaching techniques with the progressive developments in education and drama and to constantly assess the effect of their work in the schools. They built up a good system of collaboration with the teachers, so that the work could be understood and properly used. The teams were committed to the work, and this is reflected not only in their attitude to its development but also in their length of stay. This gave the team continuity, a very important factor that was greatly helped by the system that developed of taking the new director from the TIE team itself and not bringing in someone from outside.

When Stuart Bennett left David Pammenter took over. He had been in the team since 1969. The work moved to a new stage. The work is essentially fluid, developing and changing according to the interaction of the Director, the team, the teachers and pupils and the political and social state of the country. Just as Stuart Bennett had begun by establishing certain points:

> A group of people define an aim, devise material to communicate that aim, then present the project using drama and theatre skills. It's advantage is that it can develop original material suitable for the needs of its area and relate to particular types of local school organisation.[30]

so did David Pammenter:

> Theatre in Education is a theatre company which defines an aim and
> then devises a programme, a structure, a method of achieving that aim,
> involving the interaction of the actor and the pupil.[31]

There was a great deal of continuity in the nature of the work when David
Pammenter took over. It did shift slightly towards more theatrical elements,
as his definition suggests. The company began to use more technical aids,
like inflatables, settings, complicated sound tapes, and to concentrate far less
on the drama sessions. The company ceased to offer teachers practical drama
help in the form of such programmes as "Noah". However, by 1972 more
teachers were aware how to use drama in the school and drama teachers were
being appointed. The company used three-part presentations but these were
often three facets of the same subject in presentation form, not via a drama-
teaching lesson.

Obvious changes were the concentration on socio-political problems and a
shift to realistic situations in almost all the programmes. This attitude to
subject-matter did produce some very well-known and successful TIE
programmes such as "Rare Earth", dealing with environmental pollution.
Although the nature of the programmes became more realistic, their aims
were often more general than before. The aim for the Infant programme
"Ugly's Trust Abused" was "to involve the children in practical problems of
trickery and trust". The most obvious change came in company structure.
David Pammenter changed this from a hierarchical or pyramid structure
(which had allowed for a great deal of "worker consultation") to a democratic
unit, introducing equal pay and responsibility. As directors and teams change
the work at Coventry shifts in emphasis, but it has never changed its basic
function.

It was in Coventry that the concept of Theatre in Education developed.
The methods, techniques, approach, philosophy, personnel and programmes have spread out to other teams, influencing the whole area of
Young People's Theatre, and setting the pattern for a new and exciting
method of work.

Notes

Much of the information in this chapter is based on the Belgrade TIE teams' Annual Reports
and personal interviews with Gordon Vallins, Stuart Bennett and David Pammenter.

Since the writing of this chapter, Gordon Vallins has summarized his period at Coventry in
Learning Through Theatre, editor: Tony Jackson, Manchester University Press, 1980, pp. 2–15.

1. Gordon Vallins, personal interview, 13th June 1978, at South Warwickshire College of
   Further Education.
2. "Coventry sets the stage", *Plays and Players*, May 1958, p. 9.
3. Gordon Vallins, *Theatre in Education* II, October 1964, p. 1.

4. Gordon Vallins, personal interview, 13th June 1978.
5. Gordon Vallins, General Notes, July 1965.
6. Gordon Vallins, personal interview, 13th June 1978.
7. Gordon Vallins, Coventry TIE Interim Report, End of 2nd Tour, Nov./Dec. 1965, p. 1.
8. Gordon Vallins, personal interview, 13th June 1978.
9. Gordon Vallins, Coventry TIE Interim Report, end of 1st Tour, 1965, p. 1.
10. Gordon Vallins, Coventry TIE Interim Report, end of 2nd Tour, 1965, p. 1.
11. Coventry TIE Report on Drama in North Coventry Schools, Spring 1966, p. 2.
12. Gordon Vallins, Coventry TIE Interim Report, end of 1st Tour, 1965, p. 3.
13. Gordon Vallins, Interim Report, end of 2nd Tour, 1965, p. 2.
14. Gordon Vallins, Interim Report, end of 2nd Tour, 1966, p. 4.
15. Gordon Vallins, Appendix to Interim Report, end of 2nd Tour, 6th Jan. 1966.
16. Gordon Vallins, Interim Report, End of 2nd Tour, p. 4.
17. Stuart Bennett, Coventry TIE, "Belgrade's Bones" Annual Report, 1969–70, p. 4.
18. *Op. cit.*, p. 6.
19. Stuart Bennett, "Belgrade's Bones", 1969–70, pp. 7–8.
20. Stuart Bennett, "Belgrade's Bones", 1969–70, p. 11.
21. *Op. cit.*, p. 13.
22. Rosemary Birbeck, Coventry TIE Annual Report, 1968–9, p. 10.
23. *Ibid.*
24. Rosemary Birbeck, Coventry TIE Annual Report, 1967–8, p. 4.
25. Rosemary Birbeck, Annual Report, 1966–7, p. 5.
26. Stuart Bennett, "Belgrade's Bones", 1969–70, pp. 21–24.
27. Samuel Broadbelt, "Simulation in the Social Studies: An overview", *Social Education*, February 1969, p. 177.
28. Stuart Bennett, "Belgrade's Bones", 1969–70, p. 5.
29. *Op. cit.*, p. 24.
30. *Op. cit.*, p. 6.
31. David Pammenter, Coventry TIE, 1972–3, p. 3.

Chapter 3

The Development of Young People's Theatre

One of the most important factors in the development of Young People's Theatre and therefore of TIE was the changing policy of the Arts Council:

> When the Arts Council originally elected, as a matter of policy, to exclude Children's Theatre from its circle of beneficiaries, it unconsciously set a pattern which has influenced the development of theatre for young people ever since.[1]

In those early days the Arts Council of Great Britain had little money available for subsidy and they hoped that in the area of Theatre for young people that the Education Authorities might help. However, aid of this kind was rare, and virtually absent on any full and continuous basis. Authorities such as Glasgow and Nottingham did give small sums of money, but they were the exception.

Most of the Children's Theatre companies working in the 1950s survived by box-office takings, charitable trusts such as the Gulbenkian and the Nuffield and a great deal of hard work on little pay. Due to this lack of support, wages were very low, and Children's Theatre had a poor image.

In contrast, Children's Theatre abroad in the 1950s was often accorded a high degree of importance and received direct and substantial grants. For instance, in 1952 Denmark was running the Dansk Skolescene in Copenhagen. An organization consisting of five sections that were financially independent of each other: The Copenhagen School Theatre, The School Cinema, The Provincial School Theatre, The Amager Cinema, and the School Theatre House. The Copenhagen School Theatre played to the 11–16-age range with a repertory of classical and modern works performed by professional actors. It was funded partly by a subsidy from the Municipality of 20,000 crowns and partly by children's subscriptions. The Theatre's educational and artistic policy was entrusted to a committee of fifteen members chosen by the Management of the Teacher's Association.

Nothing like this existed in Britain, and the need for some kind of subsidy was obvious. Brian Way, Caryl Jenner and John English began a long campaign to gain grant aiding. Their fight was helped by the impetus that Jennie Lee gave when she became Minister for the Arts, but what finally triggered the Arts Council into action was the Federation of Repertory Playgoers Societies. In 1963 they passed a resolution urging the Arts Council and the Education Authorities "to explore methods of supporting and encouraging professional theatre performances for children, including the very young".[2] This resolution was brought to the attention of the Arts Council and discussion followed. Finally, the Arts Council Drama Panel recommended the setting up of a Committee of enquiry, and in March 1965 the committee was formed with the following terms of reference:

> To enquire into the present provision of theatre for children and young people in the widest terms to make recommendations for future development and in particular to advise on the participation of the Arts Council in such work.[3]

When the Committee began work it realized the magnitude of the task, but they finally resolved to divide the Enquiry's work into three phases, investigating first the existing professional Children's Theatre companies and then the work being carried out for young people by repertory and other professional adult companies. The third phase was to look at the wider field of Drama in Education, which eventually became a separate report issued by the Department of Education and Science.

In the first section the committee found twelve professional Children's Theatre companies in operation in May 1965. They were:

Arion Children's Theatre Company
British Dance/Drama Theatre
C.W.M. Productions
Liverpool Everyman Theatre Company
Osiris Repertory Company
Scottish Children's Theatre (Bertha Waddell)
Southern Children's Theatre
Theatre Centre (Brian Way)
Theatre for Youth (Argyle Theatre, Birkenhead)
Unicorn Theatre for Children (Caryl Jenner)
Welsh Children's Theatre Company
Westminster Children's Theatre

These companies presented plays in schools and other centres, and managed, between them, to give one visit per year to approximately a quarter of the school population. They received fees from the schools or the Local Education Authorities, which varied from £150 to £240 for a week of eight to ten performances. The wage for a company member was about £10 to £15 a week. The Equity minimum being £10 which was more than £4 lower than a teacher's starting salary on the Burnham scale. For most of the companies the result was overwork, a high turnover of people, and low standards. Standards which the Committee felt to be below the level of work which it considered should be offered to young people.

The Arts Council investigated these twelve companies and decided that five of them should be given grants if funds could be made available. This decision was reached because the Committee believed that there were special potentialities in this group which even a small increase in funds may help to be realized:

> The Committee considers that these five (whether old or newly established) could be growing points whose progress can be watched. Any development which is to come must make use of the experience and skills gained in the past — long thought and study, administrative skill and knowledge of the field here and abroad all coming from years of effort.[4]

To actually fund these five companies for 1966–7 the Arts Council agreed to use the Drama Contingencies Fund, as there was no special allocation made available by the DES. It was, in the term's of the Arts Council Annual Report, a life-saving operation.

The Committee noted the work in Theatre in education at Coventry and saw it as related to the development of Drama in Education in schools. In reviewing the work for young people by the other repertory theatres the committee came to some important conclusions. They felt that many theatres would benefit very considerably in their work with young people if they could appoint someone who devoted a lot of time to the organization of activities for them and who could establish contact with schools, Institutes of Further Education and Local Education Authorities. The committee recommended that money should be made available for regional repertories to make this kind of appointment. They also recommended that money should be available for the theatres to establish a second company to play to young people both in the home theatre and in the surrounding area. It was felt that these companies should be permanent and should use actors from the main company, and that ideally these second companies should not tour schools. They should go to theatres where they exist and to well-equipped halls, to present a number of performances in one place and book schools to visit this centre.

From these kind of recommendations it is clear that the committee were thinking in terms of theatre performances not Theatre in Education work as developed by the Coventry team. What the committee or indeed the Arts Council did not do, was to define the exact nature of the work for young people which would be eligible for grants. The decision was just that a fund should be set aside for the future needs of the companies that were starting young people's work.

The special allocation was £90,000, approved by the Department of

Education and Science and to be applied specifically for expenditure in the field of Theatre for Young People. The Arts Council established a Young People's Theatre Panel to advise the Council on the allocation of this money. The Panel consisted of a mixture of people from education and drama, and the combination proved a very useful and unique group:

> This friendly confrontation combined with a close and critical interest in the matters under discussion has already germinated ideas of the greatest value to the Arts Council.[5]

Although the policy of the Arts Council is that it responds to initiative, it does not initiate, the policy of allocating a sum of money for the development of Young People's Theatre definitely initiated work. The Arts Council asked the subsidized repertory theatres to include estimates for any Children's Theatre, or youth work, that they wanted to develop for the forthcoming year, and the theatres responded well. The Arts Council report had noted a determination to go ahead on the part of the repertory theatres and in many places the Local Education Authority was offering cooperation and financial support, and even where this was not forthcoming some theatres had organized activities without any special provision of either staff or finance in the belief that it was work that should be done.

When the Arts Council offered funding for Young People's Theatre work they did expect the Theatre to request support from the Local Education Authority. The Arts Council were eager to help schemes get off the ground but they were not willing to be the only organization financially supporting the work. The late 1960s and early 1970s was a time of expansion and booming economy. The Local Education Authorities found the funds to support new schemes, and they came to play a major role in funding Young People's Theatre.

As a result of the invitation by the Arts Council many repertory theatres applied for grants to begin or continue their work with young people (see Appendix A). However, not all of them sustained the work over the years, and some dropped the grant applications. The work varied enormously in range and standard, often depending entirely for its direction on the person employed to develop the activities.

The Arts Council recognized that the sudden upsurge in activities for young people could present problems and at the first meeting of the Young People's Section of CORT (Council of Repertory Theatres) Caryl Jenner read out the following statement from the Drama Director of the Arts Council:

> The admirable enthusiasm which now appears to be sweeping the country over the promotion of theatre activities for young people seems, in certain cases, to be in some danger of out-stripping the standard of artistic achievement. In this first vital year of subsidised

children's theatre, it is vital that this work should be of the highest quality and at the very least equal to what is presented for adults. If this standard cannot be achieved, it is surely better to wait until it can be, rather than risk giving young people a poor introduction to the theatre? First impressions are enormously important, and this of course applies not only to the children, but also to teachers and educationalists. If the latter find their pupils being offered work of indifferent quality, it may do irreperable damage to the whole movement. We would rather one of our beneficiaries told us they were postponing their plans for young people's theatre activities than that they should launch a scheme the standards of which were second rate. It is improbable that anyone will disagree with this but, from what we have heard, it seems to be necessary to utter the warning.[6]

This poor-quality work was often the result of inexperience. The lack of experience amongst those initiating or running schemes is, perhaps, not very surprising. Where, after all, were they to have gained experience? Theatre directors themselves knew little of the work, and it is doubtful that many had seen the Coventry team. Where were the Theatre directors to look for suitable personnel? Very few Children's Theatre companies existed, Coventry was only just established, and there were few trained team members there. Drama teaching was developing, but teachers did not necessarily have any theatre experience. John Allen at this Young People's Theatre Section (YPTS) meeting in 1967 underlined the dangers of lack of expertise in dealing with young people, particularly when holding discussions with them. He felt that there was a need for a longer conference or indeed a special course about the work to broaden people's knowledge.

During discussions at this meeting certain pertinent problems were raised: the need for co-operation and liaison between all members of CORT working in Theatre for Young People; the overlapping of different types of work for young people should not be avoided, a variety of experience was valuable. Liaison between the specialist companies and the repertory companies was important in promoting a greater understanding of the importance of theatre for young people in the profession generally. There were companies with low standards of work and companies who "pirated" bookings, that is companies who encroached on to an established company's area without informing them, and gained school bookings that would normally have been given to the established team. Of these points two have been achieved, but the last three still present problems. The theatre profession still finds it difficult to accept work with young people as of the same importance and quality as adult theatre work, there are still Children's Theatre companies of low standards, who pirate bookings; most of these work commercially and do not receive any subsidies.

In spite of lack of experience, the enthusiasm produced a prodigious quantity of work. In 1967 Bolton, Bristol Old Vic, Canterbury, Chesterfield, Coventry, Dundee, Exeter, Farnham, Glasgow, Ipswich, Leicester, Lincoln, Liverpool Everyman, Salisbury and Watford were planning or had begun some kind of work with young people. By 1973, however, well over half of the regional repertory theatres in Britain were doing some kind of work in schools.

Much of the early touring work to schools used established scripts, by people like Brian Way or Caryl Jenner, and were performance-based. The tours were often intermittent and on a one-off, flying-visit system, which meant there was no close liaison with the schools. For instance, Colchester took out a group of four actors from the main company in February of 1969 to visit Infant and Junior schools. The plays to be performed were: "Caradoc the Cat" by Allen Cullen, "Feathertop" by Wilfred Harvey, and "The Mirror Man" by Brian Way. Not all the tours were of children's plays, some were devised by the director on local themes, or the history of the theatre, and some were back to the old faithful — Shakespeare. In Dundee in 1968:

> A director and one or two actors and actresses would come to a school, and using the class members, approach a key scene from a play being studied for exams, employ professional theatre rehearsal methods to bring alive what is so often for children a dull and dusty academic text, as a piece of living drama about real people.[7]

There was no common factor linking any of these presentations, other than the fact they were to be taken into schools. They varied in subject-matter from the most frivolous to the educationally serious, and in presentation from the most entertaining to the very dull.

There developed from these early beginnings a mass of different aims and approaches. Two examples of this are the Flying Phoenix company attached to the Phoenix Theatre in Leicester, and a scheme at the Gateway, Chester. The Flying Phoenix was formed in 1967, but by 1969 was still suffering under financial difficulties. It received a grant of £1500 from the Arts Council and additional income from the Leicestershire County Council Education Department which paid the team as part-time teachers, for the sessions provided in country schools. However, this meant that the team were on a lower rate than full-time teachers and a lower wage than the theatre's company of actors. At that time the Leicester City Education Department was not giving any money, so the company required subsidy from the theatre's funds. However, the nature of the work developed was closely linked to the schools and to drama in education:

> The Flying Phoenix does not present a scripted play in a school. Through the means of a series of drama workshops the team helps to

create an environment in which the child may develop imaginatively
and individually through play and experiment.[8]

The method was that the child, not the actor, created the play, but to
stimulate work the team drew up various projects which they printed and
sent in advance to teachers concerned with drama, to allow for some
preparation. Examples of the kind of subjects they used are "Pirates" and
"Senses".

The company also acted in the main theatre at times, but in fact the scheme
was a stimulus for drama in education in the school: it was not a theatre-based
presentation approach. Over time the company's work changed, but in 1969
it had a specific educational aim.

In contrast the Gateway Chester set up a pilot scheme in 1972 for a period
of 13 weeks to "provide a foundation of fact rather than speculation,
considering a full-time theatre in education programme". In 13 weeks this is
a difficult undertaking, and Peter Leech comments on the team's inexperience: "The programmes that were presented were the result of a combination
of theory, idealism, ignorance and compromise rather than of knowledge and
experience."[9] The types of programme were theatre-based but were aimed to
link with school curriculum, and to be of use to teachers. For the Secondary
schools various scenes of *Julius Caesar* were presented to 'O' Level English
Literature pupils to examine the text as something to be performed. Then the
company performed a selection of extracts from Modern Drama (Osborne,
Wesker, etc.) for sixth-formers and a programme called "What is theatre?" to
stimulate an interest in theatre among the less academic pupils. The Infant
programme consisted of a variety of items, songs, stories, etc., and the Junior
programme developed into a drama workshop.

There is an obvious difference in approach between these two companies.
One firmly based on theatre (The Gateway scheme), presenting plays which
are of use to schools; whereas the Flying Phoenix company aimed at
stimulating drama in schools. Theatre in Education can in fact cover this
whole spectrum.

There were very specific reasons why schemes took on a particular
approach to the work. The emphasis on theatre, which occurred in some
companies, was often there right from the inception of the scheme, and had a
real influence on the nature of the work. Almost every aspect was affected:
the form of presentation and relationship with the pupils, the method of work
both in rehearsal and in performance, company structure, terms of contract
and so on. The Citizens' Theatre for Youth Company provides an example of
the development of a theatre-orientated Young People's Theatre scheme.[10]

The scheme at the Citizens' Theatre began because the theatre responded
to the Arts Council's offer of grant aiding for young people's work. In 1967
the Directors of the theatre (Michael Meacham and Michael Blakemore)

asked the Theatre Board to consider the application for a one-year grant to employ someone to explore the possibilities of starting a "Theatre for Youth" Scheme. The application was sent in, and the Arts Council made a grant to the Theatre. The exploratory year showed that there was a real demand for such a scheme amongst the local schools, and that the Local Authorities might be prepared to offer grants.

At the beginning of the new season in September 1968 the company was properly funded by the Scottish Arts Council and the Local Education Authorities, plus £1500 from the newly founded Duncan Macrae Memorial Trust. The money from the Glasgow Education Authority was a direct transfer of the sum given to Bertha Waddell and her Scottish Children's Theatre, first granted in 1937. When Bertha Waddell retired in 1968 and her company ceased to function, the Citizen's Theatre for Youth became the recipient of the grant aiding that she had fought so hard to receive.

The full scheme got under way in 1968 based on certain policy decisions. The programmes should be free for schools. The company should visit Secondary schools, not Primary, within a 20-mile radius of the city. These decisions were the result of discussions with teachers, and with various Advisers in the Education Offices, particularly the Drama Adviser, Miss McKechnie.

The reason for the choice of Secondary schools only was the vast number of schools within the city boundary — over 200 Primary schools and nearly 70 Secondary schools. In the large area the company were to visit there were 200 Secondary schools alone. It could be argued, therefore, that the area was too large, but against this the company needed the extra grants given by the other districts and no one knew exactly what the response would be. As it turned out the response was somewhat overwhelming, and meant that each programme was fully booked with a number of schools being disappointed.

The choice of performing only to the 12–18-year age group also had a significant effect upon the work. Due to the rigidity of the Scottish Education system and the strict timetabling of subjects it was extremely difficult to present a programme that lasted more than one hour (fitting into a double period). A half-day session was sometimes introduced, the second part being for discussion, which could be omitted if the school had no time, or no inclination, for it. This limitation meant that the presentations had to be effective within the one-hour span. They were therefore performance-based and such programmes as "Modern Drama" and a documentary on the history of Scottish Coalmining relied on the performing skills of the actors. The exclusion of the Primary and Junior age ranges meant that no programme could be devised to link in with the "centre of interest" projects, where the company could work very closely with one or two classes. Therefore the company was not able to develop material for one of the most exciting and flexible areas, where the programme can be of real use in a school providing the base or climax of a term's work.

The scheme was on a fairly small scale, the total company consisting of three actors, one actress, one stage manager, and one Director. The theatre provided rehearsal and office space. It had been hoped that the Theatre for Youth would exchange actors with the Citizen's Theatre company. In the end this proved impossible, and led to an inevitable separation between the two companies.

The performances in schools were played to 100–150 pupils at a time. Participation was, therefore, limited, although it was attempted. For first and second years the audience numbers were reduced to 80, and sometimes just to two classes. This enabled the company to introduce a much more satisfactory and flexible form of audience participation, working with the pupils in groups. The form of presentation was kept very simple and played always on the floor of the hall or gym, using a theatre in the round, three side or traverse staging. Costumes and props were kept to a minimum, and a tape recorder was used for music and sound effects. There was rarely any set. The company could not afford a designer, and at the time this did not seem really necessary.

The size of company and simplicity of presentation were very typical of much of the early work of the various companies performing in schools in the late 1960s.

For the Citizen's Theatre for Youth the performing-based policy meant that the kind of programmes offered to schools were very similar to the Gateway Chester scheme. For the higher age groups, plays were performed which related to the school curriculum, such as Shakespeare and Modern Drama. For the lower age groups, the programmes were documentary in approach and examined the history of Scottish coalmining, the workings of a newspaper, and such themes as the adventures of the brothers Landor in their search for the termination of the River Niger in 1830.

The company were fortunate in being able to use the Close Theatre, a 150-seater studio next door to the main Citizen's auditorium. Over the Christmas period the company performed a children's play for 5–8-year-olds, which had been developed through improvisation. For this occasion a designer was seconded from the Citizen's company, and the Theatre for Youth were able to utilize all the theatrical aids available.

The subject-matter of the schools programme was decided by a system of consultation with teachers and advisers, and was, therefore, always geared to the needs of the schools. Due to timetabling in Secondary schools, however, it was often difficult for teachers to do any continuous follow-up although a background information in the form of Teacher's Notes on the programmes were sent to the schools in advance.

The programmes were first researched by the director and partly scripted, the company then improvised upon this material, shaping it and adding their own ideas. The end result was very much a group creation, but the actual company structure was basically hierarchical. Being a small group, ideas were naturally exchanged but short- and long-term policy decisions were ultimately the responsibility of the Director, in consultation with the Theatre Board, the Theatre Director and the Advisers.

The grants did not provide sufficient funds to keep the Theatre for Youth company running over the summer period. Contracts were therefore for one year, although some members of the company did return for the following session. The Director worked through the summer preparing next season's programmes. This kind of contract arrangement is typical of companies whose policy tends to be play-performance based. The Marlowe Mobile in Canterbury worked in this way.

Over the next 3 years, 1968–71, the company's work developed along these lines. A writer–researcher was employed for a short period, and a second company worked in Special schools for a 10-week period. The Close Theatre was used for a Children's play at Christmas, and on occasional Monday nights, where the company prepared special shows for fifth- and sixth-

FIG. 7. Citizens' Theatre for Youth, "The New Age", scenes from the *Life of Galileo*, 1969.

formers. They developed such themes as "The Responsibility of the Scientist", which was linked to the company's performance of scenes from Brecht's *Life of Galileo* in schools.

The Citizen's Theatre for Youth, in its early days, is an example of how a performance-based company developed. This kind of company, however, does raise some major problems. Unlike Theatre in Education it can, and frequently does, happen in a vacuum. If it is treated entirely as a performance, then it may entertain and it may well introduce theatre to some hundreds of pupils, but it in no way provides a satisfactory educational resource. To introduce theatre is not necessarily a bad thing, but, alas, in a school situation it can be inordinately frustrating. It is frustrating for the team because their role in the education system is unclear. As a provider of a theatre experience, would it not be better for the pupils to come to a theatre to see the company, where all the theatrical aids can be put to use?

The questions that arise are: Why are we doing it? What use is it? In performing to hundreds of pupils and seeing them perhaps, only once during their school careers, the work does not have any foundation to build on. To tour around, doing as many one-off performances as possible, is highly unsatisfactory, both for the schools and the company. The schools have no close liaison with the team, and little reason for building one. Many people would say that the one-off performances are better than nothing and that the theatrical event can, for a few pupils, be a satisfactory and lasting experience. Yet the companies role in a school is unclear.

This is one of the fundamental differences between theatre-orientated young people's work and TIE. The latter is educationally-motivated, closely linked with schools, the programmes are usually well followed up and fit into the school curriculum. Their preparation is often the result of some form of collaboration with teachers, and the whole purpose for being in a school is clear. The itinerant role of the Young People's Theatre company with no close liaison with schools and no clear educational purpose can lead to muddled thinking in the preparation of programmes; actors unused to performing to children; unsuitable presentation; a reception as merely an entertainment, and a resulting lack of impact in a school.

It is not surprising, therefore, that many Young People's Theatre companies have broadened the scope of their work outside the school situation and relate themselves to the whole community. They can then be seen as performers offering relevant material to all age groups. The schools work becomes only part of their total commitment, and they see themselves as Community Theatre companies. This is what has happened to the Glasgow team (although financial difficulties, with doubts about the grant from the Education Authorities, provided the impetus for the major change). It seems a logical step for these companies to take, and has given them a clear purpose in their work.

The example of the Citizen's Theatre for Youth in its early days does, I hope, show the real contrast between the nature and approach to the work. Theatre-orientated Young People's Theatre companies still found their work on recognizable theatre working methods of presentation. The programmes, although they may be researched and written by the company, are more likely to be in the form of plays. The company tends to be hierarchical in structure and to perform to a large audience of about 100 pupils or more at a time. Examples of these kind of companies are Derby Playhouse Studio and schools company, the Marlowe Mobile at Canterbury and Billingham Young People's Theatre. (The Mobile Company have now ceased work, a victim of the 1980 cuts.)

Those companies that adopted a definite Theatre in Education approach when first starting up almost always drew their directors from Coventry. Thus the work, initiated and developed at the Belgrade with its educational aims, moved outwards to Watford in 1968; Bolton, 1969; Edinburgh, 1969; Leeds, 1970; Cockpit, 1971. Appendix B shows the actual spread of the Coventry personnel to other teams in Britain.

The ex-Coventry members were often actors and teachers having had experience in both areas of work. As team members they had worked together to devise programmes which had specific educational aims and use for the teachers and pupils in Coventry. It is not perhaps surprising that when the Coventry team members moved on they took more than the TIE philosophy with them, they also took programme structures.

For instance: the Edinburgh Royal Lyceum Theatre in Education scheme was started in September 1969 and two of the four team members came from Coventry: Sue Birtwhistle (Coventry 1968–9) and Gordon Wiseman (1966, 1967–9). Many of the aims of the new Edinburgh team were similar to Coventry:

1. To expand the experience and learning of the child through imaginative involvement.
2. To promote the use of Drama as a teaching method.
3. To run courses and workshop sessions for teachers and students, encouraging the use of drama and giving opportunities for discussion and exchange of ideas.
4. To devise programmes in co-operation with productions running in the theatre.[11]

The first programme that the company devised bore a striking resemblance to one devised in Coventry in 1967. The Edinburgh programme was "The Blew Blanket" for Primary 7 (11–12 years), two classes, and its subject was the quarrels of the merchants and craftsmen in fifteenth-century Edinburgh. The "Conflict in Coventry" programme was devised for 9–10-year olds, two classes, and was about the conflicts between different groups over the

payment of market tolls in Medieval Coventry. Both programmes begin with
a session in the classroom, where the pupils were involved in building up a
picture of the life at the time through the learning of facts and through
drama. There was a short break, after which the classes moved to the hall. In
both programmes this was set out as a market-place, and in this setting the
opposing groups were brought into conflict. This conflict led on to discussion
on how to improve matters. Both programmes ended with some kind of
theatre event, the Coventry one with a Mummer's play, the Edinburgh one
with a procession. In both programmes the team worked in character,
wearing period costume either working with the pupils or taking over the
action. There were differences of course in plot and factual information, but
there is a clear resemblance in structure and aim. As the Edinburgh team had
to find a way of working together quickly the use of a successful programme
structure seems sensible. It is actually quite a common occurrence, certainly
in broader structural terms. The use of the same programmes by different
TIE teams is also becoming obvious. Many of them began at Coventry: "Pow
Wow"; "Example" (the case of Craig and Bentley); "Ice Station Zero One",
all of them have been presented by other teams: such as The Bowsprit,
Cockpit, Peterborough. New Theatre in Education schemes that got off to a
successful start were often those where the TIE Director, the theatre and the
Local Authorities knew exactly what was wanted and why, and provided
sufficient funds to see that it happened. Leeds Theatre in Education began in
this way.

The development of the TIE company was associated with the opening of
the Leeds Playhouse in 1970. Bill Hays, the Artistic Director, was eager to
introduce some youth work into the playhouse activities. He knew Roger
Chapman, then working in the Bolton TIE scheme, and was interested in
asking him to work at Leeds. First of all Bill Hays approached Miss
Woodward, the Chief Adviser, and she expressed real interest in the scheme.
Roger Chapman, Bill Hays and Miss Woodward met the Chief Education
Officer for Leeds, and from this meeting there was sufficient encouragement
for Miss Woodward to go to Bolton to see the work. She was very impressed
and wrote a paper to support the starting of the Leeds scheme. This motion
was passed at just one meeting, and Theatre in Education was to be set up for
a trial period of one year, attached to the Playhouse. The first grant from the
Local Education Authority was small, in the region of £4000, but it was
increased annually until in 1976 it was £12,500. This money was matched by
a grant from the Arts Council, running a little higher — approximately
£5000 in 1971 and up to £14,860 for 1976–7.

With this backing and support Roger Chapman was able to call a meeting
of all the Head Teachers in the area, and have them addressed by the Chief
Education Officer. At this meeting the basic premise of the TIE scheme was
made clear. It was to be part of the Local Authority service to schools, the

teachers were to be involved, and not treat it as a time to go off to the staffroom. The teachers were advised that they should avail themselves of this service and they did. Even the teacher's workshops were made compulsory before each programme.

So, for the Leeds team, everything was made clear, official and respectable right at the beginning. An ideal way to begin work. The relationship with the Local Education Authority was excellent. Roger Chapman set out his aims:

(a) To extend the imagination and personality of the child through creative drama.
(b) To be the nucleus of a Children's Theatre company.
(c) To work with young people in their leisure time and through creative drama develop an appreciation of the theatre as an art form.[12]

The company was not to offer infrequent visits to schools but give a real educational stimulus as well as a theatrical experience to which work can be built up and followed on. This education stimulus was certainly an aim that David Morton, the Drama Adviser for Leeds, approved of. In 1976 he saw the company as:

A team teaching unit which generates thinking and feeling in the children, by particular use of the theatre techniques they have, but they are also using considerable teaching skills at the same time.[13]

Although the relationship with the Education Authorities remained good, the relationship with the theatre was not as satisfactory. The Artistic Director Bill Hays left in 1972, and links with the theatre slowly fell away. Although the companies existed side by side amicably enough, there was no real interaction. As a consequence the TIE company moved nearer to the Education Authority. Roger Chapman found this lack of interaction with the theatre a real loss:

I see TIE very much as part of a theatre's policy for a region and that part of a theatre's policy that works outside the theatre building. If it is not linked to the theatre, or one can't find out what the theatre's policy is, then you evolve your own policy and it may well be that you find that you are clashing at a number of particular points with the theatre, on what the function of theatre is in a society; what theatre is about. We don't have an on going debate with the theatre, which I find sad.[14]

Eventually the team moved out of the Playhouse and into premises in a school, found for them by the Education Authority. This break away from the theatre building was accompanied by the setting up of a sub-committee of the Board of Governors for the TIE team. Amongst these Board members were a local Headmaster, Miss Woodward, the Chief Adviser and Roger Chapman.

FIG. 8. Leeds TIE, "Watch Out", 1973.

The team became artistically autonomous and the only administrative link with the Playhouse is the paying of wages, still done through the theatre, and the theatre's box office deals with the bookings for the TIE's Children's Theatre production in the Playhouse in the summer.

The company expanded from five to eight members, but growth was slow. In fact Roger Chapman's original plan was on a much larger scale. His first stage was the group based on the Playhouse and working within a 3-mile radius of the theatre, with local schools. A further scheme was for expansion with five TIE companies working in major areas in Leeds. They were to work from local community centres, all offering different kinds of community theatre plus TIE work in schools, each with its own director. The first year of the one company was very successful, but while they had total support from the city in words, they never received the kind of grant aid that would make this size of scheme possible. In fact it never looks like becoming a possibility. The team now cover a much wider area than the 3-mile radius, but they work only in schools.

One of the important elements of the Leeds team, is stability of personnel. By 1976 three of the team members had actually been working together in TIE for 9 years! This stability, experience and excellent relations with the Education Authority allowed the Drama Adviser to rely on the team's judgement when choosing and presenting a programme in schools. The nature of the work the company presents in schools varied from total participation where a programme can be dependent on the children's responses, to a straightforward documentary about Quarry Hill Flats. Initially the company made contact with the schools through the English and Drama departments. Yet neither the company nor the Drama Adviser see TIE as an extension of these subjects. To try and establish this the company made attempts to explain and discuss with other Advisers, and to try and find a method of making sure that the relevant department in the school actually handles the booking and uses the programme.

Since 1970 the company have been accepted in schools by both teachers and pupils, and the pupils no longer ask questions like "What's it like to be an Actor?", but talk about the subject material of the programme.

At the same time as the Leeds TIE company was beginning to develop its work, a Drama Adviser for Leeds was appointed: David Morton. The position of drama in education in schools began to improve. Before 1970 there was one specialist drama teacher in the whole of Leeds and one drama studio. By 1976 over 80 per cent of Secondary and Middle schools had drama teachers which is way above the national average; and a large number of drama studios had been built. David Morton felt that the growth and acceptance of drama in schools was not only the result of his appointment, but came from the combination of his work with teachers, and the TIE team's work in schools. This is an example of a well-established TIE team that had all the advantages of the understanding, aid and support of both the theatre and the education authorities in its initial stages. Consequently it began with a firm base, a clear policy and a definite role in schools. The result of this was a continuing high standard of work, continuity of personnel and a close liaison with schools.

Not all TIE teams began in such favourable circumstances. Some, like the Greenwich team, had to struggle for many years to find both proper funding and a satisfactory approach to the work. In so doing Greenwich TIE met some of the basic problems that concerned teams struggling to do Theatre in

Education work in schools in the late 1960s and early 1970s.

The Greenwich Theatre in South-east London opened in 1969. Ewan Hooper, the Artistic Director, envisaged a community theatre involved in many aspects of the local area. As part of this scheme he wanted a company to work in schools. Rather like the Coventry scheme, it was to be the schools' work which flourished, leaving the community aspect undeveloped and mainly limited to the presenting of plays in the theatre building.

The three original members of the school's company consisted of a Director and two actor–teachers. Not only did they work in schools but they also took part in main theatre productions. This proved an impossible pressure and the team concentrated solely on their work in schools.

In the early days the team members had to be qualified teachers and received a proportion of their salary from the education authority. The Inner London Education Authority (ILEA) gave a small grant, but there was no other money and it had to be generated by the company itself. So they travelled outside the ILEA area and went to the schools who were interested. A fee of £30 was charged and this helped to generate the income needed.

The team increased to four people, one actor, one actress, and two teachers. They worked in pairs as actors and teachers, neither pair really encroaching on the work of the other. The morning consisted of drama work in role with one class and the afternoon was a performance to an audience of 200 at a time. This proved highly unsatisfactory for the team, but as the school was paying a fee, they were happier if as many children as possible could see the performance. Playing to so large a number it was often impossible to include any participation, but the split drama and presentation did mean that contact was made with some pupils. The financial background to the split working day was that the ILEA paid for the morning and the Arts Council for the performance in the afternoon.

This split in the nature of the work and the way it was funded exposed a fundamental problem in the development of Theatre in Education. The two areas of theatre and education were to work together, not as separate elements. This is what Gordon Vallins envisaged, and what the Coventry team were to promote. However, many Local Education Authorities and teachers did not trust, or could not imagine, this new combination.

The Greenwich team could not change the way they worked in schools until they joined forces with the Greenwich Youth Theatre and formed a new limited company: The Greenwich Young People's Theatre Ltd. The new company moved into premises in Plumstead, a converted church hall, and renegotiated their finances. The Youth Theatre had been formed in 1966 and its income had come from the local Youth committee. When the grants were renegotiated the Youth grants were dropped and instead the company was funded by ILEA and the Arts Council. As ILEA provided 98 per cent of the money to operate the whole scheme it expected the TIE company to work exclusively inside its area in schools and educational establishments, and the Youth work to continue offering a range of drama and art workshops for the local community.

For the TIE team, the new organization meant important changes in their way of work. June Mitchell, a member of the team from its early days, and then its director, explained the difference:

> When schools were paying fees the pressure on them and on the company to provide programmes for the whole school was strong, while as a Theatre-in-Education team we, and many teachers, realised the need for in-depth working with one class of children. An unhappy (we felt) compromise had been to work for a day in a school with one class in the morning and a presentation for 200 in the afternoon. Since January last year we have, we feel, arrived at a better situation. We have tried over the last year to balance out the type of programmes offered

FIG. 9. Greenwich TIE, "Tribe", 1975.

and to provide participatory programmes for larger numbers so that schools can select for themselves the quality of experience and numbers involved.[15]

The programmes changed and the teaching and performing became more integrated. The subject-matter covered a wide range of historical, social and scientific material, and was usually structured through improvisation. The programmes were half- or whole-day sessions in schools or at the Stage Centre, the company's new premises. The educational aims could become more specific, and the work much more specialized. For educationally sub-normal children of 8–11 years the team prepared a programme in 1974 which aimed:

> To provide the children with an interesting, stimulating experience and the satisfaction of solving several problems using varied skills. Each child should contribute individually in a group to achieve a collective aim. The emphasis will be on communication, co-operation and using the ideas suggested by the children. The framework is ours, the substance the children's.[16]

The company increased in size until by 1976 the TIE team consisted of nine actor–teachers and a director, and at the Stage Centre were a Schools Liaison Officer, a musician, a designer, and stage staff and personnel for the Youth work. With nine actor–teachers the TIE team, known then as the Bowsprit company, could work as two separate units, and therefore cover a much larger number of schools. Even so the company encountered a major problem with their Secondary school work, for they covered the whole of the ILEA area. This meant that close and continuous contact between the team and the schools was difficult. By 1976 there was a continuous debate as to whether the company should concentrate on only a few schools or carry on spreading their work so thinly. In the Primary and Junior work the team concentrated on a smaller area, but that still meant there were about 250 schools to contact. To cope with this the team tried to concentrate on a few schools at a time and select an area to work in. By 1975 the problem of contact with schools was acute; as June Mitchell pointed out:

> We have existed as a Theatre in Education team for six years but we still feel that we do not have adequate communication with teachers working in the schools we visit, and we still feel that our work is not totally understood or integrated. We are, by the nature of the experience and by the size of our catchment area, a drop in the ocean of the pupil's learning life.[17]

This illustrates one of the major problems of a company working in too large an area. To combat it the Greenwich team tried hard to improve liaison with schools by teachers' meetings, teachers' notes, questionnaires and discussions with children. A local association of teachers, set up in 1975, helped in this operation and offered to help in the devising of follow-up material for other teachers. Liaison began to improve by these methods, and by the work of the advisory teacher attached to the Stage Centre. As an extra measure a Schools Liaison officer was appointed, and this gave the teachers a point of reference for contact and information.

However, by 1978 the TIE company had reduced itself to a team of six actor–teachers, one stage manager, one team leader and the Schools Liaison Officer. The reason for this change was so that the same money could be used to pay better wages to fewer people, and the team went on to the much improved rate of Grade One Salary scale for Lecturers. The team was also reorganized in structure and this led to a closer democratic unit.[18]

The larger company with two teams working side by side had encountered difficulties, as Pam Schweitzer observed in her study of the team for the Arts Council:

> Clearly there are too many projects on the go for the Artistic Director to oversee them all, and therefore each one is handled by one of the more experienced company members, but even they are relatively green, having worked only two or three years in TIE. There has been quite a high turnover of team members over the last three years and this too seems to fit in with the pattern that the higher the degree of democracy, the greater the commitment of the individual members to their team. Where so many are combining their efforts it is difficult to ensure any degree of unanimity of purpose.[19]

For the Greenwich TIE team then, the decreasing of its personnel was another step in its development. Any TIE team has to adapt to the circumstances around it whilst retaining its central purpose. The examples of the Leeds and Greenwich teams show just how differently these companies developed, but once TIE is established the companies have several elements in common: their aim is mainly educational; liaison with schools is strong; they use acting and teaching techniques and devise their programmes as a team; the companies usually have a democratic structure which helps a great deal in building commitment.

The contrast in the development and methods of work in the case of the Citizens' Theatre for Youth and the two TIE teams is quite apparent, and these differences were often there at the moment of inception of the schemes. From these diverse beginnings have emerged a wide range of work all coming under the general heading of Young People's Theatre. At one end of the scale are the very drama-based companies such as the Clwyd team; at the other end are the Community Theatre groups who present plays for children and young people as part of their total work. Within this range there are still companies concentrating upon what can be called a Theatre in Education approach trying to integrate the two elements, such companies as Greenwich and Leeds, or the Cockpit team in London, or Lancaster TIE. Whilst other teams such as Peterborough have evolved a policy that aims to perform to, and work with, all sections of the local community. Their work in schools, however, follows the principles of Theatre in Education.

It is, therefore, a rather diverse and somewhat confusing scene. Theatre in Education began to emerge, not as a neat set of so many companies, but as a way of approaching work in schools, a form of programme devising and performing which could be translated into work in the Community.

The late 1960s saw the beginnings of a number of Theatre in Education and Young People's Theatre companies, often starting in different circum-stances and taking time to be recognized, or to find a satisfactory approach to the work. By the 1970s Local Education Authorities seemed to be more aware of the possibilities of TIE. Grander schemes were undertaken, well funded by the LEAs themselves. The Cockpit TIE and the Curtain Theatre Company were started by ILEA in 1971. The Clwyd Drama in Education team began in 1970.

The Clwyd team resembled the early Aberdeen scheme, in that it used teachers who worked in schools as well as taking out TIE programmes. It was formed in 1970 by the local Drama Adviser, Derek Hollins, and was then known as the Flintshire Drama in Education team. For 3 days a week the drama specialists were timetabled to teach drama in the County's Secondary schools, and for the remaining 2 days they were responsible for Theatre in Education projects in Junior and Secondary schools. The process of presenting programmes in schools was carefully worked out:

(a) A panel of teachers decided on the theme for the Project and a research team was appointed to compile a dossier on the background and data necessary. The dossier was printed and issued to schools.

(b) Class teachers used the folder as a basis for academic and creative work.

(c) A Drama Specialist would then visit the schools for two separate sessions and work with the children through movement, language and improvisation.

(d) The Team would then visit the school with a Theatre in Education programme based on the topic under investigation.

(c) The individual specialists would again visit the schools for a follow-up session. This visit also provided the opportunity for discussion with interested class teachers on ways of continuing Education through Drama until the next visit by the Team (usually about a year later).[20]

This is the format that the Clwyd team still use. They spend 3 days teaching in schools and two taking out TIE programmes. The company increased from four members in 1970 to ten by 1976. This meant that they could work in two groups, and visit both Junior and Secondary schools, offering a range of work. For example, for Infants they devised "Doctor Drip" (summer 1976), a science programme about steam using the fantasy character of Doctor Drip. For Juniors they used history: "The Fire of London", and for Secondary pupils they devised a programme about the family. Although apparently more orientated to teaching, some of their earlier presentations for Secondary schools consisted of shortened versions of Shakespeare plays: *The Tempest* in 1973, *Henry V* in 1974.

The team do see themselves as providing an educational service. The presentations in schools being viewed as a physical resource for teachers, as one member described:

> If someone wanted to do a Medieval Fair, or Medieval life in general, the Chief Librarian (in the Mold Centre) would be able to give them a list of tapes, books, video cassettes, and audio cassettes. In addition, she can say, there is a group of actor–teachers who could give a small performance about a family going to a fair in Medieval times in which there's a large amount of teaching material, which requires follow-up work by the teacher.[21]

Unlike Clwyd, the Cockpit team in London, although paid on teacher's salary scale by the ILEA do not teach drama, they concentrate upon Theatre in Education. The Cockpit Arts Workshop opened in London in January 1970, offering a number of integrated arts and schools project days. In March 1971 the Director, Alec Davison, initiated a professional TIE pilot project. Gordon Wiseman, an original member of Coventry TIE, was in charge and introduced the principles of work developed at Coventry. The project received a tremendous response from schools, and the ILEA made the company official. It was offered to Secondary schools only and usually to pupils of 14 upwards. By 1976 the team consisted of six actor–teachers, a stage manager and a Director. Like the Greenwich team the premises were used for a whole range of arts and drama workshops. The Cockpit, however, has a well-equipped and fairly flexible studio theatre which the TIE team make full use of. Pupils usually come to the Cockpit rather than the team going out to schools, and the mixing of different schools on the half-day or full-day sessions was very much part of the TIE team's policy in its early days. The company often use the theatre by presenting a play as part of the whole TIE programme. Such documentary-style presentations as "Marches", about the rise of Mosely, and "Example" (the Coventry team's programme on the Craig and Bentley case) used lighting, slides, set and sound effects to the full.

The number of pupils is usually limited to two classes per day, or half-day, thus enabling the team to work in depth. The policy is basically educational. Geoff Gillham, present director of the team, described the policy as concerned with: "how children learn, we're taking up that problem and what that implies for us, in how we teach".[22] The Cockpit team are in sympathy with an integrated curriculum in schools, and are interested in bringing as many subject disciplines as possible into their programmes.

FIG. 10. Cockpit TIE, "Marches", 1977.

At the opposite end of the scale to the Drama in Education teams are the Young People's companies or Community Theatre companies presenting plays to young people. Sidewalk Theatre company based in Islington is a Community Theatre group, which actually does about 90 per cent of its work for children. This work, however it is written or devised, tends towards the performances of a play, as one of the company explained:

> What we always aim to do is to tell a story as simply, as clearly, and as excitingly as possible. So we really use all the skills we have which best fit the images we want to put over. So we wouldn't say the end product we want is a pantomine, or a documentary. But what we tend to do is use our skills to best serve the story. So that the end product actually comes out to be a very tightly worked play. And it often is a play — a colourful play.[23]

Peterborough Key Perspectives is a group that relates to a wide age range in its local community but presents Theatre in Education work in schools rather than the "colourful play". Unlike the Leeds and Cockpit teams the Peterborough company had a hard struggle to begin at all. They were graduates from Bretton Hall College determined to begin a Theatre in Education scheme of their own. They wrote around to see if any county would accept them, and the Drama Adviser for Peterborough, John Boylen, did so. They were based at the Key Theatre, which already had a repertory company, and received £4000 which was the only money John Boylen could offer. Nine months later, April 1974, the team had run out of money, and no extra subsidy was forthcoming. They were given notice. They made a real effort to rally support and raise some money but to no avail, when quite suddenly the team received an anonymous donation of £5000, which was immediately followed by a deficit grant from the Arts Council for £3200.

The Key Theatre repertory company was also in severe financial difficulties, but could not be saved, and was disbanded in July 1974. That a Community Theatre and a TIE team should survive whilst its "host" repertory company ceased to function was, to say the least, a rather unusual turn of events!

The Key Perspectives team received grants from the City Council and the Arts Council, whilst the Key Theatre itself changed Directors, but could not revive a full-time repertory company. The team had deliberately developed their work as a service for the whole community, and they felt sure that this policy was crucial to their survival:

> One lesson that may be drawn from our struggle is that a democratic company offering a theatre service to a community whose needs it understands surely gains the political strength essential for its survival in a testing economic climate, where a straightforward repertory company is failing.[24]

The Key Perspectives had applied the principles of Theatre in Education to their work for all age groups and in so doing had pin-pointed the essential difference between their approach to their work and their local community, from that of the Key Theatre Repertory Company.

Once Young People's Theatre was properly established the Arts Council decided to re-examine its policy, and make certain changes. In 1971 the Young People's Theatre Panel that had brought together such a unique combination of people was amalgamated with the Drama Panel. The reason for the move was:

> That the Young People's Theatre Panel has established to a certain extent what the Arts Council's thinking was but there was a danger that the Young People's Theatre Panel might become too much of a separate

thing. They had to be separate at the beginning to get established but then it was felt necessary that it should become part of the whole[25]

The Arts Council took a major policy decision. In the light of the theatre's increasing awareness that young people's work should be a natural part of their activities, the Council decided to stop "earmarking" grants especially for Young People's Theatre teams. Instead, that grant would be included in the total grant to the theatre. This was a definite move to hand the responsibility for the work back to the Theatre Directors, and then, the Arts Council suggests: "Ideally the responsibility of apportioning resources to their various areas of activity, including that of young people's work, should be accepted by the theatres themselves."[26] This policy decision caused quite an outcry amongst teams who were afraid that they would lose their grants as a result. As it happened their fear was unfounded. Very few companies actually closed as a direct result of the decision, although the total amount of money granted from the parent theatres to their TIE companies did reduce.[27] In fact should a Theatre Director decide to cease any work for young people, and leave this out of his grant application, the Arts Council would reduce his grant accordingly. Certainly by 1974, Theatre Directors were much more aware of the value of the work than they had been in the mid-1960s.

The Arts Council had wanted companies to use their policy statement to seek more funds from the Local Authority, the Education Authority and the Regional Arts Association. However, the statement coincided with Local Government reorganization, which caused many problems. Companies applying for grants were faced with the dilemma of which Authority to actually contact — the City or the District. Thus the policy statement did not have the impact the Arts Council wished for and its timing was unfortunate.

By 1974 many Young People's Theatre companies included some Community Theatre as part of their work. The performances in schools had become part of a general community service for all ages. The Key Perspectives in Peterborough took their community role very seriously as the range of services they offered in 1976 illustrates:

   (i) Workshops for teachers.
  (ii) Theatre workshops for young people.
 (iii) Help with in-service training for the local Samaritans.
 (iv) Road Safety promotion for the Cambridge County Constabulary Accident Prevention Department.
  (v) We have made ourselves available as a resource to aid the work of local Community workers.
 (vi) A programme for schools has been devised in conjunction with local town planners.[28]

This change was recognized by the Arts Council and the Young People's Theatre committee from the Drama Panel decided to meet from time to time with the Fringe and Experimental Drama Committee. This was a reflection not only of the broadening of Young People's companies but of the move of some fringe groups towards work with young people. This general broadening of work had caused subsidy anomalies, and the joint meetings were, and still are, an attempt to rationalize the situation.

By the mid-1970s Young People's Theatre was well established. The Arts Council's change of policy in 1966 had initiated a quite extraordinary proliferation of work with and for young people. Amongst this range of work a particular approach to "performing" in schools was adopted by some companies, often based on the principles developed at Coventry. This was an approach which used theatrical and educational techniques to work in depth with one or two classes of pupils at a time: Theatre in Education.

Notes

1. Arts Council of Great Britain, *Report on the Provision of Theatre for Young People*, 1966, Arts Council, p. 7.
2. *Ibid.*
3. *Ibid.*
4. Arts Council, *Report on the Provision of Theatre for Young People*, 1966, p. 15.
5. Arts Council, *Annual Report*, 1966–7, p. 22.
6. Drama Director, Arts Council, quoted in Young People's Theatre section of *CORT Bulletin*, 14th May 1967.
7. M. Barry, "Players with a purpose", *The Stage*, 20th June 1968.
8. Flying Phoenix Young People's Theatre, Leicester, *Report*, 1969, p. 2.
9. P. Leech, Gateway Theatre in Education, *Pilot Scheme Report*, 1971, p. 1.
10. I was appointed Director of the Theatre for Youth scheme at the Citizens' in 1967, and stayed until 1971. (Returning again from 1976–8.) This book is, in fact, the result of my interest in Young People's Theatre and of the questions that I began to ask myself about the development and form of the work.
11. Theatre in Education, Royal Lyceum Theatre, Annual Report, 1969–70, p. 1.
12. R. Chapman, "Theatre in Education in Leeds", Leeds Playhouse Souvenir Brochure, 1970.
13. D. Morton, personal interview, 14th May 1976, at the Education Office, Leeds.
14. R. Chapman, personal interview, 13th May 1976, at TIE offices. (Left Leeds TIE in 1976.)
15. J. Mitchell, Greenwich Schools Drama, A Newsletter, 1975.
16. Greenwich Young People's Theatre (Bowsprit TIE company), *The Boy who Lost his Money*, Information to teachers, 1974.
17. J. Mitchell, Newsletter, 1975.
18. The TIE team also dropped the name Bowsprit for the company; and Stage Centre for the premises. Everything is now under the one general name of Greenwich Young People's Theatre, which has reduced the confusion that arose from the multiplicity of titles!
19. P. Schweitzer, "The Bowsprit Company", *Report on Theatre in Education for the Arts Council*, May 1975.
20. Survey of Clwyd Drama in Education scheme, 1975, pp. 1–2 (mimeograph).
21. T. Robshaw, member of Clwyd Drama in Education team, personal interview at Mold Arts Centre, 7th June 1976.
22. G. Gillham, personal interview at the Cockpit Theatre, 12th March 1979.
23. Sidewalk Theatre Company in interview, *Community Theatre*, B. Gleede and T. Goode (eds.), Drama Board Association, Occasional Paper, 1976, p. 7.

24. Key Perspective, "A history lesson", *Theatre in Education Directory*, G. Chapman (ed.), T. Q. Publications Ltd., London, 1975, p. 14.
25. J. Bullwinkle, Arts Council Drama Officer, personal interview, 26th June 1978, at the Arts Council Offices, London.
26. Arts Council, Young People's Theatre, Policy Statement, 1974, p. 1.
27. See Chapter 4, p. 136.
28. Key Perspectives, Peterborough, Policy Statement (1975).

Chapter 4

Changes in Theatre in Education

Since 1965 Theatre in Education has inevitably changed, and it has done so as a result of both internal and external pressures. The strongest push for change has come from within the movement itself. TIE companies have developed their techniques and philosophy by continuously evaluating the way they work.

Changes in the theory and practice of TIE since 1965

Brian Way commenting on the change in TIE pointed out that there have been "fantastic changes in the way it's received, the early part — the suspicious stage — is all gone".[1] This suspicion, from both theatre practitioners and educationalists, stemmed from fear and hostility towards the new technique. In pioneering Theatre in Education the Coventry team had been made well aware of those feelings as Stuart Bennett explained:

> Initially we had been subject to the theoretical criticism by theatre directors on the grounds that actors should do what they are trained to do — act in a conventional relationship, and by educationalists who believed only teachers should exploit teacher–child relationships.[2]

To counter such criticism the team worked hard at making everyone, particularly teachers, aware of the nature of the work. So that, after a year the team knew that they could arrive in a school and not meet with misconceptions.

In spite of the work of the Coventry team in the 1960s, any new TIE company starting work still had to fight its own battles against suspicion and misunderstandings. The personnel from Coventry TIE helped to start a number of new companies (see Appendix B), yet each new company had to develop its own policy depending upon the local circumstances. Coventry's policy had changed within 3 years, from an emphasis on being an "animated visual aid" in 1965 to a much broader range of aims stated in their 1967–8 Report:

> The aim of the scheme is to provide a service to schools which will explore the educational value of drama in the development of the child's

111

personality, experiment in teaching methods using drama and theatre
techniques, and stimulate an interest in theatre in adult life.

This concern with the educational value of drama in developing the child's
personality was common to many teams who began work in the late 1960s.
Drama in Education was little known in schools, the 1967 DES Report on
Drama describing it as a "young and growing subject". At the time of this
report there were only about 50 out of the 300 Secondary schools in ILEA
which included Drama on the timetable. In Coventry there were no drama
teachers in schools when the TIE team began work. In the mid-1960s in
Dundee there was no Drama Adviser and only one Drama teacher. In Leeds
there was one Drama specialist in the local Secondary schools by 1970.

This lack of drama in education in schools led some new TIE schemes to
place their emphasis on stimulating drama rather than offering a theatre
experience. The Ipswich Theatre began a scheme of sending actors into
schools in 1967. After consultations with teachers they offered a drama in
education stimulus, working with classes of 14–15-year-olds for one hour
sessions in each of the seven Secondary schools chosen, every week of the
year. The subject was to be the history of drama, but the method used was to
consist of improvisations by the children without an audience. The company
also introduced short courses for teachers in conjunction with the Ipswich
Education Authority on the subject of Child Drama in the Secondary schools.
The Coventry team had also found itself involved in offering teachers
courses, and taking on the work of a Drama Adviser. The Flying Phoenix
team at the Phoenix Theatre, Leicester, had begun with a similar emphasis.

In these early years there appeared to be a polarization between those
teams which wished to establish themselves as of educational value, and those
which retained theatre as the basis of their work. The Bristol Old Vic began
in the 1960s to send actors into schools presenting plays; although these could
be especially written for the occasion, they were performance-based. The
Theatre also introduced Play-plus Days, where school children came to the
theatre for the day. In the morning they explored aspects of preparing a
production, with particular reference to the play running at the theatre, and
in the afternoon they watched a performance of this play. This was then
followed by discussion. A number of other repertories offered similar
schemes. The education-based companies had to find an acceptable formula
for schools. If they were not offering a play why should actors be allowed into
schools? Drama in Education, a developing subject with no set curriculum
and no exam system, offered an ideal opportunity. By emphasizing this
aspect "theatre people" could be seen to be making a valid contribution to
education. Although many companies have now shifted away from this
approach they are left with the administrative structure associated with these
early days. For instance, it is still the drama teacher who books a TIE team in

a number of schools. Unfortunately it is often the drama teacher who is the only one to watch a TIE programme in the school, and the only one who attempts to use the material.

Where education was the TIE company's main concern the exploration of new teaching methods using drama and theatre techniques was an essential part of the work. Theatre in Education was a new combination of these two areas and it *had* to experiment to develop at all. To be of use in schools it had to be very aware of all the changes in education: such as the ending of the 11 plus, the introduction of Comprehensive schools, the use of project work in Primary schools and the development of inter-disciplinary work in Secondary schools. Rosemary Birbeck had seen the Coventry team's contribution as a dynamic force in the school, not a cultural frill. The team succeeded in introducing ways of work that were quite new to many teachers. Stuart Bennett believed that one of the most effective techniques that the company introduced was the use of Primary projects with a drama base into the first and second years of Secondary school.

TIE developed during a period of proliferating educational reports, Schools Council Inquiries and the publication of books critical of the educational system. In his book on Theatre in Education, John O'Toole noted that:

> Like many subject disciplines and teaching techniques, TIE was born in and of the flux, and the majority of companies are strongly committed to the idea of 'progressive', open-ended education and propagate its ideals with missionary zeal.[3]

It was exactly this kind of zeal that influenced teachers like Peter Asquith in Coventry. Experiencing a TIE programme opened up a whole range of new teaching possibilities for him:

> I could see that instead of having a subject basis I could have an open day, could say, do personal writing, transactional writing, etc., all under the heading of this one activity . . . I no longer needed a class structure.[4]

Cliff Beloe, Drama Adviser for Derby, also emphasized the impact a programme could have in a school: "We have had examples of schools who have completely changed their emphasis as a result of the performances taken into schools".[5]

The concern in the early days of TIE was rather with the method of work than the content of the programmes. This method was shaped by the team's experiments and the ability of the schools to use the material and the techniques. In the first year or two at Coventry teachers did not do a great deal of build-up work before the team came into the school, and this affected the programme structure, as Sue Birtwhistle explained:

At Coventry there was definitely a teaching part of the programme and a performance part. I think that format has gone. We always used to start with long teaching sessions in costume working as a teacher covering the work the teacher should have done. Now, I think, teachers are very keen and interested and ready to do it. It is very time consuming for the team.[6]

This particular structure was necessary in Edinburgh when Sue Birtwhistle and Gordon Wiseman introduced TIE into schools in 1969. In the early days at Greenwich the TIE team were forced to separate the teaching and the performance elements because of the split nature of the funding.

With the development of the Teachers' workshops and the greater liaison between the team and the teachers, the first part of the programme in the classroom could be used to introduce character and situation as well as facts. For instance, in "Pow-Wow" Mr. Tex is concerned with getting the pupils on his side, showing them the kind of man he is, and putting over his view of the Indians.

The emphasis on the use of drama techniques also meant the participation of the pupil in the programme. The early Coventry programmes, such as "The Lunt Fort at Baginton", reduced the performance element for the actor–teacher and emphasized the drama-session approach with the TIE team member often working as a team leader, or teacher, stepping in and out of the action. In Coventry's "If it were not for the Weaver", presented in 1968, the pupils were asked to assume the characters of the weaving community during the time of strife and poverty. The first part of the programme consisted of drama sessions exploring the historical situations, and the involvement of the pupils was directed towards speech improvisations.

Although this form of participation was very popular in the late 1960s, TIE companies did not feel bound to include it in every programme. The more their experience grew, the more able they became to analyse how and why such participation should be used. Stuart Bennett commented on this in the Coventry TIE Report, 1969–70:

> It is important to realise that 'participation' is not a fashion we strive to include. If you have an idea and you wish your audience to experience it emotionally and intellectually a form of involvement emerges. Some projects pick up methods from previous projects but they never work unless they proceed from a central need on the part of the group to communicate.

It was this need to communicate that began a shift in TIE companies' approach to their material. In the early 1970s teams became much more conscious of the need to say something about the social and political situation, and this affected the methods they chose to use. The Bolton team in 1976 explained the change in their way of work:

> We've started to do other than participatory programmes, because there has been a drive by members of the company to use their performing skills in a much more presentational way. This is reflected nationally in all TIE teams — Coventry, the Cockpit; not sure why, because it's over the past five years. When we came here the method was using actors in role, with kids in role. In a sense what you were looking at (i.e. the subject) was secondary. Now its turned on its head. You start with a real social issue and you're going to come to grips with that — not easy to do with participation. It lends itself much more easily to theatricalisation.[7]

The increased political consciousness of many of the TIE companies in the early 1970s produced three definite changes: a concern with reality, "real social issues" rather than fantasy; an increased desire to put over a point of view to "audiences" and a greater emphasis on the theatre elements rather than on drama in education techniques.

By the 1970s TIE companies were relatively stable financially. They had developed methods of work which had proved successful. Only at this point could they look outwards, and what they found was a period of increasing social and political unrest, with the conflict between the Conservative Government and the Unions coming to a head. The Conservative Government declared a State of Emergency in November 1973, following an overtime ban by electricity and coal workers. Then the 3-day working week was introduced. Finally, the Conservative Government lost the General Election of 28th February 1974 to Labour. TIE began to define itself as the propagator of ideas, as the reflector of society and the environment, and to look at the relations between people, from the point of view of class. Many team members were left wing, and some held Marxist views. Romy Baskerville, in her Paper to Conference in 1973, set out the dilemma that was beginning to face companies with a strong political stance:

> Historical perspective, seeing the present in terms of the past, becomes very important. And this, of course, is where some TIE companies are getting their, (justified), left wing reputation from. We want to show the kids what their own history has been, not that of their "superiors", but the bits that are always left out. We want them to have some understanding of the real nature of racialism, of a woman's role in society, of trade unionism, of pollution, of old age. It is necessary to understand that politics is not a dirty word; it involves, expresses and influences every emotional and material condition of our lives, and it begins with a small 'p', not a big one. Of course TIE is political. It

would be political whether or not it had a tendency to be left wing, because it has to be a mouthpiece which communicates values. And the question has to be, whose values? Thence comes the almighty one, is TIE propagandist? Or even party propagandist?

Although many members of TIE companies were left wing, and some joined the Workers' Revolutionary Party, propagandist material was not apparent in TIE programmes. The work had been observed by a number of people from the early 1970s and propagandist material had not been noted. Bert Parnaby, (Her Majesty's Inspector, with responsibility for drama) preparing a report on Theatre in Education declared that: "He hadn't seen a single programme showing overt political bias, although there is over-simplification sometimes, but no worse than is seen on television."[8]

Yet TIE programmes certainly dealt with political problems, with pollution ("Rare Earth"), the police, and revolution. Coventry's historical programme on the English Revolution was followed by a discussion in which society today was examined "in the light of these revolutionary events". The TIE companies' approach was to tackle such issues and ask questions, yet the teams were well aware of the limited effect that such programmes would have on pupils:

> In terms of effective change we can pose an opposite which might cause a question mark in the kid's understanding of what is pumped into him from all sides. But not much more than that.[9]

Yet this political attitude did lead to outside criticism of a particularly undesirable kind. The *Daily Express* printed a "Column of Disclosure" in June 1974, which dealt with "the misuse being made of a movement called Theatre in Education (T.I.E.) for which taxpayers and rate payers are footing the bill". The newspaper accused "the ever-vigilant Left wingers" of infiltrating the schools and getting at children "of all classes with their revolutionary ideas".[10]

Luckily such criticism did no lasting damage to the movement, and in fact 1973 was probably TIE's overt political period. After this companies began to integrate their political views into their work in a much more acceptable fashion. With the rise of the National Front in the mid-1970s companies were able to tackle the issue more calmly and form a clear and better balanced point of view. Bernard Crick, writing on the Cockpit's programme, "Marches", which dealt with the rise of Moseley, commented that "the play was, in fact, marvellously balanced, 'fair' and empathetic". He concluded his article with a warm support for the team in undertaking such an important political issue:

> It was not just a day out. It should not have been. Here were the very roots of theatre and of political understanding intertwined. Dramatic

political issues need an imaginative understanding of the plausibility of all relevant viewpoints. Since they exist in society, how can we possibly "exclude" National Front ideas from schools even if it were desirable to do so? We can, however, combat them effectively by making pupils more politically literate. Would that more schools could spend time in the Cockpit.[11]

By 1979 TIE's political maturity was observed by Chris Vine, who has worked in Theatre in Education since 1973:

> I think that now there are more companies who in terms of their work are more political, but that has in certain circumstances become better integrated into the overall work of the company. At one end of the scale it's been toned down a little in terms of proseltysing, which is a very irritating attitude that some people have, but on the other hand it has fed back through the work and people have got to recognise that. You've got to decide what you are doing. I realise better work is coming from companies who have gone through that process. You've got to ask fundamental things about what you're expecting from society and what young people are coming to expect. It is a very difficult one, no point in preaching. You need a focus in those areas where young people take responsibility for what's going on.[12]

The increase in the amount of performance in TIE programmes is, perhaps, a natural outcome of a company trying to present a point of view. A play, or documentary approach, enables the TIE team to explain facts, develop characters, and present an argument. When pupils are totally involved in a programme, in a physical sense, this can lead to a lack of clarity in their understanding of the totality of the problem presented. Yet this move towards performance is more true of the Secondary school programmes. In these, the play and the pupil's participation have tended to become separated. The Cockpit's presentation of "Marches" the Greenwich team's "Race Against Time", and Coventry's "The Rise of Hitler" all follow this structure. One part of the programme was a play, properly presented and well acted, the plays are often very dramatic and emotionally powerful. The other part of the programme can vary, but five main forms of work have developed: the group discussion, the hot seating of characters, the simulation, the drama workshop and the pupils acting out their own play.

In the Infant and Junior school work some programmes still use the same format developed by Coventry in the early 1970s. The Coventry programme "The Navvies" presented in 1978 for top Infants began with a session in the classroom with a navvie explaining the problems of building a railway line to the pupils. They agreed to become navvies and were shown how to use a pick and shovel. The class moved to the hall, and the story of digging the Kilsby tunnel unfolded, the children participating the whole time. The action moved on by a series of story-telling episodes, dialogue between the characters, and work sessions in the tunnel.[13] This structure is almost exactly the same as Coventry's "Penhale" programme presented in 1976, and has many similarities in form with "Pow-Wow".

Many of these Junior programmes tackled political and social problems: Coventry's "Rare Earth" dealing with pollution and looking at the mercury poisoning at Minamata; or the Lancaster programme "Travellers", which looked at the problem of travellers and gypsies, and the Council's responsibility.

Those companies who became more overtly political began to move away from their educational, drama in education role in schools and adopted a much more theatrical approach to their work.

> What has happened through the development of TIE means that performers, writers, designers etc. have the opportunity to be fully responsible for the content and form of what they produce for a particular audience. That's what the thing called TIE boils down to, and I believe, that's the nearest to a definition that can be found.[14]

The organization to which most of these companies belonged, the Standing Conference of Young People's Theatre (SCYPT), ran a yearly conference, which allowed companies to exchange ideas and suggest ways in which TIE should develop. The 1976 SCYPT Conference produced a great deal of political discussion. One seminar group's conclusion neatly summarizes the prevailing attitude amongst the teams:

> That, although our work is *not* revolutionary, one has a duty to maximize wherever possible the impact of experiences which increase objective awareness of what society is about and make this real and emotionally and morally challenging, through the power of direct 'theatrical' experience.[15]

At this period TIE saw itself as standing outside the education system, offering alternative ideas, and attempting to make the pupils question society. To maximize their impact in schools teams placed greater emphasis on their theatrical skills.

Out of this increased political awareness there emerged a change in thinking on company structure. For it was becoming increasingly apparent that those teams with a coherent policy based on a political commitment and a democratic group structure were producing the best work for schools. Teams like Coventry, Peterborough and the Cockpit had been working as a group democracy for some time, but a number of other TIE teams still retained their original structure. This meant an Artistic or Administrative Director, who controlled policy, was on a permanent contract, and employed a company on short contracts. The SCYPT Conference in 1976 allocated a whole day to discuss company structure, the Cockpit team posing the questions: "Is creative democracy the best process for devising a programme?" and "Does the existence of a political democracy for the purpose of carrying out the ongoing organization of a company necessarily dictate its existence for the purposes of programme devising?" In answer to these questions one seminar group felt that an administrative director tended to produce a "creeping paralysis in the work", because the director and not the actual company controlled policy. As a result of this discussion a number of companies returned to their base and rethought their company structure. At Greenwich this produced a complete change from a hierarchical structure to a group democracy. The motion passed at the end of the SCYPT Conference actively encouraged this process.

As the political aspect of TIE companies' development became more integrated, the work shifted again. Due to the increase in the number of Community Theatre groups in the 1970s, and a move by some teams towards a mixture of presentations for different age groups, TIE teams began to examine their aims more closely. Having explored and developed their techniques, method of work, political commitment and company structure, many TIE companies began to reconsider their role in education. In so doing some of the major companies have started to create a more effective working relationship with schools. They are beginning to develop a closer liaison with teachers, work in greater depth with fewer schools, and are pushing to have TIE programmes accepted and used across the curriculum. Chris Vine of the Greenwich team summarized the team's moves in this direction in 1979:

> We are in a transitional period. We had a major breakthrough with this programme and the last (i.e. "Unemployment" and "Race Against Time"). There was a time when it was always Drama (who used the programme). Now Social Studies, history departments and so on, have come to realise the value and that programmes are much more applicable to what they're doing than it is to drama departments. Also the cross-curricular approach is beginning to develop, with a number of teachers being involved with what's going on; and we're getting closer relationships with a few teachers in specific schools.[16]

The Greenwich team continued to develop their work, but introduced much closer consultation with the teachers, both on programme construction and on educational philosophy.

Over the past few years Greenwich, like a number of TIE teams, have been asking themselves basic questions about their function in society and education. Questions such as: "What is important to know? What do children learn? What should they learn? How do they learn?"[17] To try and find some answers to these questions, and to involve the teachers in the whole process of TIE programme preparation and presentation and incorporating it into a scheme of work, the Greenwich team introduced two pilot schemes. The team sent out a letter to Secondary schools who had shown a continuous interest in the work of Greenwich TIE, asking if any teachers would be prepared to book all the Secondary programmes for the next 2 years. Ten schools responded. The teachers involved undertook to encourage cross-curriculum use of TIE in schools and to work with the team from the outset on planning a new programme. The company held a series of meetings and workshops with these teachers, and then organized a one-day Conference. The Conference gave everyone a chance to discuss the broader issue of "what is education for", and to apply some of their deliberations to programme preparation.

Although the reason for Greenwich's pilot scheme grew out of frustration within the team rather than from any specific educational theory, the team had in fact begun to adopt a different method of approach to programmes. This approach was based on the use of a concept as a starting-point rather than an issue. In 1978–9 the team had concentrated upon such issues as racism and unemployment for their Secondary school work. By 1980 the

FIG. 11. Greenwich TIE, "Living Patterns", 1980. Part One, the simulation.

FIG. 12. Part Two, drama workshop.

team had shifted to the use of the concept applied to a topic as a much better starting-point for cross-curricular work in schools. Much of this new thinking was stimulated by the 1979 Standing Conference for Young People's Theatre held that September.

For their Primary school project the Greenwich team asked if any schools would be interested in undertaking the same commitments that had been requested of the Secondary schools. Nine schools responded. The teachers of these schools decided upon concepts that they felt were important learning areas for third- and fourth-year juniors. They were co-operation, inter-dependence, and power relationships. Four meetings were held between the team and the teachers to plan a scheme of concept project-based work. Both the programme preparation and its presentation were to be a co-operative effort.

FIG. 13. Part Three, the play.

The final result was a three-part programme with a week's gap between each part based on the concepts first suggested by the teachers. The topic was a comparison between power structures on British and Chinese building sites. The first part of the programme consisting of a simulation on a British Council house building site, the second part a drama workshop using the pupil's own choice of work place, and the third part a play about a Chinese building site. This particular programme was the result of an enormous amount of effort on the part of the team and the teachers both before and during the programme. An effort that appears to have been worthwhile. This is only the beginning as Sue Bennion points out in an article in the *SCYPT Journal*:

> What we have embarked on at GYPT is only the beginning of a struggle that has to continue both in terms of developing our educational framework as a group of people with specific theatrical skills and in conjunction with teachers as fellow educationalists.[18]

Greenwich are not alone in this new effort to liaise closely and creatively with teachers. The Cockpit team has taken a very definite stand on the policy of working with fewer teachers, concentrating on the same group and working with them over and over again. By this means they hope that teachers will take a much greater part in deciding what areas of work need to be developed. The team is also interested in an integrated curricular, and to put this into practice their recent programme was on the concept of change, using as the subject-matter the English Revolution in the Seventeenth Century. This programme, "The Ways of Change" (1979), set up specific areas for consideration:

> WAYS OF CHANGE attempts to examine the questions of how change occurs. In our programme, we have concentrated on two aspects of change: (1) how social and political change occurs; and (2) how change is experienced by individuals in periods of economic turmoil.
> Both of these are examined in the context of the 17th Century English Revolution, for the pupils to compare and contrast with the contemporary world and their experience of it.[19]

By experiencing ways of change rather than the historical event, the company hoped that "any teachers of any discipline could approach that question within the sphere of their discipline".[20] As the programme was booked by teachers of history, English, social studies, geography and drama, this policy appears to be successful.

In response to TIE team's increased educational concern, more teachers are recognizing the value of TIE as a real resource. They are more willing to alter school timetables and follow up the programmes and to work closely with the team. As a consequence teams have been able to increase the depth and range of their programmes, and teachers are building them into an overall scheme of work. The Junior two- or three-part programmes are appearing again, but teams are more careful in their structure, so that the period in between visits can be used carefully and creatively by the school. TIE teams have begun to realize that the flying one-off visit is not as useful as programmes integrated into the school's scheme of work. Companies have also begun to bring programmes back, sometimes after a year has elapsed. This is only possible when the team stay together over that period. Coventry has used this policy for many years; Greenwich brought back "Race Against Time" with a different play, and have brought back their unemployment programme, with a new simulation. Bringing programmes back allows time for evaluation, rewriting and restructuring. It therefore helps in raising the standard and effectiveness of the work in schools, and means that teachers who missed booking the programme first time round get a second chance. With "Race Against Time" some schools booked it again when it came back after a year.

The development of TIE has taken an interesting, almost circular course over the past 18 years. When many TIE companies began work they

FIG. 14. Coventry TIE, "Have a Nice Day", A programme for Top Secondary
pupils, on Northern Ireland, 1980.

associated themselves closely with the local schools, and offered their work as
part of the education service. After several years they are now returning to
this position, but with a much greater awareness of how to use the techniques
developed, why they are in schools, and the effectiveness of their work.

During the first few years of Theatre in Education in many smaller teams
there was a reaction against the use of specialists such as designers and
administrators. This was partly due to the companies' finances, but it was
also part of a move towards the team having responsibility for, and doing, the
range of work required.

Over the past few years more TIE teams have developed the maturity and
self-critical ability to realize their own limitations and to see the benefit that a
specialist could bring to the company. This move has been particularly
noticeable in the employment of designers and musicians, some of whom
have joined a team as a full member sharing in company decisions and
programme structure.

A questionnaire on design was sent out to a range of companies doing TIE,
YPT and Community Theatre work in 1977 and from this:

. . . it appeared that most teams have managed to include a designer through an increase in overall budgeting, together with either increased awareness of the need for design and/or an increase in studio- or theatre-based work. Although within the present climate, expansion is not exactly encouraged, design could be seen, in many cases, to have contributed to the raising of a team's overall standard. In certain community theatres it is felt to have contributed to box office and consequently, in terms of Authorities, it can be used to show an improvement in the product for which they are paying.[21]

Just as the actor–teachers in TIE felt the need to meet and talk about their work, at the annual SCYPT Conferences (the Standing Conference of Young People's Theatre) so have the designers and musicians. The Designers organized their own Conference to facilitate this discussion:

Conceived out of the Aberystwyth Conference, and nursed into existence through the very active support of Peter Brinson and the Gulbenkian Foundation, the SCYPT Designers' Conference finally emerged at the Key Theatre, Peterborough on April 12th 1977. Seen as an opportunity for Designers within the Movement to meet and exchange ideas for the first time, it was very definitely intended, not as a separatist movement, but as a means of providing another service within the SCYPT Organisation.[22]

From the discussions at the Conference grew a clearer understanding of the specific problems of design for this area of work, and the realization of a need to improve certain elements. The Conference elected a working party to explore a number of the ideas that emerged during the day. These consisted of the creation of a data-information service; the investigation of the possibility of teams obtaining designers through job creation and 'design fellowships'; the establishment of research grants to fund research into specialist technical areas, and to look at ways to promote design generally, e.g. through exhibitions and the SCYPT conferences.

From this also grew the Designers' Scheme, backed by the Gulbenkian Foundation, which would help teams to employ a designer, who could not normally afford to do so.

The musicians began a similar process and set up a Conference for Musicians involved in the work. This took place on 20th May 1978. The aim of this Conference, and the Working Party which came out of it, was:

We weren't aiming, as the designers had, at the inclusion of a musician in every team but more at 'opening out' and demystifying music so as to extend the possibilities of its use in TIE and YPT.[23]

The Gulbenkian Foundation also backed this Conference. From this meeting a number of suggestions were to be taken up by the working party such as the need for a list of musicians who could help teams; the need for Regional Music workshops; the possibility of enabling companies to employ musicians; and possible ways of introducing music training related to Community Theatre requirements in colleges, or Drama schools. The fact of specialists within the Movement forming their own demands, making specific proposals, and developing their own philosophy within the context of the work is indicative of how inherently different the work is from any other form. It makes very specific demands and requires special skills, many of which can only be learnt once a specialist has started to work within the team.

The changing philosophy of TIE is not only based upon its relationship with education, or the specific skills of the company members, it is also based on TIE's relationship with the theatre, both in a philosophical and a practical sense.

Many people working in TIE reject main-stream theatre. David Pammenter stated his feelings in the Coventry TIE Report of 1972–3:

> Theatre has failed as a forum, it is seldom a living force in a community. I am not here criticising the entertainment value of theatre except in that it seldom entertains young people, rather I am questioning its purpose and looking at its effect. It is, in the main, irrelevant.

This attitude is often obvious in the gulf that lies between the attached TIE team and its 'parent' theatre. The setting up of a TIE team was often the result of initiative by the Theatre's Artistic Director. The TIE team would then be treated sympathetically and offered office and rehearsal space, and an interest would be taken in the development of the work. However, a change of Artistic Director could mean that the TIE team found itself ignored and unwanted. There are in fact basic differences in philosophy, method and working schedules, that inevitably separate the TIE company from the Repertory Theatre. Fred Hawksley at Coventry pointed out this problem:

> We are in a sense very different, exercising two very definite skills that puts us not higher or lower, but a distance from a main house actor.[24]

In the early days many main house actors certainly regarded the TIE team as second-class citizens, thus helping to increase the gap between the two companies. As one TIE company member wrote in answer to a questionnaire on Drama Training:

> "Community Theatre and TIE were most definitely a 'bit off'. It was regarded very much as a second class occupation."

This statement referred to the early 1970s. Now there is a much greater awareness within the Theatre profession of the nature of TIE work and the particular skills it requires. However strong the support for its TIE team, the parent theatre can experience difficulties in coping with it. The main problem is usually one of space: this arose at the Citizens' Theatre in Glasgow and the team had to find rehearsal and storage space elsewhere. Another difficulty is the actual lack of connection between the two areas of work. Giles Havergal, who is most sympathetic to TIE work, and initiated the scheme in Watford, found that with the Watford TIE team in its early days:

> The effect on the theatre was curiously negative. Because of the way the theatre developed it didn't allow us to plug into the work they were doing in schools. What was on at the theatre wouldn't have appealed to the child watching "The Tay Bridge Disaster" in his school hall.[25]

With these problems forming a barrier to any real interaction between the TIE team and the main house theatre, many people working in TIE relate more easily to Fringe and Community Theatre. This was certainly Roger Chapman's feeling in 1976:

> I've become more and more disillusioned with Regional theatre. Even more disillusioned with the National Theatre. How relevant and important are they? More and more I have felt that the real excitement was going on in companies like "Belt and Braces", touring companies that worked outside theatres, but worked in the community much more. I always felt that TIE had a valid part to play in this process, and while our policy depends on the sources of our finance . . . probably 80% of work that I do is in schools. I think the feelings that we have about the theatre are the same as a number of fringe theatre groups outside theatre buildings. I do see us as part of this whole new stirring in the English theatre, which is much more towards . . . performers being able to perform something anywhere at any time. Highly skilled performers who can write, devise and research their own material about subjects which are very important to a particular community[26]

Many TIE companies such as Glasgow, Nottingham, Bolton (M6), and Dundee began to introduce some element of Community Theatre touring into their schedules. Companies such as Bolton were forced to move away and change their identity with the discontinuance of the LEA grant. Now, as M6, they combine Community Theatre with TIE. The Harrogate company gained Man Power Services money and with this introduced Community theatre productions. This feeling of a need to move into the Community was explained by Stuart Bennett:

> I worked in schools, and got to know the Community, and felt that we should work there. Logically the parent company should do it, but it didn't.[27]

There are few repertory theatres that actually involve themselves in the Community in this active way, the Victoria Theatre, Stoke, and the Phoenix Theatre, Leicester, being some of the few exceptions. In fact a few theatre directors still think that part of their TIE companies' role in the community is to encourage people to come to the mainhouse theatre.

The natural step for many of those leaving TIE is not to move into the main-stream theatre but into teaching or into Community theatre. For TIE has helped to create a new type of actor, as Sue Birtwhistle described:

> Actors leaving TIE are not as prepared, as they might have been just to be given a script and rehearse. They are often looking for something more, a different sort of relationship with an audience.[28]

Edward Peel, once a West End actor, who joined Leeds TIE company, recognized the effect TIE had on performers: "They are people who are looking for more than doing just a play, they are looking for content, and for some say in the policy of the place."[29] It was this kind of person he wanted to employ when he became Director of the Humberside Theatre, not those with conventional main-stream theatre backgrounds. This, however, is rare.

Many TIE companies have moved away from their "parent" theatres, both physically and philosophically, such as Greenwich, Leeds, Billingham YPTC, Ipswich, Bolton and the Key Perspectives, Peterborough. Both the Bolton and Peterborough teams have moved away from their home base, and set up totally separate organizations.

TIE has developed into a different method of work, which uses theatre and teaching techniques as an educational stimulus. Many of these techniques can also be used in Community Theatre work, particularly those of programme devising. Thus, given the nature of the TIE method, and the kind of people it attracts, Theatre in Education has a natural alliance with the developing Community Theatre movement, rather than with main-stream theatre.

In the early 1970s, however, this natural alliance was not so apparent. Companies were only just beginning to define their policies, find a form of work and discover their 'audience'. During this period of development companies were isolated from their parent theatres and from each other. They became increasingly aware of the need to break through this isolation.

The Standing Conference of Young People's Theatre (SCYPT)

Pressure from within the TIE/YPT movement for some kind of unity of purpose and a chance of sharing ideas and problems led to the formation of SCYPT in 1976. However, many years of disunity and confusion preceded it.

During the late 1960s both Drama in Education and Theatre in Education in schools were developing rapidly. However, very little information was available to teachers and Local Authorities as to the nature and application of

TIE, and the use of Drama in Education was limited and not well understood. Consequently confusion was rife. For instance, Gavin Bolton, in an article for the 1970 edition of The British Children's Association magazine *Outlook*, was asking "is Theatre in Education Drama in Education?" He gave an example of the confusion that could occur: "A comment by a Director of Education when asked about drama in schools was 'We have Brian Way's company every year' ". This assumption that one kind of activity can replace another is indicative of the real problem these "specialists" faced in trying to clarify their work and have it properly used.

Exactly this kind of confusion was also noted by Hilary Ball during her study of Theatre in Education in the late 1960s and early 70s:

> Neither teachers nor actors are entirely sure of what they want from their liaison, apart from more money. The theatre has not yet fully grasped the nature of the role it has to play in education, and the content area of drama as it is currently understood by teachers still stands in need of clarification.[30]

Attempting to develop this new technique, which rested uncomfortably between theatre and education, TIE companies felt increasingly isolated. Teachers were concerned at the introduction of TIE into schools and often puzzled as to how best to use the programmes, and many actors and directors in the main-stream theatre just did not understand the difference between Theatre in Education and Children's Theatre.

In 1969 an editorial in the first edition of the British Children's Theatre Association magazine, *Outlook*, pointed out that some kind of "coming together" of all these areas was definitely needed:

> It seems reasonable to assume that where theatre meets children, both actors, directors and educationalists should come together to share what they know of their art, for the benefit of the children and young people involved. Aims and values should be assessed and re-assessed. Perhaps even a survey of various approaches used, views held, etc., should be made by the Arts Council so that some kind of broad unity of philosophy and intention may emerge. Certainly it is not enough to experiment in a vacuum without first examining the knowledge and variety of experiences already accumulated by others.

Attempts had already been made by organizations to try and help the development of Young People's Theatre. The Council of Repertory Theatres (CORT) undertook to act as an umbrella organization for Young People's Theatre in 1957. In 1969 it began a Young People's Theatre Section Bulletin to aid the exchange of information, and teams such as Coventry regularly contributed to this. The National Council of Theatre for Young People (NCTYP) had started a regular Dairy of Activities in Theatre for Young

People "for the benefit of all those, including particularly the Arts Council Young People's Theatre Panel and foreign visitors, seeking this information".[31] Companies working in Young People's Theatre and TIE had met in 1967 for a one-day discussion, because they felt that co-operation and liaison between all members of CORT working in Theatre for Young People was essential. This early meeting, however, was concerned with practicalities and not so much with the exchange of ideas. Discussion arose on the overlapping work of different specialist companies; low standards; the need for specific clauses in the repertory contracts; fees for extra work and the need to encourage writers for this area.

By 1970 the YPT and TIE movements were gaining strength and showing some unity of purpose. As a result of a confrontation with the CORT executive by four YPT delegates, led by Caryl Jenner and Brian Way, it was agreed that a YPT sub-committee of CORT should be elected. The election took place on 4th March 1970. This new sub-committee represented the interests of Young People's Theatre, TIE, and specialist companies such as POLKA.

Over the next few years the sub-committee dealt with some very important practical matters such as the negotiating of the new Equity TIE contract, which acknowledged the totally different working schedule of most YPT and TIE companies.

However, the debate on the real nature of TIE work and its difference from YPT and Children's Theatre had not been tackled on any large scale. The fact that there was a difference was made obvious at the International Children's Theatre Festival in 1971. The performances and discussion at this Festival opened up questions on what kind of entertainment do children want and what is suitable for them? In attempting to answer these questions a sharp division amongst those present became very obvious:

> Roughly, they comprised those who favoured the traditional approach to children's theatre; story-telling, simple language and controlled participation — versus the more experimental use of realism, improvisation and not 'talking down' to the kids.[32]

Yet it was not until the National Festival of Young People's Theatre in 1973, held in London, that the quality and clarity of good TIE work fully emerged:

> However, as the Festival wore on, and the more mediocre programmes had to stand up to comparison with some more exciting work from the established companies, bigger questions were asked about aims and methods.
>
> What emerged was that the Coventry and Bolton teams seem to be the only ones who had a very clear idea about what they were trying to

do and where they were trying to go. Their convictions showed in their presentations.[33]

In spite of the Coventry teams standard the Belgrade TIE commented on the Festival in their 1972–3 Report:

> The most obvious fault of TIE nationally that became apparent at the Festival, is the lack of unity of purpose. It is still, unfortunately, not possible to talk of TIE as a movement.

To attempt to improve on this situation and to aid the contact between teams, a series of meetings were organized by various TIE companies. To these all the TIE teams in the country were invited. This gave TIE teams an opportunity to begin discussion in depth on the nature of Theatre in Education work and its relationship to education. As a result of this series of meetings The Standing Conference of Young People's Theatre (SCYPT) was formed.

The need for SCYPT was unanimously agreed at the Leeds Symposium in 1974. This gathering was the first which really attempted to bring together those inside and those outside the TIE movement, for it continued over the weekend with a 2-day Conference for Local and Financial Authority representatives. Time was set aside during the week to work out a method of approach to these representatives, and a way of presenting TIE and its particular needs. The emphasis of the Symposium itself, expressed in the General Symposium Plan, was to be on "sharing and comparing experience, and exploring together our common needs at present and in the future". The areas chosen for discussion are indicative of the fact that TIE teams were attempting to grapple with the more fundamental problems of Theatre in Education rather than with the practical day-to-day affairs. The issues to be raised were listed in the Symposium plan as:

> . . . relationships with teachers, authorities, children and so on; the internal organisation of groups; the uses and abuses of participation — a specifically practical session this — financial and union status, etc. A most important aspect of these sessions also will be an attempt to investigate common ground, and move by the end of the week towards a definition of a TIE and some coherence within the movement.

Over the past 2 years TIE teams had become increasingly aware of the need to establish a more formal co-ordinating body for its activities. Once having voted to actually set this organization up the teams had to define its policy. This was set out as:

> The aim of the organisation is to encourage the improvement of current artistic standards in Young People's Theatre and Theatre in Education in the devising, writing, designing, directing and performing of work

for young people. It will also represent YPT/TIE companies in Great Britain and liaise with other appropriate bodies, especially those concerned with the growth of Drama and Theatre for Young People.[34]

This dual function of keeping member companies in touch with each other and of promoting the work on a national scale was to present continuous problems over the next few years. The idea of SCYPT was encouraged by the Gulbenkian Foundation, which offered £9000 for 3 years after which the organization should become self-sufficient. After further conferences at Leicester and Peterborough SCYPT finally came into being in 1976.

It was to be run by a committee elected from the members. A new committee would be elected each year at the AGM. An important part of their work would be the organization of the Annual Conference. A base theatre was to be selected each year, which would take on the responsibility of collecting and sending out SCYPT information, and the Newsletter.

A constitution was drafted, much discussed and eventually ratified. This constitution set out a whole series of aims, which are worth quoting in full:

Objects: The advancement of education of young people through the theatre and dramatic arts and in furtherance of the above but not otherwise:

(a) to encourage and promote the creation and presentation of programmes in schools, youth clubs, theatres and in the wider community which will stimulate and be of benefit to young people;

(b) to arrange the collection, collation and dissemination of information in the field of theatre for young people;

(c) to provide guidance, information and other assistance to organisations, institutions, authorities and persons working in the field of theatre for young people particularly to raise current artistic standards;

(d) to consult and co-operate with or make representations to Central and Local Government and International, National and Local organisations to do all lawful acts and things as are incidental to the attainment of the primary Objects of the Conference and so far as may be necessary or desirable to do such acts and things in collaboration with any other Body, person, Constitution, Authority or otherwise;

(e) to foster, promote and increase the interest of young people in the theatre and dramatic arts;

(f) to receive, hold, administer and raise funds for the use of the primary Objects of the Conference.[35]

Once SCYPT had begun to function as an organization, the members decided to broaden the membership beyond the confines of TIE to enable SCYPT to be more representative of Young People's Theatre and Community Theatre. This move reflects the development of the movement as a whole where work for young people was being presented by a number of different groups, many of the presentations being based on TIE principles.

SCYPT also developed liaisons with a range of organizations associated with the work, such as NCTYP and Equity. The main function of the organization was, however, to set up the Annual Conference, and this it has done every year since 1976. The conferences last 4½ days and a large number of member companies attend, the whole company not just representatives. This time together gives the members a chance to debate their philosophy, to thrash out problems, and sometimes to see each other's work. These Annual Conferences have proved very important for the development of TIE teams understanding of their work. They frequently provide a stimulus for change in the individual company's ideas, methods of work and educational philosophy. In addition to these Conferences, local meetings have been organized by teams, so that problems relevant to the area can also be raised.

In 1976 SCYPT began a Newsletter to facilitate that exchange of information. The committee recommended that it should be an outward-going publicity and information service. However, the Newsletter also became subject to one of SCYPT's continuous problems: how to reconcile the desire to advertise itself outside the movement and need of its members to discuss and explain their work amongst themselves.

To aid the dissemination of information about TIE/YPT work a SCYPT journal was started with a £1500 grant over 3 years from the Gulbenkian Foundation. The aims of this journal were:

> To provide a forum for general discussion of areas of specific interest to TIE/YPT with a view to:
> (a) promotion of the movement through publicity;
> (b) more thorough discussion of the aims and progress of the work than is currently available;
> (c) extending the links of the movement with fields of allied interest and corresponding groups abroad.[36]

The journals are published twice a year and at first tended to concentrate on presenting programme outlines. This has now changed and the journal is moving towards being a forum for discussion. In 1983 the SCYPT journal represents the only publication dealing exclusively with TIE, YPT and Community Theatre work, and offering informed information and comment. It is, therefore, a very important part of SCYPT's fight to explain itself to those outside the movement.

Since its creation SCYPT has discovered a fundamental problem; whether it should just be a forum for internal debate, or whether it should also try and be a disseminator of information about the work of SCYPT members and liaise with the various other organizations in the field. After much debate SCYPT decided to concentrate upon its internal functions: the development of the work of member companies. In so doing it has dropped many of its external functions such as representation on various committees.

Chris Vine of the Greenwich Young People's Theatre strongly supported this internal movement. He pointed out that because of the way SCYPT is set up at the moment the members do not have the time to sell TIE to the outside world. His view in 1979 was that:

> The best way to sell yourselves is to make the standard as good as possible, and for individual companies to deal with the authorities on that basis. It is the classical mistake of a lot of funding to feed it in at the wrong end — for administration, or paying for research — yet there is no money to actually do the work. The other big problem is if you put the emphasis on going out selling TIE and you get interest, what do you do with it? Already a problem has arisen with people in Higher Education wanting to bring students to Conferences.[37]

The decision to turn inwards to raise standards, and sell TIE by this means, appears to disregard the need for communicating on a wider scale than just to local teachers. Without this communication it is possible the hostility that met TIE in the early days could return, or that the grant-giving bodies could show a lack of understanding of the nature of the work. Any effort involved in increasing the information on TIE for the general public would surely bring real returns in terms of understanding and support. In fact *not* to attempt to raise interest appears to disregard TIE's interests in both the short and the long term.

One of the most important areas of communication for TIE teams is with their funding bodies. In the present climate of cutbacks the more the Local Education Authorities know about their local team the more informed will be their discussion on its grant.

Theatre in Education has always been subject to the external pressure of the grant system. TIE is labour intensive and very susceptible to cuts. On many LEA budgets it appears as a separate grant to a group outside the education system itself, and could be classed as a "fringe benefit". The need to seek, and keep, funds has exerted a real influence on the development of TIE.

Funding

Since Theatre in Education began in 1965 some major shifts have occurred in the nature of its funding. For many companies the Arts Council was the first organization to offer money, and only when some sort of liaison with schools and a detailed scheme had been worked out, or even tried out, did the Local Education Authority contribute.

Where the LEA began, or took over the financial responsibility for, a scheme, the companies tend to be well established and respected. The obvious examples of this policy are the Coventry team, and the two London teams, the Cockpit and the Greenwich Young People's Theatre. Sometimes the Local Education Authority supports the TIE company by paying the team's wages as teachers, and then seconding them to do full-time TIE as in Edinburgh. Or the team are teachers, but divide their time between teaching in schools and preparing and taking out Theatre in Education programmes, such as Aberdeen and Clwyd.

Most companies are in receipt of an Arts Council grant, which often matches that from the LEAs pound for pound. These kinds of grants mean that many TIE companies do not have to charge schools. They are providing a service of educational value to the pupils and teachers during school time. Neither schools, nor pupils, should therefore have to pay for this. There are a few TIE companies, however, who do not receive sufficient money in grants and must charge schools to survive.

There are teams, such as Watford, who actually combine a number of these forms of funding. The Director and the Assistant Director receive Lecturers' salaries through Watford's Cassio College, and the TIE company itself are paid from the income created by charging schools and by the grants received from the Arts Council and the Local Authority. This mixture of funding can be very unsatisfactory as the Lecturer salaries are on the Burnham scale and the companies' wages are sometimes linked to the Equity TIE minimum, which tends to be much lower. In a very small company where work and responsibility are fairly evenly shared if such wage differentials do apply they can seem very out of place and could be a potential source of friction.

In 1975 John Greatorex, Drama Adviser for Powys, predicted that: "Within ten years a company . . . run by the authority, will be a normal part of education services."[38] In the present economic climate this looks very unlikely indeed, but in 1974 the Arts Council were suggesting exactly that:

> . . . it seems reasonable, as a guide, to suggest that in general the cost of work for children and young people within school hours (whether in school or in the theatre) should be sought from the local education authority, and that subsidy for work presented outside school time should be sought from both the Arts Council and the Local Authority.[39]

In fact the funding for Theatre for Young People is still fairly evenly balanced between the Arts Council (approximately 46 per cent) and the Local

Authorities (approx. 40 per cent), with the Regional Arts Associations contributing the other 14 per cent.

From 1974 to 1978 the actual number of companies performing for young people had greatly increased. By 1977 there were about ninety companies doing work for children, and the Arts Council funded just over half of them. However, in the past few years the total Arts Council grant has decreased in real terms running below the level of inflation. The Arts Council needed a 22 per cent increase in their total grant for 1980/81 just to keep pace with its commitments and meet inflation and wage settlements. This would have taken it from £61 millions in 1979 to £73 millions in 1980. In fact it received £70 millions. For 1981/82 the Government has given the Arts Council £80 million. This represents a 14 per cent increase, but £2½ million has been earmarked for capital projects and this will leave just 12 per cent more for clients. Yet that figure is only 1 per cent higher than the projected inflation rate. Many theatre companies are already seriously in debt; only substantial grant rises would help. This is very unlikely. In fact the Arts Council have warned that some clients will have their grants axed completely, believing that its first priority is to give money to those of its clients in whose creative strength and vitality it has confidence. This does not bode well for the small companies, who are struggling to keep going.

The increase in the Arts Council's grant aiding to Young People's Theatre from 1974 to 1978 has not kept pace with inflation. In 1973/4 the grant was £594,000 and by 1977/8 it had risen to £700,000, an increase of £106,00 or 18 per cent. Inflation over the same period, however, was much higher.

Another factor which affected the actual amount of money available for Young People's Theatre was the end of the 'ear-marking' of grants by the Arts Council in 1974. In 1973/4 the proportion of grant spent on young people's theatre work by the various repertory theatres was 13.8 per cent; by 1977/8 it had dropped to only 12.5 per cent.

The Arts Council is well aware of its inability to meet all the demands made by the companies working with young people. They suggested in the 1974 Policy Statement: "The problem of adequate subsidy is likely to remain in respect of Young People's Theatre as in all areas of the arts. Therefore it is vital that money should be sought from as many appropriate channels as possible." Companies certainly have made an effort to tap any and every source. The Greenwich Young People's Theatre, with its large range of activities, have received money from such sources as: the Community Relations Commission, the ILEA Youth Service, the Committee for Racial Equality, the Arts Council new play grant and the London Schools Drama Association. This is in addition to their usual larger sums from ILEA and the Local Borough.

Companies doing some Community Theatre work also add to their income with box-office returns, or fees. Yet charging schools for TIE work is very undesirable, and against most TIE companies' policy. There are curious pockets to be found in Local Authority funding, the major one being the Leisure services. In 1975 the Serpent Theatre company in Sussex received money from the National Playing Fields fund. This kind of discovery requires ingenuity, a knowledge of the nature of Local Authority funding divisions, and the right kind of presentation to offer at the right time. The amounts raised in this way are usually very small and are often granted for that one occasion or programme only; thus giving no continuity or security. Grants from industry are very rare indeed, and these are usually given to Community Theatre or touring companies rather than to TIE companies. The Solent Company, who do no TIE work but do work with young people outside school hours, received money from Duplex, and Esso. However, to raise even small sums of money in this way takes a great deal of effort for very little, if any, response. This kind of funding is much more likely to be offered to the large and prestigious organizations such as the Scottish or Welsh Opera companies.

Money from Trusts is another source of income from TIE, but few Trusts contribute to this kind of work. Theatre Centre was helped by a capital grant from the Nuffield Foundation when it first began touring. The Citizen's Theatre for Youth received money from the Duncan Macrae Memorial Trust for the first 3 years of its existence. The Calouste Gulbenkian Foundation is the one trust which has really helped the TIE movement, and it has done so in a variety of ways over the past few years. In 1976 it helped to start the Standing Conference of Young People's Theatre (SCYPT) and continued to contribute to the running of the organization for 3 years. It has recently launched a Theatre Writer's Scheme for which it had allocated £10,000 for 1979–80. The scheme provides money for the attachment of a writer to a SCYPT company for a period of up to 6 months. The Gulbenkian Foundation interest in TIE began in 1973 when it helped to found the Everyman Priority Community Theatre Project in Liverpool. The Gulbenkian provided most of the money for this project and contributed quite a lot to its overall philosophy, which meant a new kind of development for the Foundation. Peter Brinson, Director of the UK Branch of the Gulbenkian, commented that this:

> . . . reflected major policy revisions which had taken place since 1972. One result was to shift the emphasis of the Branch's work much more towards social change and social action.[40]

With the adoption of this new policy it is perhaps no surprise that the Gulbenkian Foundation should have found the TIE movement worthy of support. It has recently offered a grant to the Theatre in Northumberland Schools, which was formed with money from the Man Power Services Commission in 1977. The Foundation has, however, spread its support across a wide range of work with young people and helped companies such as Medium Fair, Theatre Mobile, Moving Being, Half Moon and Polka Puppets.

In spite of its desire to help TIE, YPT and Community Theatre the Gulbenkian Foundation has insufficient funds to support more than a few companies and the umbrella organization, SCYPT. A number of TIE schemes begun in the mid-1970s relying upon the two main grant-giving bodies, the Arts Council and the Local Education Authority, are finding it difficult to survive. Plymouth TIE, formed in 1975, was unable to keep a company running and had to disband three teams in the first few years.[41]

The only new source of funding for TIE and Community Theatre work in recent years is the Man Power Services Commission, MSC. Set up by the Labour Government in 1975 to help curb unemployment, it has become a major factor in the creation of several new companies and a method of saving other companies from closure. The Citizen's Theatre was able to begin its Theatre about Glasgow, as a Community Theatre scheme with MSC money, in 1976. Without this source the company would have had to close down until the money came through from the Local Education Authority for the team's work in schools. The Leicester Phoenix Community Company was supported by £32,000 from MSC for 1978–9. The Harlow Community Theatre was set up in 1978 with MSC support, and is now supported by the Local Authority. Action PIE in South Glamorgan, begun with MSC money, managed to continue with grants from the Local Education Authority and the Welsh Arts Council, when the MSC funds ran out. The Man Power Services Commission funding is essentially short term, providing money for one, or at the most, 2 years' salaries. Yet a large number of schemes from TIE to Community Arts work were created with the help of this funding, not all of them will survive when their MSC money stops. In fact the MSC itself will have less money to offer with the present Conservative Government cuts.

Yet, in spite of the gloomy economic situation in the last few years, new companies are still being set up. A new professional company began work in 1980 in Easterhouse, Glasgow, funded by the Man Power Services Commission under the Special Temporary Employment programme. The company specialize in schools and Community Theatre work.

Some Local Education Authorities have attempted to set up schemes but these have been on a very limited basis. Wakefield Education Committee initiated a Drama in Education project in 1977, but at first could only make two of the original four appointments.

Other ways of starting up a company are still possible. Paul Harman, the original director of the Everyman Priority Community Theatre Project, has recently set up the Merseyside Young People's Theatre Company with funds from Merseyside Regional Arts Association and from charging schools.

Against this seemingly hopeful scene must be placed the closures of already established TIE and YPT teams. Nottingham TIE Roundabout company, established since 1973 and one of the largest groups in the country running two TIE teams, had its £31,000 grant from the Nottingham County Council cut in 1979. The company was just one item in a list of economies made by the County Council to save £1.9 million 1979/80.

It is too early to tell how the government cuts and the present recession will affect TIE in the long term. There is no doubt that it is in danger. Whilst the Man Power Services Commission has increased the number of TIE, YPT and Community Theatre companies this is essentially short term. There is little guarantee that LEAs and the Arts Council can take over the responsibility for funding such work when the MSC funding period is finished.

This economic uncertainty can lead to companies concerning themselves principally with money raising rather than with their work. It can lead to the dilution and virtual disappearance of the TIE work as companies begin to perform to the community and visit special touring date theatres to raise box-office income, fees and grants from other Local Council pockets.

TIE has become a recognized way of working with pupils and teachers but only continuous co-operation with a limited number of schools offers any stimulating and effective contribution to education.

As TIE teams realize the need for their work to be absorbed by schools in depth and across the curriculum, they are becoming much more concerned with the effectiveness of their programmes. This can only be judged by feedback from pupils and teachers through constant evaluation of the work.

This desire to evaluate is enhanced by the worsening economic climate and the consequent need to present to the fund-giving bodies the value of the work in schools. As Chris Vine pointed out, to survive TIE teams must prove "that we're not dabblers, that there is a very clear, beneficial educational policy developing".[42]

It is the problem of evaluating Theatre in Education which forms the second part of this book.

Notes

1. B. Way, personal interview at Theatre Centre offices, 7th May 1976.
2. S. Bennett, Belgrade TIE, Annual Report, 1969–70. *Belgrade's Bones*, p. 6.
3. J. O'Toole, *Theatre in Education*, Hodder & Stoughton, London, 1975, p. 37.
4. P. Asquith, personal interview at the Belgrade Theatre, Coventry, 12th July 1976.
5. C. Beloe, personal interview at Area Education office, Derby, 9th June 1976.
6. S. Birtwhistle, personal inteview at Roundabout offices, Nottingham, 14th June 1976.
7. Bolton, TIE, personal interview at TIE offices, Bolton, 24th June 1976.
8. B. Parnaby, in an Open Forum of Observers of TIE, SCYPT Conference Aberystwyth, Sept. 1976, Report of the Conference for SCYPT members.
9. R. Baskervill, paper to Conference, 1973.
10. *Daily Express*, "Column of disclosure", 14th June 1974.
11. B. Crick, "The play's the thing", *Times Educational Supplement*, 9th December 1977.
12. C. Vine, personal interview at Stage Centre (GYPT), 22nd March 1979.

13. This script is now published in *Theatre in Education; Five Infant programmes*, Pam Schweitzer (ed.), Methuen Young Drama, 1980.
14. R. Baskerville, paper to Conference, 1973.
15. SCYPT Conference Report, Aberystwyth, September 1976.
16. C. Vine, personal interview at Stage Centre (GYPT), 22nd March 1979.
17. S. Bennion, "Working with teachers", *SCYPT Journal*, no. 6, 1980, p. 43.
18. *Op. cit.*, p. 48.
19. Cockpit TIE, *Ways of Change*, Teachers Pack, 1979, p. 1.
20. G. Gillham, personal interview at the Cockpit Theatre, 12th March 1979.
21. R. Bourke, "Talking about design", *SCYPT Journal*, no. 1, 1977, p. 22.
22. *Op. cit.*, p. 21.
23. SCYPT, Minutes of Music Conference, 20th May 1978.
24. F. Hawksley, personal interview at the Belgrade Theatre, 22nd June 1978.
25. G. Havergal, personal interview at the Citizens' Theatre, March 1978.
26. R. Chapman, personal interview at Leeds TIE offices, 13th May 1976.
27. S. Bennett, personal interview at Rose Bruford College, 17th June 1976.
28. S. Birtwhistle, personal interview at Roundabout offices, Nottingham, 14th June 1976.
29. E. Peel, Director of Humberside Theatre, personal interview at the theatre, 21st June 1976.
30. H. Ball, "Mapping its growth", *Drama in Education, Annual Survey*, no. 3, J. Hodgson and M. Banham (eds.), Pitman, London, 1975, p. 14.
31. Report of a meeting of the Young People's Theatre Section of CORT, Sunday, 14th May 1967.
32. *NCTYP Bulletin*, Sept.–Oct. 1971, no. 14, p. 1.
33. P. Schweitzer, quoted in *Belgrade Coventry TIE Annual Report, 1972–3*, p. 64.
34. Standing Conference of Young People's Theatre, Information Leaflet.
35. SCYPT Constitution, 29th May 1976, p. 1.
36. SCYPT Committee Minutes, 16th–17th October, 1976.
37. C. Vine, personal interview at Stage Centre (GYPT), 22nd March 1979.
38. J. Greatorex, quoted in Peter Fanning's article: "Tied to the purse strings", *Times Educational Supplement*, 6th June 1975.
39. Arts Council of Great Britain, Policy Statement, 1974.
40. P. Brinson, "The Gulbenkian Foundation and Theatre in Education — a personal view", *The Theatre in Education Directory* C. Chapman, (ed.), T.Q., Publications, London, 1975, p. 9.
41. Plymouth TIE, Information to SCYPT, March 1976.
42. C. Vine, personal interview, 22nd March 1979.

Chapter 5

The Evaluation of Theatre in Education

Due to its unique position straddling the areas of theatre and education TIE is susceptible to judgements and criticisms based on widely differing criteria. Anyone watching a programme will make some kind of personal assessment, from "That was well acted" to "It was a very useful educational stimulus".

Personal assessment is not sufficient for the needs of a TIE team or a grant-giving body. To understand properly and judge the value of the work clear criteria for evaluation have to be found.

A TIE team's work is a dynamic process. With each new programme the team begin with more information, more self-knowledge, more awareness. They learn about their work, themselves, each other and about the world around them through the process of programme preparation and presentation. Thus, the team, the pupils and the teachers learn with each new programme. This learning process relies, to an extent, on the team's understanding of what the programme has done, or is doing, and its effect in a school. To move on to the next programme the TIE team must evaluate their work, both during and after the presentation. Some teams work 4 days a week in schools and spend the fifth day discussing the present and future programmes, or researching and rehearsing. This discussion period provides a forum for a continuous debate about the effectiveness of the work, but it is basically inward looking. To gain an overall picture of the effect of a programme for proper evaluation the team need the opinions of their consumers — the schools.

Theatre in Education companies have established some methods of gathering this information. They hand, or send out, questionnaires to teachers after a programme, and organize teacher-team meetings. Few teams have the time or the personnel to follow up their programme in schools themselves and talk to pupils about it. Therefore, teams have to use a fair amount of intuition and guesswork when assessing the programme's effect. For an experienced team with a sound knowledge of the area this method can work, but for an inexperienced team it can be disastrous. It can lead to bad work and an increasing distance between what the team offers the schools and what the schools actually require, or find useful.

Teachers can be reticent about criticizing team's work, and unsure how to do so. The philosophy of "Oh well it's better than nothing" can prevail, with the accompanying fear that too much criticism might lead to the withdrawal of the service altogether. As many grant-supported teams have no fee system or 'box office' they have no way of discovering their failings. Only continuously bad or outrageous work would lead to the schools ceasing to book what is in some cases a free service.

Local Advisers, of English or Drama, often keep an eye on the team's work and try to create a link between the team and the Local Education Authority. Some Advisers can recommend the withdrawal of a grant if they feel that this is justified. However, most Advisers would try to improve the team's work rather than to stop it altogether. In the present economic climate it is doubtful that an LEA would renew a grant that had been withdrawn.

In a time of economic cuts the grant to the local TIE team is in danger. It is a small but defined amount of money to be struck off the budget, and the TIE service can look like a dispensible 'fringe' benefit. This is exactly what happened at Bolton where, in spite of the pleading and the letters from numerous teachers, the LEA decided to stop its grant to the team. Where a LEA pays the teams as teachers this grant cutting can be more difficult.

What criteria does a Local Authority use when considering the value of a TIE team's work? If Bolton can be taken as a typical example they do not use criteria based on the opinions of the customers — the teachers in the schools. There is a great danger that the LEAs try to impose a cost-effective value.

TIE is labour intensive, and works in depth with few pupils. It can present two- or three-part programmes to one or two classes at a time. Any use of criteria based on the numbers of schools and numbers of pupils visited will be emphasizing the quantity rather than the quality of the work produced and shows a basic misunderstanding of TIE.

The attitude of considering the cost-effectiveness of a TIE programme is certainly a threat in the present economic climate, when LEAs are searching their budgets for places to cut expenditure. In so doing a Local Education Authority may well ask itself: "Is this TIE company worth the money we spend on it?" The answer to "Is it worth it?" cannot be found in the number of pupils who have seen the programmes, or the number of schools visited. The worth of a TIE team's work can only be ascertained by evaluation of their programmes, preferably taking into account the team's long-term effect in schools, and on their local area.

However, this cost-effective approach has made itself felt by imposing an increasing pressure on teams for accountability. The team must justify their cost by showing the positive effects they have made spending the money they have been granted. To enable a TIE team to demonstrate these positive effects some clear method of conveying the value of their work is needed. To convey this value, the work must be evaluated; but what exactly is meant by evaluation? It can be seen as "The estimation of a degree of value: of a work of art: of a scientific discovery, or . . . the efficiency of a learning process."[1] Evaluation looks at the value, or worth of the process that is offered to the pupils, not at the pupils' own ability, or achievement in learning. The pupils' achievement is studied by assessment of their work, and judges their actual and potential performance within the education system. Evaluation, on the other hand, is to do with the education service itself, as Ken Robinson points out in his article in *Learning Through Theatre*:

> Evaluation . . . looks at a programme in terms of the opportunities which it provides for learning and not only at what children may or may not have learnt as a result of it. Evaluation looks at the *teaching*, not just at the children.[2]

The TIE team's method of sending out questionnaires to gain information on the value of programmes has its limitations as teams are well aware. The questionnaire cannot be too long, or detailed, as teachers will not find time to answer it. The questions the team ask tend to be general and not related specifically to each programme.

This is usually because the same phrased form is used for every programme. In fact the Cockpit questionnaires, in 1976, were very simple, allowing the teacher freedom to select and discuss any aspects of a programme. The forms had a large space just headed "Teacher's Comments", and one other heading related to the programme: "Pupils' attitudes and reactions to the project at the time and in the discussion after." Whereas the Curtain Theatre TIE questionnaire of 1976 was a much more complex affair consisting of eleven questions:

> Please comment on the relevance of the programme — its content — presentation — pattern of work — demands and expectations — length:

> Were the material and approach at the right level for the children it was aimed at?

> Did the programme achieve its stated aim?

> What were the children's reactions to the programme?

> What were your reactions to the programme?

> How useful was the Teachers' Workshop?

> Would you have liked to participate more or less in the programme?

> Were the follow-up suggestions useful?

> Have you done any follow-up work? If possible, outline it briefly:

> Can you give us any feed-back of children's comments or work:

Was the attitude and organisation of the Curtain TIE Company satisfactory?

None of these questions was allowed much space, unlike the Cockpit form, consequently on the Curtain form answers tended to be brief: and not always very analytical, or they consisted of one word, such as "Yes"! The Cockpit forms were usually fully completed, but of course the comments were not necessarily specific. The Coventry team's questionnaires of 1976 (still in use) were a happy medium between these two extremes and consisted of five questions on the programme. These followed the same kind of pattern as those of the Curtain team:

Do you think the subject material of this programme was suitable for your children? Please comment:

Was the form of presentation suitable for your children?

What, for your children, was the educational value?

Do you anticipate doing any follow-up work or not?

Comment on the programme or your children's reactions.

The Greenwich team worked out a specific questionnaire for "Race Against Time", as it was an especially requested and rather delicate issue. Even so, the kind of questions asked were along similar lines to the Coventry and Curtain questions:

1. "Could you comment on the suitability of the material for this age range?"

Unlike the general forms, it asked specific questions on the structure of the programme:

2. The programme attempted to relate the experience the pupils had in the morning session to the issues raised by the play in the afternoon.
   (a) Do you feel that the links between the two sessions were understood by the students?

From this range of questionnaires it can be seen that there are certain basic questions which each team ask:

1. The suitability of the subject matter for the pupils.
2. The suitability of the form of presentation for the pupils.
3. The pupils' reactions to the programme.
4. Whether the school has done any follow-up work.

Does this kind of questionnaire actually produce useful information? In trying to answer that question an example of the range of comments made by teachers on one programme might be helpful. The local teachers' comments on Coventry's programme "Pow-Wow" were varied and fairly full. "Pow-Wow" was a very successful programme, performed by many other TIE teams, and worked on by a number of people over a period of 5–6 years. It has now been published.[3] To place the teachers' comments in some sort of context I will briefly summarize the programme.

Its aims and method were presented in Coventry's Annual Report of 1972–3:

Aim: Traditionally in the cowboy and Indian games that infants play, cowboys are the 'goodies' and Indians the 'baddies'. However innocent this may appear, it is a prejudice. And, as such, it has much in common with those extreme forms of prejudice which lead to race riots and pogroms: like them, it is fostered by ignorances, myth and fear. Potentially, it is dangerous. 'Pow-Wow' aimed to overcome this prejudice at grass roots level.

Method: The programme was intended for one class of top infants and their teacher, and was in two parts with a break between them. The first part of fifteen minutes was in the classroom, and the second half of an hour and a quarter took place on the school field. The actor–teachers involved were seen by the class 'in character', and complete belief in the situation was encouraged. There was no preparatory work with the teachers although follow-up work was supplied.[4]

Mr. Tex, an American showman, walks into the classroom and talks to the children about the white man and the Red Indian and about his "Black Elk" Show. He tells the class Black Elk is a savage Red Indian, like his ancestors who killed the white man in America. After the break, the children go to the school field, or to the hall, and find there a teepee in a circular wire cage. Black Elk emerges and does his "show" acting out how Indians lived, with Mr. Tex providing the commentary. When Mr. Tex leaves to make some phone calls the children are left alone with Black Elk. Slowly he gains the children's confidence until, eventually, he gets them to release him from the cage. He then works with the children to create a Red Indian village, and to fish and hunt the buffalo. They have a Pow-Wow, and smoke a peace pipe. Mr. Tex returns and is furious to see Black Elk out of his cage. He demands to be given the peace pipe and the tomahawk which Black Elk has been showing the children. Mr. Tex then asks the children to vote on who should have the tomahawk and peace pipe. For the voting the children must decide whether to stand by Mr. Tex, that he should have the two items, or by Black Elk. There are then, two possible endings depending upon the way the children vote.

In reply to the Coventry team's first question on their questionnaire about the *suitability of the subject matter* for the children there were twenty-six replies from different schools, and fourteen of these thought that the subject was suitable. Of the other eleven the range of criticism or concern was as follows:

> Two schools were worried about the moral problem in the programme.
> Two schools found the programme too sophisticated.
> One school thought the structure too complex.
> One school felt that the children did not understand the red man vs. white man problem.
> One school suggested that the background information on North America, presented by Mr. Tex, was covered too quickly.
> One school found Mr. Tex's accent difficult.
> One school thought the children found the settler problem difficult to understand.
> One school felt that the children really had not yet developed a sense of history.
> One school said the children were scared.

As an illustration of the kind of things the teachers actually wrote here are two quotations:

> Suitable for children of this age — it's a natural form of play. They already know a little about Indians less about the settlers. From always thinking about the Indian as "baddie" they were able to see the primitive skills of hunting, fishing, etc., alongside the power of the guns of the white settlers.
>
> Yes, but would benefit from much simpler presentation, maybe having the 2 characters explaining themselves at the same time might have been better. To see Mr. Tex first gave him the advantage and made a bigger impression than Black Elk.

These are two of the longer quotes, most were only two lines long, the favourable ones just saying yes, and that the subject was a popular one. As can already be seen by the second quote some of the comments are not always written under the appropriate question, which for this quote would have been the one on the *suitability of the presentation*. On this question there were twenty-five replies (one school not filling in that section) and eight were totally in favour, the seventeen criticisms were mild and usually pin-pointed one element of the presentation as unsatisfactory such as the fact that the preamble in the classroom was rather too long, or the children had to sit for rather a long time and the programme could have had more participation. Examples of these comments are:

> Some of the children are so impressionable and Mr. Tex stamped his opinions on them so firmly that any possible enjoyment value or

involvement during the rest of the show was lost for them in their violent fear and dislike of the Indian or worry of possible retribution from Mr. Tex for having anything to do with Black Elk.

This is one of the severest criticisms; others were more mild:

> Both Mr. Tex and Black Elk's presentation were presented very well. May I suggest Mr. Tex uses some form of visual aid as his 'quick talk' sometimes lost the children of my class.

OR "Thought the presentation was very good and suitable."

The question on the *educational value of the programme* produced a range of responses,

> A great stimulus for language development, and insight into a different life style.

OR Gave them a sense of history, and made them realise that Indians are not simply baddies who appear on the TV all too frequently.

Only one school thought that the programme had no educational value. Of the rest, eleven schools thought that it helped the children understand the life style of the Indian, six suggested it helped language development and another seven felt that it aided the children's ability to make moral decisions. There is no doubt that the programme stimulated the desire to learn more in the children, as the answers to this question, and the one on follow-up work, show. The most interesting comments came under the last section, which allowed the teacher to add to the questionnaire their own thoughts not covered under the other questions. Although the programme was a successful one, in fact perhaps because of its success, many teachers wrote at length. They often repeated points they had made earlier but many of them commented upon the final vote that the children had made:

> On further thought and discussion the children 'thought through' the implications much more seriously and formed some more 'moral' judgements on Tex's unkind actions and Black Elk's trust and kindness.
>
> Had the vote been taken on the following Monday I feel the result would have been quite different with far more voting for Black Elk. (They found the concept of voting very difficult.)
>
> From the discussion afterwards it was evident that the children had been thoroughly "brainwashed" with regard to cowboys and Indians. They voted for the cowboy because: "Cowboys are good." Some voted for him out of fear. Four children regretted their decision to vote for him when they later realised the consequences.

For one teacher this comment section allowed a reflection on a problem which TIE teams have been wrestling with for years:

> I feel that we are taking an unfair advantage of the children if we don't let them realise beforehand that it is a 'play' in which they are asked to take a part. Even knowing this many will become so involved that they 'live' the situations. But I feel in some way we are humiliating them by letting them take part believing that all they see is real as it is happening. Children of this age often have difficulty in distinguishing between fantasy and reality and I believe we are doing them a disservice by playing on their gullibility merely for effect.

The information from this set of questionnaires could certainly be of use to the team, but how much use? The criticism was made about several different points and did not emphasize one particular element that should be changed. However, if a team were worried about a particular part of a programme then one or two criticisms by teachers on that point would be sufficient to confirm the team's suspicions. Otherwise the questionnaires tend to offer a range of disparate views.

In the comment section at the end the teachers tended to review what the children said or did, rather than reflecting upon the programme's structure that made them respond in that way. The teachers are assessing their children's performance, where the team wish to evaluate their programme's performance. Also teachers tend to be rather protective of their class. To a certain extent both they and the class are on show to the team, and the teacher is worried whether the children will respond, or behave. This concern and protectiveness becomes apparent in the questionnaires with many teachers starting comments with the phrase: "My children . . ." In spite of this, of course, the teacher is giving his or her own opinion, and that of the children is not asked for, and rarely given. Unless the follow-up work is sent into the team, which does happen occasionally, the details of what the teacher and the pupils actually did with the stimulus of the programme remain a mystery, apart from the brief descriptions in the questionnaires.

As the teachers often fill in the questionnaires soon after the team's visit, there is no information available on the long-term effects of the programme, or how soon the children forgot the experience. Also it is usually the "keen" teachers who are in favour of TIE, who fill in the forms. Their comments, therefore, tend to be supportive and only mildly critical. Due to the amount of space after each question, and also due to the teacher's timetable, replies tend to be brief, and often general and unanalytical. In fact, unless a teacher is well versed in TIE techniques, problems and concerns, it is difficult for them to analyse why sections did, or did not, work.

TIE teams read the questionnaires and do adjust and rethink elements in the programme in response to the comments. If, however, a lot of information is forthcoming, as with the "Pow-Wow" returns, it tends to be confusing. Unless the information is properly correlated and the pressure of opinion noted, it tends to remain a mass, or a mess, of impressions with the team remembering only those points which first caught their attention.

The Greenwich TIE team are lucky in being able to employ a schools liaison officer, part of whose job is to make a report from the returned questionnaires. Therefore the information is ordered and points are brought out for the team's attention. Both the Cockpit and Coventry teams have recently appointed a Schools Liaison Officer.

The general comment forms, such as the Cockpit's questionnaire, present immense difficulties in the actual sorting out of all the information offered. For instance, here is a teacher writing about the Cockpit's version of "Coriolanus" (they did not try and present the whole play but put it into a modern setting using speeches from the play mixed with other dialogue):

> Given a firm knowledge of the text, the programme was a useful exploration of political motive in the play: the demagogue aspect to the Tribunes came off particularly well as did the less astute Brecht-type folk-play, which showed more fairly the legitimate concern of the people of Rome — this was a high-spot in the day. The passions of Coriolanus were less clearly shown, but of course these are more evident in the text itself, especially in the family scenes.
>
> The controversial question of whether Coriolanus is a tragic hero or not is, in my opinion, best left for classroom discussion: the final scene of the programme seemed to me admirably constructed to leave this question open for later argument — at least a day later, when the dust has subsided . . .

That is only half the teacher's comment. It is very helpful, thoughtful and analytical, but to make sure that the ideas are placed in relation to other teacher's comments so that some overall picture can be gained, requires someone to read each questionnaire, split it into different headings and correlate it with comments from other teachers. When the comments are long, and many on the "Coriolanus" programme were, then this is a real time-consuming task.

Questionnaires are helpful, but not entirely satisfactory and certainly, they do not give a clear picture of the total effect of the programme.

Information gathered at teacher-team meetings, after a programme has finished its run, can fill in many of the gaps. However, it is probable that only the "keen" teachers will attend these meetings which are held after school hours. To make sure that the discussion is constructive, the team need some sort of agenda, or points for discussion drawn up in advance, and someone who can guide the discussion. Also details from meetings like this tend to be forgotten unless the discussion is recorded, and the main points noted.

Greenwich TIE team recorded the discussion after "Race Against Time", but I wonder how many valuable ideas have gone unnoted, or are half-remembered, because no recording is made, or no one was taking notes during the meeting.

This kind of evaluation is obviously internal, for the team only, but there is a case for external evaluation. Few teams have the time to follow up a programme by visiting schools after the "run" of the programme is complete, and as had been said, even sorting out the information that does come in via questionnaires and meetings can be too time consuming. TIE teams have neither the time nor the money to check, in detail, upon the effect of their work in schools.

The more TIE teams work with only a few schools, and get to know the teachers well, then it is probable that the exchange of information will be sufficient for them to feel that they know what is happening and whether their programmes work. Few TIE teams can do this. The London teams are certainly trying to develop such a policy but for most teams the pressure to visit more than just a chosen few schools is too great.

Who should, or could, evaluate TIE work in schools? Should it be someone who is considered part of the company, or a seconded teacher, or someone totally outside both the worlds of theatre and education? Few teams can afford to employ someone to do such a job full time, there is no doubt that the role of the Schools Liaison Officer is an extremely useful one for any team to have, but even so this involves far more than just evaluation: it is essentially an administrative post. A seconded teacher would appear to be an answer, but few LEAs are going to think of seconding teachers, when even these working in schools are facing the possibility of losing their jobs.

The advantage that an outsider could bring is that of objectivity. There should be no bias or axe to grind! It might, also, prove easier for teachers too, for they are not offering opinions and criticisms straight to the team, but know that their ideas will filter through. In the present financial circumstances the only way a team could undertake full evaluation themselves would be for one of them to drop out of performing for a while. This already happens with writing and programme research.

Whoever it is who is evaluating the work, what do they actually do? The research needs some shape, and purpose. The writers of a paper on evaluating adult education have drawn up three points to be used as criteria for assessing research of this kind:

(a) *Objectives*:   Are these clear, practicable and useful?
(b) *Methods*:   Are these systematic and effective in pursuit of the objectives? Are they not excessive in time and not prohibitively expensive?

(c) *Applications*:   Are these of practical value both in the short term and in the long term? Can decisions be directly based upon them?[5]

This provides a useful set of guidelines to help in the search for a suitable evaluative model for TIE. The model provides a practical and philosophical framework with which to approach the work to be evaluated.

One of the most popular models used by evaluators is the Goal-attainment or Objectives model. This is defined as "evaluation as measurement of the degree of success or failure encountered by the programme in reaching predetermined objectives".[6] To use this model the goals, or aims, must be clarified, and the evaluation consists of trying to determine whether these goals have been achieved. An obvious example of the use of this approach appears in the Curtain Theatre's 1976 Questionnaire: "Did the programme achieve its stated aim?"

To use the objectives model on a TIE programme would mean that the team must have worked out the aims clearly, and to have borne these in mind when structuring the programme. Not all teams, however, work out clear aims. They can be rather nebulous, or just very difficult to check whether they have actually been achieved. For instance, the aims of the Lancaster team for their "Travellers" programme:

> Secondly we wished to look at some of the cultural differences between Travellers (romanies, potters, tinkers, vagrants) and the settled urban population to highlight and contrast values and differing patterns of family and social interdependence and loyalties, e.g. the single and the extended family unit. At another level we wanted the children to understand the effects of some of our more barbaric laws relating to this traditionally persecuted minority, and through their own identifying with the characters (presented as real) to question and challenge and seek alternatives.
>
> Thirdly and lastly, by making a two-visit programme we wished to show the children a real development in the events affecting the characters as a result of the decisions made jointly with the children on the first contact, i.e. to recognise a pattern of consequences.[7]

In the first part of these objectives the key words denoting intent are "to look at", "to highlight and contrast". To see if this had been achieved, a researcher would need to study the programme structure to see if this has been done. Had the company actually "looked at and highlighted" the various elements they had chosen? This could be generally ascertained but it is very doubtful that it could be measured as the elements described are too vague "differing patterns of family and social interdependence". The next aim is that the children "understand" a particularly difficult concept of the workings of the law in terms of a minority group. What exactly is meant by understanding in this context? Against what criteria should the pupils' success or failure be judged? For the third aim the recognition of a pattern of consequences is also a very difficult concept and its success or failure hard to judge.

Thus the kind of aims that Lancaster drew up may well help in the clarification and structuring of the programme itself, but would prove very difficult to measure in terms of success or failure in the schools. Also the children will respond differently in each school, and would therefore produce contradictory results for each objective. The concentration on aims excludes all the other effects of the programme: the emotional response of the pupils, the learning in other spheres, etc. Often the side effects are extremely important. As it employs a far too limited perspective the Objectives Model is a very unsatisfactory method to use when evaluating a TIE programme.

Ken Robinson, in his article on evaluating TIE, points out that there are in fact two types of educational objectives, the expressive and the instructional: the latter hopes to teach specific skills, whereas the former describes an educational situation and task.[8]

Theatre in Education certainly sets both kinds of objectives but the expressive objective cannot be evaluated via the objectives model. The real danger of this model is that if evaluation is based on whether the objectives are achieved it takes a very narrow view indeed of the learning process, and disregards many of the most important, more subtle methods of learning that may take place. These could be found in the side effects that had not been considered when the objectives were set up.

One of the difficult factors in trying to find a satisfactory way of evaluating TIE is that the programmes frequently consist of different dramatic and educational forms such as simulations, plays, discussions, drama sessions and so on. Would it be of value to use different methods of evaluation for the different parts of the programme? The simulation, as a teaching method, has been evaluated by Dale Garvey. The result of his research proved to be: "A catalogue of judgements, findings and hunches."[9]

He decided to evaluate how a simulation could be used by teachers to achieve their teaching objectives. His approach indicates a possible method for TIE evaluation: "the evaluation of simulation must be essentially a subjective judgement of the technique as a motivational device".[10] He chose five categories to describe the use to which simulation could be put:

(a) As a device for motivating students.
(b) As a means of affecting student attitudes.
(c) As a means of facilitating the acquisition and retention of knowledge.
(d) As a means of developing social skills.
(e) As a means of providing laboratory experiences.

He summarized how he evaluated each category. For point (a) he used his own experience based on observing students' increased motivation in a simulation situation. Category (b) involved an attitude assessment using the Thurston scale. This is a method of measuring attitudes and consists of about five levels of attitude usually under "strongly agree, agree, not sure, disagree, strongly disagree". The students register their opinions on the subject on this scale both before and after the particular educational programme which is to be evaluated. Garvey also used a control group here to check attitudes. This is a method of comparison. The control group does not experience the learning programme, but is often taught the facts in a straightforward manner. For this research the control groups' attitudes would be checked on the Thurston scale. The results would then be compared with the students who had been involved in the simulation. Garvey found that in this research the data was tenuous. For (c) Garvey used tests on the knowledge gained, and graded them. He also used control groups. For this part of the research he discovered that:

> In actuality, the control group, which did not experience simulation, indicated that it acquired more factual knowledge and the experimental group, using simulation, indicated it retained more conceptual knowledge.[11]

For points (d) and (e) Garvey again employed observation. His research led him to the conclusion that:

> Present instruments for measuring achievement by students are constructed to measure their performance after exposure to conventional instructional methods. Such measurements probably do not assess all types of changes which may occur such as a result of participation in a simulated situation. Effective evaluation of simulation as a technique would require the design of measuring instruments which assess the students' acquisition of skills, their changes of attitudes and behaviour as well as the amount of knowledge gained.[12]

Thus, although Garvey can claim that "Simulation possesses some solid advantages for use in education", he has to admit that this statement is not fully backed by empirical evidence.[13] Garvey's conclusion of simulation evaluation could also be applied to the problem of TIE evaluation: the methods of measurement available are geared to the conventional instructional forms.

TIE programmes offer much more than a few facts. In "Pow-Wow" two sides of the argument are presented: that of the white man, and that of the Red Indian. The pupils are placed in a moral dilemma and asked to choose who they support. Through the programme they experience fear, distrust, disbelief, loyalty, disloyalty, enjoyment, etc. The pupils' experience and learning covers the whole area of the cognitive, effective, social and imaginative spheres. Measurement in these circumstances becomes difficult, and Garvey makes the point that: "Precision of measurement is difficult at best and frequently impossible in education."[14]

Garvey's research used a mixture of objective measurement tests and subjective observation. Although objectivity is considered to be important in evaluation, in any area other than strict factual testing it becomes difficult to maintain.

An evaluation model for TIE must allow for the inability to measure effect and the subjectivity of response of the observer. It is in the area of the arts, and drama particularly, that a more suitable model can be found. In an article on researching drama C. Gordon Brossell suggests the use of humanistic research:

> Humanistic research begins with the subjective knowledge of experience, and discovery is its characteristic mode of enquiry. While it has no standard methodology, its advocates share a common attitude concerning the nature of the investigative task. This attitude has three recognisable aspects:
> (1) A problem-centred orientation.
> (2) The use of 'heuristic' methods of exploration.
> (3) The holistic analysis of experiential data.[15]

"Holistic" analysis of the data concentrates on the organic unity rather than the separate parts of the process being evaluated. However, within any one TIE programme there can be numerous different forms: a drama session, a simulation, the performance of a play and so on. Therefore to evaluate the overall effect of a programme in a school it is necessary to allow for the varying effects of these elements and to draw on information from as wide a source as possible. New evaluation models have been suggested which are much more flexible and which take into account the situation and nature of the learning process to be evaluated. The terms used to describe these models have been clarified by D. Hamilton in his book *Curriculum Evaluation*.[16] They are "responsive", "holistic", and "illuminative". As their titles suggest, these models seek to respond to the process being evaluated, and are not limited to the original plan or objectives. To do this they look at the educational programme as a whole, and by this means they seek to open out the situation to informed analysis and criticism.[17]

Adopting a holistic approach allows for a broad-based method of collecting, sorting and analysing data, and incorporates a range of opinions. However, this should be done systematically, as Brossell indicates:

> An ideal investigative technique would use the concrete experiential

data of personal discovery as a basis for later systematic analysis and classification.[18]

The other elements of humanistic research noted by Brossell do have some application to the evaluation of a TIE programme. The heuristic method is one of discovery by doing, and this could apply both to the pupils experiencing the programme and to the evaluator who uses this experience. The problem-centred orientation can be seen in the same way. Most TIE programmes have problem-solving as an essential part of their structure, and the evaluator would also use it in preparing the evaluation.

Having found more suitable evaluation models there is still the question of the methods to use for collecting the information. Evaluation methods used by Educational Televison could be of use. The Swedish Educational Television and Radio Service employ a special group concerned exclusively with research and development questions. Their emphasis is on the "non-traditional" approach and they discard traditional research methods. The method they use is to take the generally phrased questions that are the result of contacts between the researcher and the producer and the production team and split them up into more concrete questions. In the next step they try to define how to get answers to the questions by choosing methods to be used for the evaluation project. They try to interfere as little as possible with the daily school work. However, they have found that there can be a problem with this approach, for answers to their questions can, in some cases be rather vague. They, therefore, try to cover the questions in several ways. Even attempting to maintain a natural atmosphere in school work the evaluation suffers from the "Hawthorne effect". This effect was named after the experiment on worker productivity at the Hawthorne plant of the Western Electric Company in the late 1920s. Here the experimental situation itself "modified social relations, group moral and individual motivations among subjects in ways such as affected their performance, in most cases for the better".[19] The Swedish team select particular schools rather than visit a random group. Their answer to the criticism of this method is:

> What we want to know through our research is not whether all teachers and students in Sweden look at our learning aids in a certain way. Instead we want to go deeper and describe how one particular learning aid or one particular program functions in a number of classes.[20]

There is much that is relevant for TIE evaluation here. Covering TIE programmes in a wide variety of schools would produce only generalizations. To be of use it would seem better if the evaluation were specific, and related to one TIE programme only, presented by one team. The formation of concrete questions would appear to be a good method of clarifying exactly what information is required from the schools. These questions could be asked directly to the pupils and teachers who have experienced the programme. They could be in written or verbal form.

With the use of the holistic model for evaluation, information could be gathered in as many ways as possible. Therefore any form of written, verbal or visual information on the programme could be of use. It is important to establish the timing of the evaluation, whether it is to be formative or summative. Formative evaluation can be used to help shape a programme and maximize its effectiveness by pre-testing ideas and methods in schools. In 1968 Coventry TIE team went into schools to improvise with pupils and from this to discover the most suitable material for a children's play (see Chap. 2, p. 69). When preparing a programme teams sometimes talk to pupils and teachers to gather ideas and attitudes. The Greenwich team did this for "Race Against Time" and for "Living Patterns" (1980). Preliminary teacher's meetings also provide some form of evaluation when a new programme is discussed. The main difficulty for TIE is that due to the group-devising process, material is not always available to try out until the end of the rehearsal period.

Summative evaluation (i.e. after the programme has finished its run in schools) has the obvious value of being: "directly based on the real situation; it is assessing what actually happened".[21] Time is less of a pressure, but the problem is that whilst a lot of effort may go into this form of evaluation, results may only be of value to the one programme evaluated. The information gathered may be of use if the team wish to set up a similar programme for the same age group. In addition there are always unlooked-for effects which can be of value to the work as a whole.

Teams also evaluate during the run of a programme. Teachers' comments and their own doubts and dissatisfactions will be discussed and fed into the programme whilst it is still in schools. This constant evaluation helps the dynamic, evolving nature of the work. Programmes are not "fixed" once they are running, but are under constant scrutiny, and will be changed. By the end of the run a TIE programme can sometimes have undergone a number of real alterations. However, any "major surgery", such as the reworking or rewriting of a play, or a simulation, often has to wait until a programme is brought back after a period of time.

Has any attempt at evaluation of TIE programmes been made before? There are two experiments that have been published. They were on the specific issue of audience participation and used arts-based evaluation techniques. John O'Toole's experiment recorded in his book on TIE was to question the findings of an earlier experiment written up in the BCTA magazine *Outlook* No. 4 (1972). The writers of the article in *Outlook* were contesting the opinion that when children actively participate in a pro-gramme they are more totally involved than when they just sit and watch. The information was collected after the plays and was, therefore, summative.

The investigators were looking at Children's Theatre performances presented by students, not at TIE. It was not meant to be a scientific study but an inquiry to see how much children can remember after a participation or non-participation performance. They collected information after a number of plays and appear to have used the checking of the children's drawings and paintings after they had seen the performances, and from these noting the accuracy or memory.

> Thus, when Main Course students devised two different plays for Junior Schools last year — one, an animal story, in which the children watched and, another, the story of the Gorgon, in which the children were actively involved throughout — we found again that the total story was best remembered by children watching the former, but there was a greater immediate depth of imaginative involvement by the children participating in the latter. Certainly in their paintings they depicted the trees, ravines and mountains of the story, rather than the climbing frames and mats of actuality, but details of story they rapidly forgot. Indeed, they often depicted events which did not in fact take place in the play, but which they had thought about afterwards.[22]

The conclusion drawn was that children who sit and watch a performance have a much clearer memory of events in the play than those who participate. John O'Toole felt that this conclusion should be challenged. To do this he set up his own experiment and worked out a method:

General aims

Theoretical: To attempt to throw light on:
(a) Whether material taught in different ways is differently under-stood.
(b) To what extent, if any, total group participation offers understanding of a dramatic story.

Practical: In a preliminary way:
(a) To see if there are any differences in response to a TIE programme which is based on surprise and unpredictability, a told story and a programme where the children are acting out a familiar story.
(b) To attempt to isolate factors in theatre in education with young children which are successful and some of the problems.

Strategy: To present a TIE programme to 10 classes of 7-year-old children and have the same material, written as a story with all elements of possible theatre removed, read by the class teacher to an equal number of parallel classes from the same schools. Both sets of classes would be asked to do the same visual and verbal follow-up work; after a week the programme would be performed to those classes who had previously had it read to them. The two sets of follow-up work would be compared as objectively as possible.[23]

The follow-up work asked the children to write down as much of the story as they could remember, and draw a picture of the children with their space machine. O'Toole notes the number of variables that arose in the way this follow-up work was carried out, such as timing after the programme, or sometimes the drawing preceding the writing.

O'Toole used control groups and percentages to compare the accurate, the unfinished and the confused stories. From these comparisons he drew the tentative conclusion that the pupils involved in the TIE programme remembered the story better, suggesting that: "total integral participation, where the children operate throughout as a group, actually enhances their comprehension of the story."[24]

These two experiments suggest some methods of gathering information, the use of specific follow-up work to judge memory. This method is not scientific for it allows for a number of variables. It is also checking on one area of the children's reactions to the programme — their memory of events. Also the research looks at only one element of a programme — the effect of audience participation, and is therefore atomistic, looking at a part and not at the whole.

There is one published example of a more overall view of the effect of a TIE programme on pupils in the text of "Rare Earth".[25] Although it is not intended as an evaluation it offers an account of a visit to a Primary school by two members of the TIE team a few months after the performance of the programme. What emerged provides an interesting contrast to O'Toole's approach and findings.

"Rare Earth" was devised by the Belgrade Coventry TIE team and performed in local schools in 1973 and 1974. It is a three-part programme for 9–11-year-olds on the theme of pollution and the need to look after the world's resources. It tackles this subject from three angles. The first part reviews the white man's destruction of North America, comparing his way of life to that of the Red Indian. The company developed a cartoon-type, broad comedy play, using the Ramsbottom family on holiday, to show the building of cities and the polluting of the atmosphere. The play begins with Wakantanka, the Great Spirit of Red Indian mythology, speaking directly to the audience, and explaining the Red Indian's way of life. The second part is also a play telling the horrifying story of the Minemata disease in Japan, and using the very stylized techniques of Japanese Theatre. The third part is a Board game which the children play, using maps of fictitious countries as the Board, and pieces of felt representing natural resources such as oil, water, food, etc. The aim was to see which country could build a spaceship first, but to do this each country had to produce certain commodities like televisions and this cost so many resources.

"Rare Earth" was used as a basis of two programmes in the BBC series "Middle Years at School" in 1975. The first BBC programme showed the actors revisiting Clifford Bridge Primary School in Coventry some 6 months after the children had seen the programme. The actors discovered that the children's memory of the three parts of "Rare Earth" was very good, and from the pupils' comments it was obvious that the programme had made a strong impression on them. Six months after, the pupils could still produce vivid paintings and drawings of what they had seen, and they could argue about, and discuss, parts of the programme, particularly the last part: "The Ramsbottom Game". The children had obviously absorbed the ideas, and their answers to the question of pollution revealed a very personal response to the problem:

> If we didn't have factories we wouldn't be able to cook our food and we wouldn't be able to get electricity from the electricity factories, and we'd have a heck of a lot of trouble. If we didn't have factories that made books and that, you wouldn't be able to read anything or if you didn't have factories that made pencils, or crayons or books that you could get ideas out, you just wouldn't be able to do anything. But with the Ramsbottoms they wanted to build loads of cities — I don't mind if you just built a couple of factories like these round here because you're not getting so much pollution — but the Ramsbottoms they wanted to build more and more. Once they've got one factory, 'Oh, that's brilliant, let's build some more', and they built more and more.[26]

The Headmaster of the Clifford Bridge School, Peter Asquith, was well aware of the possibilities of a TIE programme. He was, in fact, Chairman of the Belgrade TIE's Teacher's Advisory Panel, and had long been an advocate of the value of TIE in schools. For him "Rare Earth" was one of the high points of the team's work amongst many other excellent programmes. He thought the intellectual demands made on the pupils in this programme were very tough, but the pupils were not the only ones who were challenged:

> All the concepts were normally above 11-year-olds' understanding, and brings you into a different world (politics — capitalist government, chemical works, power etc.) This is where teachers begin to wince and step back from it. You've got to try and trust people working with it, and with kids afterwards. If anything is too much for them, they're going to bring it out.[27]

The school did not force any follow-up on the pupils, but left it optional. Here is Peter Asquith's account of what happened after the programme, and when the BBC arrived several months later:

Small groups of kids wanted to hammer it out (i.e. the programme) so I gave them a tape recorder. At first they shouted at each other, then they listened. After the third or fourth tapes they noticed a difference. They found they'd more in common than in opposition, . . . and eventually it became more of a reflective discussion. This made a great change in their relationship to each other and their appreciation of each other. The final tapes were very reflective, pointing out the different ways they had interpreted things. BBC 2 came along with cameras, doing a programme on middle years at school. They knew my kids were given a great deal of freedom to talk and discuss, and get away from teachers . . . One of the children more or less turned to the camera and said. "Of course this is the way we work here. Our teachers don't tell us what to think. They listen to us, we talk a lot, and after a while we know what we think." This was four months (*sic*) after the programme. They were talking to Sue, who played Wakantanka, quoting it right back to her. She was amazed that it had stayed so long in the children's minds, and at how they had thought about it. The kids couldn't stand the injustice, etc. They were saying the right sort of things, to do with education, rather than the safe areas of the three 'Rs'.

Before we did the T.V. we had a few days warning. I realised that no one had done any painting etc. I wondered what they would do if we let them work in whatever media: costumes, props, paintings, A Ramsbottom Super City, etc. Their work certainly showed the value of not forking over the subject by the teacher straight after the programme . . . It's possibly having a little bit of peace and time to think it over, maybe, that makes that thing settle in the children's minds in terms of changing attitudes a little, but opening a few new idea-windows to them. It's hard to be specific, I've not got a formula.

School would be a less attractive place for the teacher and the child without that sort of imput. Not many teachers have the time, mental activity, or assurance to manage a programme like that on our own. The research work itself which goes into the Project Packs, which support the programme, are very useful. I found in the late 1960s that I was in fact lifting the TIE company's ideas wholesale and was, in fact, doing programmes of my own.[28]

Amongst the various interesting points raised by Peter Asquith here, it is obvious that the stimulus of the BBC visit produced a check on what the effect of the programme had actually been, and the few months between the programme, and the visit of the BBC team, offered an excellent opportunity for some of the longer-term effects to appear.

This long-term effect was checked again later by two of the Belgrade TIE team, Stephen Wyatt and Maggie Steed. As editors of the script of "Rare

Earth" for Methuen, they went into schools 18 months after the trilogy had been performed. They visited five Primary schools and talked to groups of pupils about what they remembered of the programme. They found that in four of the five schools the children still remembered a considerable amount. During these discussions some interesting facts came to light:

> One perhaps surprising fact is that the game was far less vividly remembered than the plays. At the time a number of teachers had felt the game to be the most valuable part of the programme because it involved the children actively rather than passively in the problems of pollution, but we found hardly any children who could remember more than what country they had been. We discovered only a couple who remembered any of the transactions they had made and they remembered them because they had cheated! On the other hand several of the groups could still give a detailed blow-by-blow account of the events in Minemata just by talking it through without prompting or racking their brains. They mostly recalled enjoying the game, but it had not lingered in the memory.[29]

Although this return visit was not used to draw detailed conclusions about the value of the work, some points had begun to emerge. The theatre element of the programme, particularly the highly stylized second part "Drink the Mercury", had proved to be a very effective way of conveying the facts and ideas in the programme. The plays remained in the pupils' memory in great detail, whereas the obvious learning-by-doing game, although enjoyed, had not been retained by the pupils after 18 months. The company did in fact have some trouble in making this third part work, and it was never as successful as parts One and Two. In these the visual images and the strong story line had a powerful effect upon the pupils.

Most of the children had responded, remembered and thought about aspects of the programme. The script account ends with this comment by a 10-year-old girl:

> I think this "Rare Earth" programme was good because it shows people, shows children, what they were really doing. You don't realise what you're doing when you're building all those factories; you're more or less committing suicide in a way.[30]

This account of the effect of "Rare Earth" on the children provides a most useful example of how to go about discovering what a programme has meant to its "audience". It also suggests some pointers as to what aspects of TIE work can make the most impact.

Research Project on the Evaluation of a TIE Programme

In an attempt to work from theory into practice I set up a small-scale research project on TIE evaluation. I wrote to a number of TIE teams to suggest evaluating one of their programmes. The response from Greenwich TIE was positive and after discussions with the team, the idea and the form of the evaluation were approved.

The programme to be evaluated was "Race Against Time". This was a whole day's programme for one class of third- and fourth-year Secondary school pupils. Its theme was racial prejudice in today's society and how it is affected by the economic situation. The programme was structured in three parts: the morning consisting of a simulation game; the afternoon was a play and the last part was the questioning of some of the characters from the play by the pupils.

The general objective of the programme was "to combat racial prejudice in all its forms" but this was broken down into five specific aims:

1. To show children of all races that there are common problems which we share and that the question of 'race' is often used to divide and divert attention from these problems.
2. To point out that racial prejudice is encouraged by the creation of myths and stereotypes.
3. To dispel some of the current lies and misconceptions which inhibit racial harmony.
4. To encourage a study of the history of colonisation and immigration which will place our present problems in their time context and help to correct what is often a distorted, chauvinist historical viewpoint.
5. To show that we live in a pluralistic multi-racial society and that we must learn to accept and value all the members of that society without seeking to eradicate cultural differences.[31]

Each part of the programme looked at different aspects of racial prejudice. The main aim of the simulation was:

> To give the pupils an understanding of what it feels like to be discriminated against on a personal level, and what this means in financial terms. They will discover that in times of hardship many people suffer, regardless of race, and that common problems cannot be solved by one group blaming another.[32]

The subject-matter of the programme had first been discussed by the team as a result of the events in Lewisham in 1977, when racial undertones found an outlet in street marches and demonstrations. As the team operates in many of the South-east London schools they were well aware of the importance and relevance of racial prejudice for a TIE programme. However, at that point they did not have enough time in their schedule for the accurate research such a subject would require, and felt that they should make the topic a priority for September 1978. Shortly after the discussion the company received a letter from John Walton, head of Greenwich Community relations group, asking for their help in combating racism in schools. He believed that:

> The vehicle of theatre would make a stronger impression than leaflets or general discussion and would provide a way for teachers to a topic they find hard to approach with students.[33]

The team asked teachers at a meeting in early autumn whether they should tackle racism. Most of the teachers felt that this was a good idea, but that it should be done carefully and responsibly and in close consultation with them. The team decided to go ahead.

They felt that the content of the programme should be cross-curricular and that this approach was endorsed by a joint report of ILEA's school sub-committee and the further and higher education sub-committee. The report issued in November 1977 stated that:

> Our society is a multi-cultural, multi-racial one, and the curriculum should reflect a sympathetic understanding of the different cultures and races that now make up our society. We live in a complex interdependent world, and many of our problems in Britain require international solutions. The curriculum should therefore reflect our need to understand other countries.[34]

The team prepared the programme for the summer of 1978. As part of this preparation they had to spend a lot of time discussing the whole issue of radical prejudice and how they felt personally. During the research period several team members visited schools to talk to teachers about how they saw the issue in relation to their schools and which specific areas the company should work on. From these preliminary discussions the team worked out its aims for the programme.

The evaluation model which I decided to use was the arts-based model, that does not use measurement or goal attainment only, but allows for a response to the whole programme. The important factors for this evaluation are that the TIE programme should be looked at in its entirety, that as much information as possible should be gathered, from which some kind of overall view can be obtained, some analysis made of the effectiveness of the different parts of the programme and some conclusions drawn upon the research material which will reveal the strengths or weakenesses of the programme and its effect in schools. The arts-based models allow for the subjectivity of the evaluator, but insists on the orderly collection of data.

TIE programme: "Race Against Time"

"Race Against Time" was presented by Greenwich TIE in schools in 1978 and 1979. There were three tours of the programme altogether, two in 1978 in the summer and the autumn terms, and one in 1979. My research was based on the 1978 tours, especially the autumn one.

It was in the 1978 summer tour that the company experimented with week-long stays in three schools, and this formed part of the research. The 1978 autumn tour consisted mainly of one-day visits.

When collecting information on the programme I utilized a range of ideas already noted in this chapter, choosing as the main method the interviewing of pupils and teachers who had seen the programme. I interviewed two groups of pupils (about five or six in each group) out of a class who had seen the programme. These interviews were recorded and then written out in full. I also talked to, and sometimes recorded interviews with, the teachers of those classes. Three of the schools I visited had seen the programme in the summer, and two had received it for a week. I visited these two during the summer term. One school I visited in the autumn term had seen the programme in the summer and there was, therefore, a 6-month gap between viewing the programme and the interview. Of the schools booked in the autumn tour, I visited seven out of nine.

The interviews were unobtrusively recorded and fairly informal. I had worked out a range of questions on the programme and worked them all into the interview where they seemed appropriate. So there was a basic structure to the interviews and the questions were asked in some sort of order (see Appendix C) but could allow for flexibility. The questions were framed as a result of seeing the programme, recording it, and talking to the company.

In addition to the interviews I collected some of the follow-up work set by the teachers and completed by the pupils. I copied the information from the teams' returned Teacher's Questionnaires and from the company's reports on each performance.

I also talked to the company about the programme and attended the teachers' meeting after the first run of the programme. A report of "Race Against Time" appeared in ILEA's magazine *Contact* and this was most useful.

Problems Encountered

The problems that can arise from asking pupils questions is that the emphasis can be placed upon points in the programme that the pupils would not necessarily have considered important. There is also the danger of asking a question which is biased enough to illicit the response the questioner actually wants to hear, however, subconsciously. To try and prevent these difficulties I phrased the questions as carefully as I could, and allowed the interviews the kind of flexibility which let the pupils spend time discussing particular aspects of the programme which interested them.

Inevitably there were a number of variables. I did not see two groups of pupils in each school: out of the ten schools visited I interviewed seventeen groups. These arrangements always depended upon the teacher, and the school timetable. The teacher's availability was a problem. I did not manage to see each teacher for as long as I hoped. In some cases there was time for discussion, and this could be wide ranging. These interviews I recorded. Sometimes, however, discussion was hurried and unsatisfactory. With hindsight, I am sure that a lot of time and effort should be put into arranging a meeting with the teacher, which would allow for a full discussion. This is not easy to organize when a teacher is very busy, but it is worth being persistent. As with the pupils' interviews some definite questions should be worked out first. Where I had not managed to see the teacher for a full interview I did send them a questionnaire to complete. These were not returned. Contact with the teacher is important, but difficult, and may perhaps be easier for someone who has time to build up this liaison, rather than the flying visit.

To broaden the range of information I did attempt one measurement experiment. I worked out a questionnaire on attitudes to the race problem and included for each question the Thurston scale of "Strongly agree/agree/ don't know/disagree/strongly disagree". These questionnaires were to be given to the class both before and after the programme. The answers could then be compared to see if the programme had produced any change in attitudes.

The company read the questionnaire, but expressed some doubts whether the questions would work out of context of the programme, and this proved to be so. The experiment was not a success. Only two teachers actually gave out the questionnaires, and some schools expressed concern at the nature of the questions, which might produce prejudice rather than lead pupils away from it. Out of the context of the programme such questions could be misleading. Obviously, when the issue is as delicate as that of race and prejudice any assessment or measurement of attitudes can be very difficult, and I doubt that even if the questionnaires had been handed out that the results would have been in any way conclusive. If a change of attitudes does occur, it may not be instantaneeous. It may take months or even years to happen, and then it would be impossible to judge the part the programme had to play in the change. To visit the schools about a year after the programme, and talk to the same pupils, would, however, have made an interesting addition to information available. The research project only looked at the short-term effect of the programme.

Analysis and Classification of Material

To make some sense of all the information gathered it was necessary to write out the recorded interviews and then to correlate the answers. This I did by placing all the answers to one particular question under that question (see Appendix C). I also noted the school, and the interview group beside each response.

As extra information and opinions emerged I made new headings and put all the information under the appropriate heading.

To evaluate the programme I used the range of information under each question or heading, and analysed it to see if there was any recognizable pattern of response. This method produced a breakdown of the opinions in terms of numbers and a summary of the general ideas. This method produced detailed information on particular aspects of the programme and an overall picture of the whole.

I decided not to use a control group. This was because the nature of the programme was such that no control group could have been taught the facts in any equivalent way, i.e. part of the strength of the programme lay in its manipulation of the pupils' emotions to lead them to an understanding of prejudice. Even if I had decided to try control groups this would have led to enormous problems of organization and co-operation by the schools. Each school would have to have provided another class, which would be taught certain facts by the teacher or myself. When Secondary school timetables for the third and fourth year tend to be extraordinarily complicated such extra teaching would have proved virtually impossible to arrange. In a Primary school such arrangements are easier to make, as John O'Toole found when organizing his research on audience participation.

The method of collecting information and the evaluation model were chosen in the light of their suitability for this very particular area. They may not be totally satisfactory, but within the range of methods available, and my own experience, this approach appeared to be the most sensible. As to whether the approach was effective or not, can be judged in the next chapter.

Notes

1. J. Robinson and N. Barnes, "What kind of evaluation is useful to Adult Educational Broadcasting." In *Evaluating Educational T.V. and Radio*, T. Bates and J. Robinson (eds.), The Open University Press, Milton Keynes, 1977, p. 125.
2. K. Robinson, "Evaluating TIE", *Learning Through Theatre*, T. Jackson (ed.), Manchester University Press, 1980, p. 87.
3. P. Schweitzer, (ed.) *Theatre-in-Education, Five Infant Programmes*, Methuen Young Drama, London, 1980.
4. Belgrade, Coventry TIE, *Annual Report*, 1972–3, p. 18.
5. J. Robinson and N. Barnes, *op. cit.*, p. 126.
6. H. Schulberg and F. Baker, "Program evaluation models", *Readings in Evaluation Research*, F. C. Caro (ed.), Russell Sage Foundation, New York, 1971, p. 74.

7. Lancaster TIE, "The Duke's Playhouse Theatre in Education", 'Travellers' *SCYPT Journal*, no. 2, 1978, p. 3.
8. K. Robinson, "Evaluating TIE", *op. cit.*, p. 91.
9. This is the title of Garvey's article in *Educational Aspects of Evaluation*, P. J. Tansey (ed.), McGraw Hill, London, 1971.
10. *Op. cit.*, p. 205.
11. D. M. Garvey, "A catalogue of judgements, findings and hunches", *Educational Aspects of Evaluation*, P. J. Tansey (ed.), McGraw Hill, London, 1971, p. 218.
12. D. M. Garvey, "A catalogue of judgements, findings and hunches", *op. cit.*, p. 225.
13. *Op. cit.*, p. 226.
14. *Op cit.*, p. 204.
15. C. G. Brossell, "Researching drama — A humanistic perspective", *Teaching and Understanding Drama*, N. Stephenson and D. Vincent (eds.), NFER Publishing Co., Slough, 1975, p. 96.
16. D. Hamilton, *Curriculum Evaluation*, Open Books, London, 1976, p. 39.
17. Ken Robinson explores this subject of evaluation models in much more detail in his article "Evaluating TIE", *Learning Through Theatre*, Tony Jackson (ed.).
18. C. G. Brossell, *op. cit.*, p. 95.
19. M. Trow, "The evaluation of innovation", *Readings in Educational Research*, F. C. Caro (ed.), Russell Sage Foundation, New York, 1971, p. 89.
20. C. Frey, "A method to study the effects of media in the classroom", *Evaluating Educational T.V. and Radio*, *op. cit.*, p. 10.
21. John Robinson and Neil Barnes, "What kind of evaluation is useful to Adult Educational Broadcasting?", *op. cit.*, p. 127.
22. J. Coultas and J. Pick, "Children as audience", *Outlook*, No. 4, BCTA, 1972, p. 4.
23. J. O'Toole, *Theatre in Education*, Hodder & Stoughton, London, 1976, pp. 147–8.
24. *Op. cit.*, p. 157.
25. Belgrade Coventry TIE, *Rare Earth*, London, Methuen, pp. 57–65.
26. *Op. cit.*, p. 58.
27. Peter Asquith, personal interview at the Belgrade Theatre on 12th July 1976.
28. *Ibid.*
29. Belgrade Coventry TIE, *op. cit.*, p. 62.
30. *Op. cit.*, p. 63.
31. Greenwich TIE, "Teachers Notes: Race Against Time".
32. *Ibid.*
33. S. Bennion, "Race Against Time", *Contact*, Vol. 7, Issue 12, 22nd September 1978, ILEA, p. 31.
34. *Ibid.*

Chapter 6

The Evaluation Project on "Race Against Time"

Before presenting the results of my evaluation experiment of "Race Against Time" a full description of the programme itself is obviously necessary. My summary of the programme is drawn from watching the programme twice in schools and once as a lecture-demonstration at the 1978 SCYPT Conference. I recorded the programme when it was presented at Kidbrooke School, but instead of transcribing the whole programme word for word, I have written a detailed scenario. The description is of the programme as it was presented in its first tour in the summer of 1978.

Race Against Time

(Greenwich Young People's Theatre at Kidbrooke Secondary School)

The simulation

The team assumed definite roles from the beginning of the programme. Some of these roles were organizational such as the Employment Officer and the Mayor. Two of the company expressed anti-immigrant attitudes in character: The Social Benefits Officer and Mr. Ward, the business man. He was a more developed character portrayal. Two of the company worked amongst the pupils, one as a New Towner, one as a Saurition (an immigrant).

The hall was set up with benches, screens and tables. On the screens was information relating to New Town, a map of the area, information on houses. The tables were set out around the hall as a series of "stopping points" for the pupils. They were the Employment desk, the Cost of Livings desk, the Housing desk, and the Information desk. The team offered no introduction or explanation to the programme but started straight away by dividing the class into two sections. One group were the inhabitants of New Town, just moved there, and the others were the new immigrants from Sauritious. This division was entirely arbitrary, and often meant that a number of black pupils were in the New Town group. Green cards were handed out to the New Towners and blue cards to the Sauritions. These cards held information on

168

size of family and job qualifications. The division into two groups was done very quickly, and as the New Towners settled down on the benches in the hall to listen to the Mayor, the Sauritions, in a separate room, were addressed by the Immigration Officer. They learned something of their home country and its link with Britain.

Immigration Officer: Sauritious has belonged to Britain for one hundred years, and this has brought great benefits to both sides. You have had a great British education. You feel these ties in your hearts.

In Sauritious all is not well, the monsoon was destructive and the rubber plantation can no longer compete with the plastic industry. There is a chance for the Sauritions to find a good life in Britain's New Town. New Town has especially asked for them, their skills will be appreciated and they will have wonderful job and housing opportunities. The group is then encouraged to emigrate to Britain at a cost of £500. As the immigrants are in pairs both holding £250 it is necessary for them to put their money together for one partner to emigrate. The others will follow as soon as the partner who has emigrated has managed to pay the correct amount.

Meanwhile, in the hall, the Mayor has explained the three areas of New Town — the green belt with its good houses, Grade 1, Surbiton with its middling houses, Grade 2, and the old town with the poor houses, Grade 3. There is an industrial estate where the New Towners will get jobs. The system of getting a job then moving to the Cost of Living desk to have this

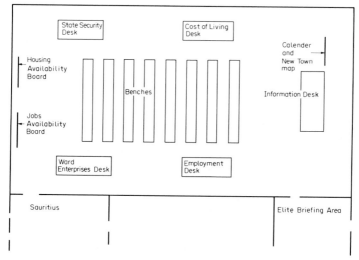

FIG. 15. Greenwich TIE, "Race Against Time", 1978. Plan of layout of hall for the simulation.

THE GOOD LIFE CARD

NAME _____

QUALIFICATIONS / SKILLS   <u>*ELECTRICAL   INSTALLATION*</u>

SIZE OF FAMILY   <u>*LARGE*</u>

To achieve The Good Life and be successful you need : a house grade 1 or 2
a job   grade 1 or 2
cash in hand

HOUSES	1	2	3	

JOBS	1	2	3	4

YEAR	1	2	3	4
WAGES				
COST OF LIVING				
RENT				
MORTGAGE				
BALANCE				
STATE BENEFIT				

FIG. 16. A "Good Life" card.

taken off the wages and then trying to rent or buy a house is explained. The Mayor presents them with the prospect of the 'Good Life'. To achieve this they must aim at a good grade house, preferably a Grade 1 in the green belt, and a good, well-paid job.

Thus, the simulation game was set up, the element of competition established, and the rules explained. The pupils had been given roles and addressed by the actor–teachers in role. The game started immediately and the pupils found themselves in the middle of it, before they had time to question what was happening. To show how the process of going round the various desks worked the team member playing the New Towner went up first, and the game got under way.

A few pupils were selected to work at the various desks; again this was entirely arbitrary. One of which was manned by Mr. Ward, as business man and Estate Agent. He offers his selected workers £10,000 a year and the prospect of a Grade 1 house in the area where he lives — the Green Belt. He also reminds them that the Sauritions will work very hard for little money. "Bear this in mind when you're advertising" he advises.

As the New Towners began to move round the desks they were treated politely and helped as much as possible. Meanwhile the Sauritions were having trouble with the Immigration Officer. They were harrassed for their vaccination certificates, and the addresses of their partners, and threatened that without documentary evidence they would not be leaving. Finally they arrived in New Town, and were welcomed. Mr. Ward said he hoped that they would settle down and assured them that there were plenty of jobs available. He told them that he was offering a number of houses, and hoped that they would be able to buy them.

At the end of year One, nearly everyone had a job, and some people had managed to buy houses. The game moved into year Two. Promotion was offered, secretaries became administrators, labourers trained to be electricians. The Sauritions were making arrangements to bring their partners over, which entailed the payment of sums of money. The pupils were involved by moving from desk to desk, but not in any enactment of the roles or mimed sequences of work. At this stage the simulation resembled a board game rather than a drama session.

At the end of year Two everything was working well: good wages, many promotions, many houses sold. Suddenly the game changed gear with an announcement from the Mayor:

Mayor: We have just heard from the Government that there is an economic crisis in the country, which means that there is a slump and there is not enough money to go round.

He warned there would probably be a rise in the cost of living but no rise in wages. The consequences of the crisis were felt immediately, and redundancies began. The Employment Secretary asked for the two Works Managers to stand up, one of them she said must lose his job because of the slump. Looking at their cards she decided that it was only fair that it should be the Saurition who lost his job. This brought an immediate protest from the pupils. It was at this point that the Immigrant dependants arrived.

A States Benefit desk was set up. The actor–teacher as the States Benefit Officer adopted a very anti-immigrant attitude, shouting at the Sauritions for being selfish and lazy and taking all the jobs. She was rude to them, and often refused benefit. This treatment produced anger and frustration in the pupils who were Sauritions. The atmosphere was made worse by the fact that she treated the New Towners very politely and never quibbled with their claims.

The actor–teacher as a New Towner talked to other New Towners about this situation, and the loss of jobs. The New Towners began to feel that it was the Sauritions' fault. As they moved into year Four, Mr. Ward made a speech:

Mr. Ward: I moved to New Town to get a job and to bring my family up here. I wanted to bring them up in a decent way. For five years I worked hard. Now I see it all being snatched away by all these wretched Sauritions coming in. (Angry protests from the pupils.) They are taking all the houses (more angry protests). I speak for the hard-working natives of New Town. The town is

in this state because of all you Sauritions. I will hold a meeting
for all those who think it is the Sauritions' fault.

At this point the actor–teacher playing the Saurition stood up and warned
everyone to think carefully, both New Towners and Sauritions were suffering
because of the economic crisis. He encouraged those who did not agree with
Mr. Ward to stay and discuss the situation. The pupils divided into two
groups very quickly and one group went off with Mr. Ward. The pupils
made their own choice here.

FIG. 17. The States Benefit desk.

After both groups had discussed the situation separately they came
together in the hall and faced each other. The Mayor assumed the role of
Chairman for the discussion and the pupils began to argue their case. The
actor–teachers made points but the pupils participated fully. One pupil
pointed out that there was not a single Saurition who had a £10,000 job. This
was illustrated by a show of hands of those holding such jobs, all of whom are
on Mr. Ward's side. Of the £4000 jobs, three only are on the Sauritions' side.
Few unemployed were in Mr. Ward's group. An argument developed about
houses, bringing protests from pupils in role as Sauritions:

Pupil: Mr. Ward said they had complaints about our house. They say we
       chuck rubbish into other people's gardens. We don't, we're just as
       clean as they are — cleaner!

FIG. 18. A pupil arguing in the simulation discussion.

After much discussion, in which it becomes increasingly obvious that the Sauritions have not been taking the jobs or the houses, the team member playing a New Towner stands up.

New Towner: I thought there must be some people to blame because of the bad times. I thought it was the Sauritions, but now I've found it isn't. So I don't really know if I can stay over on this side.

With this she moved away from Mr. Ward's side to join the others. In the performance I saw a number of pupils followed her. The discussion continued for a while, but finally the actor–teacher playing a Saurition warned everyone that if they go on pushing Sauritions around: "One day we'll push back and we'll push back harder and harder until it leads to violence and you will have caused it. It's your fault not ours!"

This was greeted with cheers. Then one of the team came out of role to thank everyone for playing the game, and to remind them that although they got quite emotional it was only a game. She then repeated the Saurition's

FIG. 19. The play (first version).

FIG. 20. A song from the play.

threat: "If things keep on like this there will be violence — see this, this afternoon".

The play in the afternoon was written for the company by Michael Maynard. He used the ideas and improvisations which the company gave him, and developed the play from these. In rehearsals there was some rewriting of his original script.

The play was a Brechtian-style presentation, with several short scenes, interspersed with songs commenting on the theme. It was played in front of screens with the audience seated facing the performance area and in the ordinary lighting of the hall. There was the minimum of costume and properties.

The play's central character, Liz, had witnessed the murder of a black youth in the market-place and identified the murderer as a young Pakistani. After the trial Liz began to doubt what she saw and is haunted by the fear that she gave the wrong evidence. The man she identified is in prison. The play followed her search to find out the truth. In pursuit of it she talks to a number of different characters all of whom had definite attitudes to race: a doctor, a stall-owner in the market-place, a youth-club worker, the New Front organizer and his secretary, and the accused Pakistani.

The play was on a high emotional level, and veered from dramatic intensity to quiet discussion. It moved fast and presented a number of characters who were social types rather than individual personalities. Finally the murderer

FIG. 21. In-role discussion after the play.

confessed. It was a young white man, whose sister had recently had a baby by
the black youth. The girl's brother was disturbed and withdrawn, and hated
the black youth for making his sister pregnant. After the play the pupils were
divided into small groups for discussion. They were to try and discover why
the murder actually took place. To answer this they could question any of the
main characters from the play. The team stayed in role as the characters to
answer the pupils' questions. After this discussion period was over, and each
group had seen at least two characters, the ideas on why the murder took
place were read out.

The day finished with a general discussion on what could be done to stop
prejudice. During the course of the day two leaflets were handed out
containing facts and figures about immigration and attitudes to prejudice.

Research Project

"Race Against Time"

A selection of the research material is placed in Appendix C, but some of
the quotes from this research have been placed in this next section to
illustrate the various points that emerge. The word "responses", which is
used during this chapter and in the Appendix C, refers to the number of
replies to the question asked. This can mean that in an interview with a group
of six pupils only two or three pupils gave a reply, or response, to a question.
Each of these replies was correlated under the heading of the question,
putting together responses from all the schools. Thus, under one question
there could be fifteen responses all varied (see Appendix C, p. 222). I
purposely did not go round each member of the group asking for an
individual response as this would have been immensely time consuming,
possibly stopped the flow of discussion and just led to pupils repeating each
others ideas. If a question got a poor response I would rephrase it, and ask it
again.

Comments and Conclusions

Build-up work

Out of the ten schools visited only one did some kind of work before the
programme came to the school and this had consisted of watching a film on
the "Sus" laws. Most teachers felt that the programme should be a starting-
point. They wanted "Race Against Time" to stimulate work or thought, not
to be a culmination of a project or a series of lessons.

Although some schools did deal with race and prejudice in social studies or
ethnic studies, the general feeling was that: "I didn't do any build-up work as
I felt that the programme itself was a launching pad." (Drama teacher:

Kidbrooke Secondary School.)

The value of this kind of programme is that it can suddenly put the pupils through an intense experience with no need of preparatory work. Coming in as outsiders the company can make a real impact, the effect of which benefits from follow-up, but does not disappear altogether if the teacher chooses not to do any further work on it.

With this kind of subject-matter build-up work is not necessary. The question whether it is desirable, or would add to the pupils' understanding of the day, is difficult to answer as there is no way to test it on this project.

The Simulation

The beginning of the simulation was well organized, the pupils being divided immediately into two groups, and then thrown straight into the "reality" of the game. However, for the participants it was a bewildering experience:

1st pupil: We were pushed straight into the room.
2nd pupil: I feel they should have told us what was coming to us.
3rd pupil: No, because it made us more surprised.
4th pupil: It was a bit quick. She said you want to go over to Britain (pupil in role as Immigrant). In real life we would have had more time to think. We had to say yes, because everyone else was.

(Pupils: Crown Woods School)

"Strange" was the most popular word used by the pupils to describe how they felt on coming into the hall; two pupils felt that more explanation would have been useful. One pupil was worried about the possibility of doing something wrong, not knowing what was going to happen. One thought it was just going to be a laugh. Another pupil felt that it was a good atmosphere in the hall, exciting and friendly.

None of the groups of pupils appeared to have done anything quite like this before so had no idea what to do or how to behave. Neither the teachers nor the team introduced the programme. However, this did not actually seem to worry the majority of pupils as they were organized as soon as they got into the hall, or where I saw the programme, into a side room, and from there were divided into the two groups. The pupils were into role before they had time to realize the fact. This produced a sort of organized chaos, which as one teacher commented: "the company utilised the chaos well at the beginning" (Teacher, Deptford Green).

Role-play in the simulation

A selection of the material gathered on this subject appears in Appendix C, pp. 219–21).

The use of role-play in the simulation is very different in nature from "building a character". The latter is usual in the acting of plays, improvisations on, or towards, creating a play, or in drama classes. The recognition of the difference between role-play and character playing is essential to the success of the game. The role becomes a way to learn, a way of giving the pupils a freedom to express themselves. Rather like the putting on of a mask it places between the pupil and the events a disguise, something to hide behind rather than something which requires the creation of a new identity. The assuming or creating of a different personality would involve the pupils in a creative activity which would divert him or her from the actual learning experience of the game.

The Greenwich team gave the pupils a number of facts about the roles: size of family, skills, etc., which they could use to play the game — like giving them a set of playing cards. These facts were written on a particular coloured card, and this colour was the key to the experience of prejudice, as one pupil commented: "The cards showed your nationality like the colour of your skin."

Without the need to develop character the pupils could respond to these roles at a number of different levels. It gave them freedom to develop the role (if not the character) further. One pupil, at the performance I saw, was defending her house and garden from criticism of untidiness and filth. This was an entirely imaginative situation she had created.

The roles helped the pupils to appreciate the relationship between skills, qualifications, experience and job possibilities. Prejudice was made very clear, when the well-qualified Sauritions attempted to get suitable jobs they were rarely offered anything which matched their qualifications, and sometimes could not even find work. Life was made extremely uncomfortable for them as the recession developed:

> I lost my job. I had been working with rubber trees in Sauritious. I couldn't get a job over here, but I got money, and I had to spend it to get my partner over. When I done that I had no money left. I wanted a middle class house, I couldn't get it. I didn't have any money and when I asked for money from the States Benefits they wouldn't give it to us because we were immigrants.
>
> (Pupil, Charlton Boys' School, interview)

The programme could be criticized for bias here, but it concentrated a great deal of truth into a limited time span, and produced, as a result, a strong emotional reaction from the pupils "playing" Sauritions.

By offering the "good life" as the ultimate achievement the pupils were motivated to try for better jobs and houses. The grading of standard helped enormously here, with the pupils aiming for a Grade 1 job and house:

In the first year, as I had no qualifications I had to make do with a third class job, which was that of a hospital porter. However in the second year I had the opportunity to train as a nurse. I also had to live in a grade 3 house, but applied for a grant to re-decorate it.

(Pupil's written follow-up work, Kidbrooke School)

This pattern is very simplistic, but effective. It is after all a simulation *game*, and the pupils need a motivation to play. The competitive element is easy to stimulate, but unlike some games the competitive element was not overriding because the opportunities to gain promotion and better housing were limited and carefully controlled by the team. The pupils were in competition with each other, but more importantly, they were in competition with society and the economic situation. By this means they were made aware of the "system", its modes of functioning and its prejudices. The simulation introduced the link between economic crisis and prejudice.

The pupils certainly gained an awareness of these factors, as their comments in the interviews made clear. Even after 6 months, which included the summer holidays, one group of pupils still clearly remembered the details of their roles, their experiences in the simulation, and the prejudices and difficulties they encountered:

Three of us were held back, because we couldn't get into the country. Suddenly there was a war, so we had to leave. We were just shoved in (i.e. to New Town) and didn't know what was going on. Everyone was arguing about jobs. We went up to get a job, they said we were skiving and just trying to get money out of the country.

(Pupil, Crown Woods School)

However, experiencing and understanding are not necessarily the same thing. Not all pupils could make a clear link between their own experience in the game and the social and economic situation that had been set up. This is where sensitive follow-up work is of infinite value. Even without this kind of follow-up the simulation did succeed in bringing elements of the outside world, and "real life" situations into the schools. This is where a TIE programme can succeed so well, and where lessons can still divorce learning from life.

Role-play in the context of this simulation proved to be a satisfactory method of leading the pupils through the learning experience. One teacher made the observation that:

It was very easy for the pupils to get into because they weren't being asked to play a part. Far easier to get into role because what was important was a good house or job. That built up frustration or self-satisfaction very simply.

(Teacher, Roger Manwood School)

Pupils' involvement in the simulation (see Appendix C, p. 221)

The pupils' involvement relates both to the use of role-play and to the structure of the simulation. Not every pupil was totally involved, and the game did allow pupils to drop out if they wished. In some schools a few pupils did sit down outside the action. Only three pupils in the interviews expressed indifference to the game, but on the whole involvement was good, as the company reports on the performances show. To involve a class of 13–15-year-olds both mentally and physically for a whole morning is very difficult. For many of them "acting" is an anathema, but simulating life is acceptable.

The pupils' involvement was a result of certain factors created by the company. These factors became obvious from the research material collected, Appendix C, pp. 219–21.

1. The creation of a recognizable real-life situation:

   "It could happen in real life".

   (Pupil, Peckham School)

2. The technique of beginning the simulation without a detailed introduction.

3. "Real" people talking to the pupils as if they were adults:

   They treated us like adults — it's important. If they'd just ordered us around, it wouldn't have been good, but because they were treating us as adults we did more.

   (Pupil, Charlton Boys School)

4. The giving out of roles to the pupils, and the practical demands on the pupils to fulfil these roles.

   You were involved because you are pushed into seeing certain things happening: saw the levels, very simple 1, 2, and 3. They (the pupils) were pushed to think that they should do better. On the level of the game there was the frustration because you'd gone down to a grade 2 house . . . It appealed at an emotional level and it was very easy to get into because you weren't asked to play a part.

   (Teacher, Roger Manwood School.
   The teacher had joined in the simulation)

5. The competitive element of the game:

   You got involved to make sure you were alright. Afraid of losing, like gambling — you want to win.

   (Pupil, Samuel Peypes School)

6. The building up of an emotional response in the pupils of anger, envy,

frustration, etc.

7. The simulation had a strong structure: the use of the desks, the order the pupils went round with their cards, and their earnings, the use of the 4 years, and the changes that occurred in the last part of the game due to inflation and recession.

The pupils' reaction to the changing economic situation in the game
(see pp. 222–23)

By creating the competitive element and frustrating that by an outside factor, a change in the economic situation over which the pupils had no control, the pupils were forced to react.

Out of this a conflict situation was created by the company. This conflict was essentially theatrical. The "characters" in the simulation suddenly removed jobs, and therefore income, and accused the pupils in role of laziness, or living off the State. The officer who had given out the jobs so politely removed them brusquely and with little commiseration. Mr. Ward, once all smiles, became an angry opponent of the immigrants in New Town. The introduction of a new character, the Social Benefits Officer, who took a blatantly prejudiced view, sparked off strong reactions amongst the pupils. Many of the Sauritions were shouted at, accused of laziness and generally frustrated.

> I lost my job, felt bad. I blamed it on the immigrants straight away. The person who doled out the money was saying it was the immigrants' fault.
>
> (Pupil, Roger Manwood School)

This did not alienate the pupils from the game, where they realized what was happening and could rationalize their reactions:

> It could upset you a bit, but always remember they were only acting. So although you got annoyed when they shouted in the back of your mind you knew they were acting.
>
> (Pupil, Deptford Green School)

Where pupils did not make such rationalizations real anger or tears occurred:

> I began to get really angry. They didn't like us, they turned against us.
>
> (Pupil, Peckham School)

The balance betwen pushing the pupils' reactions to a maximum and turning it into violence was very delicate indeed. That the situation never got out of hand is a clear indication of the team's ability to sense the correct moment to reduce the pressure. This is a very sophisticated element of TIE work, and with a less experienced team the use of such an emotional build-up could easily have resulted in some physical violence.

The discussion at the end of the simulation (see pp. 223–25)

The purpose of the discussion was to make the pupils aware of the actual facts, that the immigrants were not responsible for New Towners losing their jobs. Roughly two-thirds of the replies in this section revealed that the pupils had understood this point:

> It was not just the coloured people's fault, also the Government's fault. The Sauritions were losing their jobs, just because of what they were. They're different, so people were saying its their fault.
>
> (Pupil, Crown Woods School)

One teacher pointed out that having to choose sides quickly and with little explanation often placed the pupils on the "wrong" side:

> They asked the kids to form into groups. It became rather forced. I felt that they were obliged to follow ideas they didn't really agree with.
>
> (Teacher, Peckham School, about the first tour)

However, the point of the discussion appeared to be, not that the pupils should be on the right side in the first place, but that they should decide, after the discussion, which was the right side.

Although during the course of the discussion many pupils realized that they should be on the other side, not all of them moved over. They experienced pressures which kept them where they were: pressures such as fear of Mr. Ward, the possibility of losing a job, the need to stay with friends and not be isolated by doing something different. This in itself was a valuable learning experience:

> Some of my friends were on his side (i.e. Mr. Ward's). They were afraid that if they were on the Saurition side they wouldn't get a house. They were too frightened to stand up and move over. The look he gave you was terrible.
>
> (Pupil, Kidbrooke School)

From the length and enthusiasm of the replies in the interviews it was obvious that the majority of pupils were really involved in the discussion and enjoyed the theatrical element of confrontation:

> We were all shouting at each other. New Towners saying we took all the jobs and we're saying no we didn't. Some of us got Grade 3 houses and some of them got Grade 1 houses. They kept blaming us all the time. Then after the discussion some of the New Towners came onto the Saurition side saying this is true you know, because Sauritions haven't got good houses. Those that were left had mostly Grade 1 houses, and they started to have second thoughts.
>
> (Pupil, Peckham School)

Within the structure of the simulation the discussion was the equivalent of the de-briefing session, and, as this, worked moderately well. It was not totally successful in conveying the causes of the economic crisis, as the answers to the question on economic causes proves (see pp. 225–26).

The simulation's effectiveness in dealing with the economic issues

Questioning the pupils on what actually caused the economic crisis produced a wide range of replies. See Appendix C, pp. 225–26 for a fuller list.

Although the company were trying to relate the economic situation to the growth of prejudice this relation was not always clear to the pupils, in spite of the demonstration of facts during the discussion. (Those without jobs and houses raising their hands.)

The concept of the cost of living, wages, rent or mortgages was mapped out fairly simply in the simulation, and was understood by the majority of pupils. However, by having to demonstrate the economic workings of society plus illustrate prejudice and its relation to the economic situation the company were possibly overburdening the simulation. Although the pupils' experience of prejudice was in many cases very real their understanding of the changing economic situation was muddled:

1st pupil: Too many people.
2nd pupil: The Government.
3rd pupil: Defence cuts wasn't it?
4th pupil: Cuts — money cuts.
5th pupil: Most people were losing houses and jobs, because there was not enough money, not enough jobs. We thought it was the Sauritions coming at the beginning, but when we saw others suffering, we saw it differently.

(Pupils, Samuel Peypes School)

If after all the discussion, arguments, and the physical illustration by show of hands of who had jobs, 50 per cent of the pupils could still say it was the immigrants who were responsible for the loss of jobs, then clearly this aspect of the simulation is not working properly.

It was the Sauritions coming in. Others said there were jobs for everyone. There weren't, and we couldn't send them back.

(Pupil, Charlton Boys' School)

A lot of people coming in. There were no jobs to give because a lot of people coming in.

(Pupil, Blackheath Bluecoat School)

It was some of the third-year groups who did not grasp this economic aspect of the programme. The programme would therefore appear to be more suitable for fourth years, and is not material to be offered to the very low stream classes.

Pupils' reaction to the simulation game

As only three out of all the pupils interviewed said that they did not enjoy the game, this is obvious proof of its success in terms of entertainment.

In terms of impact the fact that the pupils carried on discussing the simulation over lunch showed their involvement. Some of this discussion (five out of twelve responses) consisted of the pupils trying to sort out their ideas and feelings, which indicated that the effect of the simulation required the pupils to attempt some kind of immediate analysis of what happened and how they felt.

> We talked about it, and said all we felt about it. If we were split up we talked about what it was like.
>
> (Pupil, Deptford Green School)

> Talking about it with my friend. He's white and I'm coloured. They were saying "Go back to your own country". It made him feel like we felt sometime, and we talked about it. I felt bad about it, when we went to the State Benefit the woman was giving him hell.
>
> (Pupil, Deptford Green School)

For drama teachers the actual simulation technique itself was of use. A TIE programme can be both an exploration of an issue and the example of a particular teaching technique:

> I've worked on the simulation role as a technique . . . It's a drama teaching technique that's most effective. It gives the kids an experience, they've got to suspend disbelief . . . but I knew that I couldn't possibly do a simulation as well as they did (the company) so I wanted them (the pupils) to have the experience.
>
> (Drama teacher, Peckham School)

On one occasion in a girls' school the reaction of the girl pupils gave rise to special analysis by the teachers. Pupils react very differently to a programme, and this reaction is often to do with the social setting, academic level, sex of the pupils and the nature of the school, rather than varying performance standard by the company.

> One interesting reaction from the pupils: they started off very bubbly, we were trying to calm them down before they went in. When they actually went in and started they became totally subdued and in fact

things were happening to them. The Saurition Head Teacher lost her job and nothing was said. At one point one of the TIE team came over and said 'They're taking it all very quietly are they alright, what's going on?' I thought perhaps in this sort of school and given the fact that they are women, they are oppressed in many different ways. Much of their life experience involves them holding back. They couldn't react, they put up with it. I had a very strong feeling that up until a certain point they would go on and on taking it.

(Drama teacher, Peckham School)

There is no doubt that this simulation was successful on a number of levels. Some of this success may, of course, be due to the technique of the simulation itself. John Taylor and Rex Walford discussed these advantages in *Simulation in the Classroom* (London, Penguin Education, 1972, p. 34):

Increased student motivation, stemming from heightened interest in the teaching and learning process is a commonly reported phenomenon following simulation exercises. Without doubt, this is the clearest and least disputed gain attached to simulation in the classroom, despite the difficulties of measuring it. It seems to apply at widely differing levels of learning.

This one quality alone is seen by many as sufficient reason for continuing to pursue simulation experiment and development. The body of opinion on this point is uniform and impressive; but *why* simulation arouses and sustains a high level of interest, enthusiasm and excitement, is relatively unresearched.

The information gathered from the research on "Race Against Time" may provide one or two clues towards why a simulation can arouse and sustain interest and enthusiasm. However, TIE simulation, and this one included, is much more likely to use emotional manipulation within its framework. Actor–teachers in role set up interaction and conflict between the pupils and the "characters". Thus TIE's use of simulation has a strong element of theatre, and it may be this which stimulates student involvement, interest and motivation so well.

The play (see Appendix C, pp. 226–27, "Race Against Time", Research material)

In a questionnaire handed out to pupils by the drama teacher at Kidbrooke School there was a question:

Which part (of the programme) did you enjoy most?
All of it? — *48* pupils underlined this.

The drama situation in the morning? — *10*
The play? — *40*
The discussion after the play — *2*

There is no doubt that the majority of pupils enjoyed the play: "Brilliant acting, I'll never forget that play, it was so good" (Pupil, Peckham School) even if they did not all rave in quite the way of the Peckham school girl.

When I asked the pupils what they thought the play was actually about this brought replies that were all basically similar. Seven pupils thought the play was about blaming black people; four said "Racialism", three "Prejudice", and two "The National Front".

Whatever the pupils' various views on the theme of the play, its meaning was generally understood. What did arouse comment and criticism was the presentation technique. Some of the pupils found the style of the play difficult to accept. The songs, particularly, came in for criticism, and obviously caused alienation amongst pupils.

> I didn't like the singing in the play, stupid. It didn't fit, made me laugh.
>
>   (Pupil, Crown Woods School)

I doubt that the words were understood at the time, and the "stop acting, start singing" technique did bewilder and amuse pupils.

The more extreme characters received criticism from one teacher and a few pupils:

> The kids coped with the format of the play alright. The characters were all stereo-types, some ill chosen. This confused the kids, and did not help what the play was about. The story was rather over complicated.
>
>   (Teacher, Roger Manwood School)

There was a tendency for pupils to dismiss these characters as "thick", or intransigent, rather than recognizing their potential danger.

> The National Front people — they were extremes. That woman, Mrs. Dexter, was so thick.
>
>   (Pupil, Crown Woods School)

The company were worried that the play was too long, particularly for the third years. The pupils, however, made no mention of this. The form of the play excited many of the fourth-year Drama Option groups, and suggested to them new forms of theatre.

> *1st pupil:*
> That play should have went (*sic*) on T.V. — that was like real life, like a musical; stop dead, start, do action, stop, use music — really good!

2nd pupil:
The way they used one table as many different things, and the table cloth. We learnt practical things.

(Pupils, Peckham School — Drama Option Group)

The Drama teachers were well aware of this opportunity to introduce different techniques of presentation to the pupils. Being stylized the play was an extreme contrast to the "reality" of the simulation. Possibly, this contrast did not help some pupils to apply what they had experienced in the morning to the afternoon, but the link was understood on a superficial level by the majority of pupils. They could see that it concerned the same subject-matter, but two teachers doubted that the ideas and experience of the morning and afternoon were sufficiently related. Certainly, the difference in the characters and the nature of the experience between the morning and the afternoon did not help the pupils to use the information from the simulation in the discussion after the play. As the pupils were not physically involved in any way there was a danger that some pupils dismissed the play, as they could not associate with it. One teacher felt that the play was actually too complex (see quote on p. 188).

The discussion after the play (see Appendix C, pp. 227–29)

Like the simulation the pupils' involvement left them with stronger feelings on this section. The more extreme characters provoked the most discussion.

1st pupil: Talking to the N.F. man, he said everyone should go back to their own country. I said what about me, I'd have to go back through several countries. He was saying it's up to you.
2nd pupil: We were all shouting at him. It was real.

(Pupils, Peckham School)

They presented extreme points of view that were easy for the pupils to argue with, whereas the more ordinary characters did not arouse the pupils' interest as strongly. Those outside the main plot line, like the Stall-holder, were less in demand during the discussion. The company's reports make this clear often noting that the character was not called to go to any of the group's during the "in role" discussion period. This was due to the fact that the character's attitudes were brought out during a long discussion with Liz, but were not revealed in any dramatic situation which would highlight their importance. In the company's reports of the discussion they noted six good discussions out of ten during the autumn tour, and no really bad ones.

It is interesting to note that one of the pupils felt that only those extreme characters stayed in role:

Liz was telling us about her wrong decision, she came out of character. Mr. Wood and the woman were the only ones who kept in character.

(Pupil, Crown Woods School)

This pin-points a difficult problem for the actor–teachers when they are being "hot-seated" in role. If the actor–teacher is using a large amount of his or her own personality, as was the case with Liz, then the "character" playing is less obvious. The further away the character is from the personality of the performer the easier it is for the pupils to see that the actor–teacher is acting. When it comes to "hot-seating" this retaining of role can become very precarious.

Strong characters, such as Mr. Ward, and the propounding of clear or strong attitudes provoke discussion. The inherent danger in this is that it can lead to oversimplification of the argument, and shouting matches instead of discussion.

The link between the morning and the afternoon

The company had expressed some concern about the link between the morning and the afternoon. They felt that the separate parts did not help the pupils to use all their day's experience in the discussion at the end. However, only two teachers expressed doubt on the link between the two sections, and this was only after the company had discussed it with them.

> I shared some of their (the company's) unhappiness. I don't think it transferred the ideas and the reactions from the morning clearly enough — for our kids anyway — into the afternoon. It was a big jump in imagination, not all the kids made it. I'd like to have seen a simpler play in the afternoon.
>
> (Teacher, Roger Manwood School)

However, in the returned Teacher's Questionnaire two teachers were sure that this link did work:

> *Question*: Do you think that the links between the two sessions were understood by the students?
> *Replies*: Not in all cases, but the majority of them made the connection and used both elements to refer to in later discussion which helped the others to grasp the links in hindsight.
>
> (Teacher, Crown Woods School)

> Totally, — the structuring made this possible. Each stage of development contributed to the afternoon programme. The 'doing' experience helped the 'understanding'.
>
> (Teacher, Blackheath Bluecoat School)

This was a case of the team's uncertainty not being fully corroborated by the teachers in the schools. One school had made sure that the pupils did make the link by talking to the class after the simulation, and before the lunch break. They felt that this discussion period would help to bridge the gap.

Follow-up work (detailed outlines of the individual school's follow-up work can be found in Appendix C, pp. 229–33)

The schools varied enormously in the amount of follow-up work actually done. During the two tours of the programme in 1978 there were only two schools that did a full range of follow-up.

It would appear that when a school makes the effort to book the company for a week, which involves them in a great deal of organization, they also try to utilize the visit to the full. This, however, carries the possibility of "overkill", and teachers need to be aware of the dangers of actually making the pupils sick of the subject!

> Good if it was just one lesson, but it was about three lessons, everyday for three weeks — horrible! Discussion would have been enough. In the end you forgot what you thought before, and just wanted to say, "Shut up, I've had enough of this!"
>
> (Pupil, Kidbrooke School)

This pupil's view is, however, balanced by the obvious value both for the school and the teachers from the week's visit by the company, and the range of work that it was possible for teachers to set up after the programme. At Thomas Tallis follow-up work was done in drama with discussion and in-role essays, Maths concentrated upon the use and misuse of statistics. In art the pupils discussed why and how propaganda posters were produced (see p. 233).

This range of work contrasts with the follow-up that could be done in the case of just one teacher booking the programme for a particular class. Then the amount of follow-up possible was usually very limited — a drama session, or a discussion. Obviously, without the backing and class time of other staff the teacher is limited to his or her own periods with that class (see pp. 230–1).

> We had the programme right at the end of term, so we didn't do much except talk. Never got cross-curricular work going but the group's tutor came with me (to Stage Centre) and found it a very valuable day, and has also had further discussions with the kids themselves.
>
> (Teacher, Crown Woods, from returned Teachers' Questionnaires to Greenwich TIE)

Two schools used the company to introduce a touchy subject that they would not have dealt with in school. In these cases they purposely decided not to follow-up the programme, but let it stand on its own:

> Little follow up work done. The programme made such an impact on them that hammering it in would have caused a reaction. Inter-curricular communication not good here.
>
> (Teacher in Questionnaire, Abbey Wood School)

One can see the logic behind the teacher's argument. The programme was certainly powerful, however many of the pupils in schools, where little follow-up work was done, actually wanted to do more:

> 1st pupil: We should have carried on after — talking. It's hard to get your own opinion at the time, because with so many people shouting, you get muddled up.
> 2nd pupil: It would have helped to have more facts after.
>
> (Pupils, Samuel Peypes School)

The pupils' own ideas on how they would like to have followed up the programme varied from making up their own play about the subject of racism to talking to people in the street about it.

> 1st pupil: I'd like to talk to people in the street, ask them.
> 2nd pupil: Ask them about the National Front, and see if they can (*sic*) change their minds.
>
> (Pupils, Charlton Boys' School)

See Appendix C, pp. 233–4 for further details.

Out of the three schools who received the "Race Against Time" for a week, two managed to arrange an interesting selection of cross-curricular follow-up work. This fed back into general planning and helped long-term aims for the curriculum.

In schools who had the team for a one-day visit only the follow-up work was limited, and very little cross-curriculum work emerged. The follow-up work tended to be limited to an improvisation or discussion session, although reference to the programme was made later and Social Studies' teachers obviously made use of the theme of the programme and, in some cases, of the Teachers' Notes.

The Teachers' Notes

These were not properly used, and their sheer size rather overpowered some teachers (over 100 pages). These Notes are of most use when they become resource material for a number of subjects, not where they are used exclusively for the class that happened to see the programme.

Few teachers seemed to have treated the Teachers' Notes as resource material for present and future work, rather they have tended to use one small section, or worse, not use it at all. I got the impression that if the teachers did not use the material properly they hid it away out of a sense of guilt, and then forgot about it.

To try and combat this attitude perhaps the company could suggest that the Teachers' Notes should be considered as resource material for continual use in different subjects, and not emphasize that they were only related to the programme.

The effect and value of the programme

For the pupils (see Appendix C, pp. 234–39)

Few pupils admitted to any racial prejudice before seeing the programme, so they could not therefore admit to it having radically changed their views! What the programme did do is to make the pupils much more aware of the effect of prejudice in different situations. By focusing the pupils' attention on the subject, the programme made them realize that prejudice existed.

1st pupil: It makes you think.
2nd pupil: It made me feel embarrassed about thinking of any prejudice.
(Pupils, Crown Woods School)

The pupils seemed fairly definite about their feelings and ideas on the value of the programme for them, and their responses followed a similar theme: the programme had made them more aware, given them more facts about racism, and made them realize that racial prejudice was wrong.

By putting the pupils through an experience of prejudice and relating this to the economic situation the pupils were made aware of their strong emotional reactions, and their frustration resulting from their inability to change the situation. From this they realized what was wrong with people's attitudes towards immigrants:

I learned that the immigrants in this country are not to blame for the economic crisis, or the housing shortage or the unemployment crisis . . . I learned how readily people blame people different from themselves for a crisis, and I understand why many resent the whites.
(Pupil's written comments, Kidbrooke School)

To get even seven pupils out of those interviewed who gave positive examples of how they used the programme in arguments with friends or relatives, shows the usefulness of the presentation:

My Dad calls them 'wogs'. I said to him you don't know anything about it yourself. I had an argument with him at home about it after the programme.

(Pupil, Kidbrooke School)

It would be foolish to claim that it radically altered the pupils' way of life, but it obviously provoked discussion and gave the pupils amunition to use in arguments. (See Appendix C, pp. 237–38 for other examples.) From the teachers' point of view the fact that an outside group could deal with the delicate topic of racial prejudice made it much easier to deal with it internally. As a teacher from Thomas Tallis School explained in an article on "Race Against Time" in the ILEA magazine *Contact*.

> Without doubt, the presence of an outside group dealing with such a delicate topic made it easier to deal with internally. It was noticeable that colleagues who had expressed considerable reservations in the beginning were pleased and encouraged by the response they had from pupils during tutor and registration periods, as well as lessons generally. It is a most valuable function of a TIE team's work to provide the external stimulus for work in this area since, through their skills as teachers as well as actors, they can create a perspective which the staff of a school can go on to develop.
>
> We found it a very stimulating and valuable experience, and as one of the pupils said: "Cor, when can we do this again?"
>
> (*Contact*, ILEA, Issue 12, p. 34)

Teachers did not view the programme as something that would radically alter the pupils' prejudices, but realized that it provided excellent material to build on.

> The programme challenged the children's preconceived ideas and prompted them to gain insight into the issues explored by the programme.
>
> The effect is not so much political more opening up avenues. The uninformed see that there is something to be said on the issues and respond to the visual demonstration of a point.
>
> (Teacher in written comment, Blackheath Bluecoat School)

However, as the follow-up information shows, few teachers used this opportunity to the full.

Learning by doing

When discussing the hypothetical question of whether the pupils felt that they learnt more from the TIE programme than they would have done from a series of lessons, the responses were quite definite. The pupils felt that the

TIE programme taught them more. Their replies revealed that it was the method of learning which was important:

> Yes, because I wouldn't have had the experience. It taught me by doing.
>
> (Pupil, Thomas Calton School)

> You learn from having done it. If I get a book and discuss it, it's not so good. I read, but I've got so many things on my mind I can't read a book and ten days later remember anything in it, but this (the programme) was two months ago and I still remember it.
>
> (Pupil, Samuel Peypes School)

Why the programme was booked and by which department
(see Appendix C, pp. 239–41)

This particular programme, with its emphasis on cross-curricular work, did break away from the usual syndrome of being booked by the Drama department. Two Social Studies departments booked, but English and Drama departments made up the rest. Where there is a long-standing contact in a school this is usually with the English or Drama departments out of tradition. Perhaps a strong indication of the balance of the programme and the possible interested departments, stated clearly on the publicity information, would help to break this tradition. Only continual emphasis of this sort and the building up of new contacts in different departments in schools is going to bring about any change in the present booking pattern.

The reasons why the programme was booked were very various, and revealed that even with such a definite and topical subject the programme could be booked for reasons that had nothing at all to do with the subject-matter.

> I booked it because I was interested in it and could use it as a dramatic discussion on shape etc. with the pupils, not just because it was about racism.
>
> (Teacher, Crown Woods School)

> It was booked because it was a subject that the teacher thought important, but not one that the school dealt with at all. So, the programme raised issues that the school would not normally have touched on, because of its policy of keeping the race question out of lessons and the school.
>
> (Interview with Teacher and Head Teacher, West Greenwich School)

The majority of teachers booked the programme because it was about racism, a subject which everyone in South-east London schools felt strongly about because of the National Front demonstrations in Lewisham. As it was an extremely delicate subject most teachers were glad that it could be introduced in the form of a TIE programme presented by a group from outside the school.

Booking and organization in the schools (see Appendix C, pp. 239–45)

One of the major factors in helping the company's bookings, especially with this delicate subject-matter, is its association with ILEA. The Authority gave GYPT a grant, and featured an article on "Race Against Time" in its magazine *Contact*. Without this "badge of respectability" some Head Teachers might have refused to have the company in the school.

> It was interesting when I talked to the Head Teacher she asked if it was the programme that was featured in "Contact". I got the impression that this meant it was a good thing.
>
> (Teacher, Peckham School)

Organizational problems in booking a programme always arise, especially for fourth-year pupils who are doing several different subjects. This is often why the teacher doing the booking uses the class he or she is working with on the day for which the programme is booked.

> It was not possible to share it because of timetabling, we used the drama classes. I was going to work with the Social Studies Department, but this was not possible, which was a shame.
>
> (Teacher, Roger Manwood School)

The school timetable frequently creates an impenetrable barrier to change or innovation. Thus in many schools any hope of joining up with other subjects, or classes, or booking the programme for a week are completely unthinkable. The lone innovator in such a school system has little hope!

Value of performing for a week in a school (see pp. 241–45)

When the company are in the school for a week they become part of its day-to-day activities. They are there to be talked to, and questioned. The spin off from this is very valuable. Teachers gain a much greater awareness of the team's work, methods, aims and attitudes. Elements in the programme that worry either teachers or pupils can be thrashed out. GYPT's other activities and the work of TIE companies can be discussed. The team can begin to associate with and understand that particular school, and make real contact with the staff and pupils. One-day, one-off performances are very tiring, and allow no time for meeting the staff, or forming any link with the school.

Sue Bennion commented on the value for the company and the school of the one-week visits:

> The three schools involved in this experimental scheme presented very different problems and the programme elicited very different responses from students. In all three though, the level of co-operation and mutual understanding between team and teachers was impressive and did much to consolidate existing links with the schools. At Thomas Tallis, for example, up to five members of staff were able to stay, all day, with the pupils. It seems a small thing but so often even in a half-day programme, teachers are not always able or willing to be there throughout. This was a break-through, and one which the team appreciated.
>
> ("Race Against Time", *Contact*, ILEA magazine, Issue 12, pp. 33–34)

From the interviews, and other information gathered (see Appendix C, pp. 239–45, 245–7), it is quite obvious that where a one-week presentation of the programme in a school can be organized its return value is infinitely greater than for a one-day performance. No fewer pupils receive the programme, although fewer schools have the chance of seeing the company. To work in depth, rather than to spread the work thinly over a wide area appears to be a far better use of Theatre in Education in schools.

Praise and Criticism of the Programme

Very few pupils expressed dislike of the programme, and even then it was indifference rather than dislike. Only three pupils out of approximately 110 interviewed were indifferent.

The criticism was mainly from one school, and was on the fact that the programme was biased. This had obviously come up during their discussions.

The teachers were positive in their praise of the programme and the company, this was clear not only in their specific praise, but also in their whole approach to the programme.

Praise

Teachers' comments

> The team had taken time, carefully and sensitively and produced one of the most valuable pieces of Theatre in Education I have ever seen.
>
> (Teacher, Roger Manwood School)

I'm interested in theatre communication a burning aspect of life. This is what the team did.

(Teacher, Peckham School)

I was quite impressed, a very well balanced programme, attempted to get to the situation.
. . . I think the Bowsprit (Greenwich TIE) are an excellent company. I don't think I've seen them do a bad programme.

(Teacher, Kidbrooke School)

Kidbrooke Questionnaire to pupils

Question 8:
Underline the phrase that describes (as near as possible) how you felt after seeing the programme:

I'm glad I saw it — 60 pupils underlined this.
It was interesting — 39 pupils.
It was boring — no pupils underlined this.
It wouldn't have bothered me if I hadn't seen it — 1 pupil underlined this phrase.

Teacher's comment in Greenwich TIE Questionnaire

Excellent day — a topic more easily handled by strangers than well known teachers. Kids are quick to sense bias in teachers, and white kids (in this class) keen to feel insults not always intended, to black kids.

(Teacher, Abbey Wood School — not interviewed)

Pupil in interview

Ask them to come back again.

(Peckham School)

The Evaluation Model

Having completed the research the success of the actual evaluation model chosen needs consideration. The criteria used by Adult Educational Broadcasting to assess research models concentrated upon the objectives, the method and the application of the evaluation model.

Objectives: "Are these clear, practicable and useful?"

The objective for the application of the evaluation model was to see whether it would produce information on the effect of the "Race Against Time" programme. This information would range across several areas and levels, e.g. the emotional and intellectual effect; the nature of the follow-up work, etc.

Although the objective was clear, the sheer range of information needed required a fairly full-time commitment to the collection of data. As the information consisted of value judgements rather than measurements the conclusions drawn rely on balancing judgements rather than measuring effect. The objective was useful for it provided a large amount of information both on the value of the model itself and, most important, on the programme.

Methods: "Are these systematic and effective in pursuit of the objectives? Are they not excessive in time and prohibitively expensive?"

The method was systematic in that I went through a definite series of moves to gain and record the material: contacting schools, interviewing teachers and pupils, writing up the interviews, gathering in other sources of information and correlating the material.

As for the effectiveness of the method, it supplied a large amount of spoken, but not a great deal of written, material. More written information was available in the form of pupils' essays, but these were virtually impossible to extract from the overworked teachers concerned. Not all the teachers were properly interviewed, and more time was needed to arrange special interviews with them.

The one experiment using some form of measurement, the Thurston scale, was not a success, and produced no useful information. This was due to the nature of the subject-matter of the programme, and the style of the questionnaire I devised. Isolating questions on racial prejudice tends to emphasize some very delicate issues, which teachers felt should not be raised in so bald a fashion as the questionnaire.

There is no doubt that the method takes up a great deal of time. The actual research in schools was spread over 2 months, and the writing up, collecting of written material and correlating the information took at least another 2 months.

To do this kind of research properly it is essential to visit schools personally and interview pupils and teachers. Obviously the correlating of the information cannot be done until all the material has been gathered and written down.

As the research takes time it is expensive, but this expense is in man hours, and therefore wages or fees. It is not difficult to put into operation, neither is it expensive in materials. However, it takes up too much time for a TIE team to do it themselves with their commitment to continuous work in schools. It would therefore necessitate the employment of an extra person. The nature of the research does not demand that one person collect all the material, but the interviews are probably more consistent and effective if only one person is involved. The actual correlation and drawing of conclusions would also be better if only one person undertook the task.

Applications: "Are these of practical value, both in the short term and in the long term? Can decisions be directly based upon them?"

The answer to these questions is definitely yes. The information from the research is applicable in a number of ways. It can discover the areas of the programme that pupils and teachers find difficult, or that work best, it can reveal failures to follow-up in schools, or administrative problems of booking and so on. These can help the team both in the long and the short term.

The application of my research on "Race Against Time" helped the team to make decisions on how to improve the programme when it came back into the repertoire. The research did not necessarily suggest the changes, but was used by the team as proof of their own doubts.

When the programme was performed again in the Christmas term 1979, certain changes had been made. In the tour of "Race Against Time" in the autumn of 1978, the simulation was not introduced, and the pupils were

FIG. 22. "Race Against Time", new play.

involved immediately in the action. In the Christmas term 1979 tour the company introduced themselves and the nature of the work they were going to do. This change has more to do with the company's alteration of policy, making sure that the pupils understand who they are and the nature of the work than as a result of the evaluation project. For this latest tour the simulation had been tightened up, so that the time span covered 3 not 4 years, thus reducing the numbers of times the pupils had to go round the desks.

The play in the 1978 tour had provoked some criticism. Pupils, teachers and the team themselves were concerned that the play did not link well with the morning simulation game, and its very theatricality, use of songs, intense emotions, etc., tended to get in the way of its message. It was also rather long. For the latest tour a *new* play had been written. It was set in a small biscuit factory and involved the conflict between some white, female workers; a Pakistani foreman; a male worker who was an NF supporter, and the owner of the factory. The attitudes of the NF were put across less forcefully than in the first play. The factory owner linked clearly with Mr. Ward, the business man, in the simulation. One of the female workers began with strong anti-immigrant views and changed her ideas during the course of the action. The play was 45 minutes long (the other play had been an hour) and was far less theatrical. The low-key presentation and the three-dimensional characters helped to make the play a more integral part of the whole programme.

During the 1978 tour the discussion after the play had tended to concentrate upon the play's themes and its characters, rather than as a starting-point to discussion on racism generally. The discussion in the latest tour was far more successful. This was mostly due to the change of play, for it enabled pupils to link their experience in the simulation to the play and to their own ideas.

These changes were not the result of my research, but the material I had gathered and given to the team did provide them with firm evidence to support their vague suspicions and doubts about areas of the programme. The pupils' quotes in the research enabled the team to gauge the kind of effect the programme was having on the pupils. Although the research was in no way a substitute for the team's own self-critical approach to their work, it did provide them with positive evidence, and a range of opinions which would not have been available from any other source.

The short-term value of the research is borne out by these alterations in the programme which the company chose to make, helping to improve the work and consequently its effectiveness in schools. The long-term value lies in the information such research can provide for future planning. For instance, the value of spending a week in schools as against a day became very clear. The research can provide evidence for grant-aiding bodies on the use and effectiveness of the work in schools. The problem here, as with drama in a school, is that no measurement is possible and the evidence is necessarily 'unscientific'.

The evaluation model did provide a good method of collecting and correlating information on a TIE programme. It did not demand trained expertise in educational evaluation such as scientific measurement. The problem with the model is that it is expensive and demanding in time and therefore in wages. A way of using the evaluation model properly would be the employment of an additional team member who can concentrate on visiting schools, and collecting information on a programme.

Greenwich, the Cockpit and Coventry teams each employ a liaison officer, whose job it is to build up contact with schools. The job also includes an element of evaluation, but this is not a major part of their work. Obviously, closer contact with schools will bring teacher's comments and criticisms of programmes to the notice of the team.

The only way that TIE teams can carry out proper evaluation is the use of an additional member of staff, such as a seconded teacher, or someone especially employed to concentrate on evaluation. Whoever does the job it should be on a continuous basis and look at both the short- and the long-term effects of the programmes. One-off evaluation projects such as mine on "Race Against Time" are of limited value to the team. This project was to open out the question of the forms of evaluation and to discover the range of information which could be collected. It would be good to see TIE teams set up their own projects and improve upon the methods used and ideas suggested in these chapters.

Conclusion

The "Race Against Time" project, although a one-off experiment, could be a useful formula for internal and external evaluation of a team's work. It is possible for one person with time available to put into operation. What is required, of course, is an understanding of TIE and of schools.

For any TIE evaluation close co-operation and discussion with the TIE team concerned is essential. This will establish the team's general ideas and philosophy as well as their specific thoughts on the particular programme. If the evaluation is to be structured by the asking of carefully chosen questions then these must come out of full discussion with the team and a good knowledge of the programme, i.e. seeing it first, perhaps more than once before phrasing any questions. Most TIE teams will give a clear indication of some information they would like to know. Certainly the Greenwich team did this on "Race Against Time". It is doubtful, however, that the team will have a clear idea for every section of the programme, and this may therefore be left to the discretion of the evaluator, who should then indicate his or her ideas to the team.

If the type of questions asked of the pupils are rather vague it is unlikely that they will produce many useful results. The response would rely on the interest of the teacher and the pupils to open out the discussion. Whilst teachers may well offer good, reasoned arguments with specific examples from the programme, it is doubtful that the pupils always will! Discussion could wander off into non-related areas, or never get under way at all. A too general approach obviously allows for vagueness, and "hobby-horses". On the other hand, too tight a range of questions, and form of questioning, might be inhibiting, and not allow for the unlooked for "spin-offs" to emerge. Some happy compromise is obviously required.

Would the evaluation method be suitable for all kinds of TIE programmes?

The "Race Against Time" evaluation format was geared to discussions with Secondary school pupils of 13–15 years, and covered a range of factual, conceptual and hypothetical areas. A 7–8-year-old would find it difficult to respond to some of the questions. In fact, in many cases, the 13–15-year-olds questioned were far more coherent and fluent when answering factual points and discussing their own experiences. Questions can be used for the younger age range if this approach is carefully thought out. It is quite possible to ask 7–8-year-olds about the story of the programme and, once the pupils have recalled this, to ask specific questions about characters, events, ideas, and what the pupils felt and did during the course of the programme. It is much more difficult with this age-range to ask the question "why?" The nature of the evaluation, then, must be on a slightly different basis for the younger age group.

To evaluate Infant and Junior programmes such as "Pow-Wow" and "Rare Earth" the method of questioning pupils can stimulate recall. By getting the pupils to remember the story, it is possible to discover *why* they remember it. The DES Report, *Actors in Schools*, used this approach on "Rare Earth" and made an important discovery:

> For more than one child in the group the delicate trigger-mechanism for recalling the whole experience appeared to have been the first motion, the first gesture, of Wakatanka, the Red Indian Goddess — stylised, strangely disturbing and unanalysable — but which had clearly communicated itself visually and emotionally to many children. This movement was described by the children in great detail . . .[1]

Such images and gestures can trigger recall of a programme, and are, therefore, most important, both in the performance and in the evaluation of the programme. If the evaluator is aware of these "keys" to memory then he or she can use them to stimulate pupils' memories. On the other hand, these "keys" could be discovered during the course of the evaluation.

"Rare Earth" is full of strong visual images. One child commented of the entrance of the Chisso factory in the second play:

> You could see this great big . . . well it was a man with this mask on with his great pointed fingers sprayed silver, he was the factory and all his fingers were supposed to be the mercury coming out of his fingers.[2]

In "Pow-Wow" the image of the Red Indian in his cage conveys the basic message of the programme. The script emphasizes the length of time necessary for Black Elk to gain the children's confidence and persuade them to let him out of his cage. This was certainly true of the production I saw by York Young People's Theatre Company. The cage was a most powerful visual symbol, and the actor–teacher playing Black Elk took a long time in gently gaining the pupils' confidence.

Mr. Tex's gun is a symbol of his authority, authority by fear, not necessarily by respect. The image of Mr. Tex pointing his gun at Black Elk when he discovered the Indian out of his cage formed a very strong impression on the children. One Coventry teacher, commenting on the final vote, pointed out that "They all went to the cowboy — he had a gun — and they felt unsafe about going to the Indian, although several said they wanted to".

Theatre in Education companies are well aware of the importance of these theatrical images. Geoff Gilham explored the subject in a recent article in the *SCYPT Journal* no. 5, discussing the use of the theatrical image in the Cockpit TIE's programme "Ways of Change" (about the English Civil War). He sees the theatrical image as "a concrete stage event which has meanings embedded in the event which go beyond the event itself".[3] Taking several examples of the use of an axe throughout the programme he explains how the context gives meaning to the object.

What significance does the theatrical image have for the evaluator? Firstly, it is a common feature in TIE programmes for all age groups. Its use becoming more subtle, perhaps, for the Secondary school pupils. In any evaluation these images can emerge in discussion or in the follow-up writing and painting. Here the evaluator must deal with the interpretation of the meaning by the pupils.

The use of such theatrical images and symbols provide valuable "short-hand" about the meaning and message, preventing TIE programmes becoming heavy sermons, or agit-prop pieces. They convey the message without the need for the soap-box. Geoff Gilham suggests that to discover whether the image has worked as hoped, the pupils would need to be sensitively questioned by the teacher on the "perception of meaning", i.e. what was a character feeling when he drove the axe into the wood like that? In this way:

> Their response would tell us how accurately they received the image, even though they would be unlikely to know what the use of an image was, what made the complexity of feelings the Father had available to them.[4]

This provides a useful evaluation method, but theatrical images are not always so obvious, and in TIE programmes using different forms such as "Race Against Time" any images that are useful come in the play. The guilty brother holding the bread knife, and cutting the bread as he talked, certainly provided a memorable stage picture, but the play contained no running images such as the axe.

Another element common to most TIE programmes is both useful and problematic for an evaluator: the use of emotion. It is essential to allow for it in the results, but difficult to discuss constructively. In "Pow-Wow", "Rare Earth" and "Race Against Time" powerful use is made of a range of emotions: fear in "Pow-Wow" as the children are left alone with Black Elk, sadness at the suffering portrayed through mercury poisoning in the second part of "Rare Earth", and anger at the treatment the immigrants received from the Social Benefits Officer, and other New Town officials, in "Race Against Time".

Kathy Joyce discusses the use of emotion in TIE from the consumers' viewpoint in *Learning Through Theatre*:

> As long as the powerful emotional reaction is modified by intellectual understanding and channelled constructively within the programme, the children are extended within a unique learning situation, providing a challenging stimulus wide open to development by a perceptive teacher.[5]

The evaluator must be able to take account of this use of emotion and its effect upon the pupils. With a powerful programme such as "Rare Earth" a gap of a few months before the evaluator talks to the children may provide the necessary time for the programme to be properly absorbed. When the emotion is too fresh it is sometimes difficult for pupils to discuss what they have seen, the same is true of an adult audience watching a very powerful and moving play.

In the case of a programme like "Pow-Wow" many teachers commented in their questionnaires that the children had felt differently about their final vote a week or so after the programme. At the time, the emotional involvement and the feeling of fear were too strong to allow them to make an objective choice between Black Elk and Mr. Tex.[6]

One of the problems for the evaluator, which is common to many Infant and Junior programmes, is the use of the "suspension of disbelief". The programme and the characters are presented as real. For instance, in "Pow-Wow", the reality of the characters is never questioned. In fact the entire programme depends upon the pupils' total belief in the reality of these people they meet. Even in a programme which is introduced as not real, pupils can become extremely involved and actually forget that it is "only a play".

Bearing this in mind how does an evaluator discuss the programme with the pupils, and should he or she actually do so, will this destroy the reality? The evaluator must obviously avoid any dismissal of the events as just a play, especially if this effects the pupils' follow-up work. The programme must be discussed as a real event.

Another problem for the evaluator is the differing programme structures. "Race Against Time" has three forms, the simulation, the play, the discussion, whereas "Pow-Wow" has the division of the first part taking place in a classroom with an element of teaching, followed by the events in the hall. Should the evaluator tackle each part of the programme as a separate unit, and employ different methods for each? Although this may be effective for each separate section it is doubtful that it will give an overall picture of the programme. This is why the evaluation model used for "Race Against Time" was holistic, to allow a complete picture to emerge, and it used the same method of fact finding for all three sections.

For all the differences between TIE programmes the one fact that they have in common is their concern with real issues. Issues that are a part of the world around the pupils, and which are presented in such a way that the pupils can relate the experience of the programme to their own lives. After "Race Against Time" a few of the pupils began to find their own voice in discussion on race outside school, others admitted to becoming aware of their own prejudices.

However, to convey the basic facts of these issues TIE programmes tend to take a particular angle on the topic to stimulate a response. Character views are often completely opposing. David Pammenter pointed out the value of this in his introduction to "Pow-Wow":

> The piece consciously polarises its participants and it is the conflict caused by this polarisation that gives rise to true education and learning.[7]

For the evaluator, however, this polarization can mean a distortion of the pupils' initial understanding of the issue itself. It is oversimplification for a purpose, and if the programme is properly structured the learning process should become clear. If the programme is not well structured the polarization can work against the aims of the programme and obfuscate the issue or genuinely mislead the pupils. This can be a useful pointer for the evaluator.

A major concern for any evaluation project is exactly what are you evaluating? Is it the programme structure, the pupils' response, and grasp of the issue, the school or even the teacher's abilities? Some programmes like Greenwich TIE's "Living Patterns" involve teachers very closely in programme preparation and presentation, so the teacher would naturally become part of any evaluation. "Atomistic" research, or concentration on just one aspect of the whole, can be of value, and may sometimes be all that is possible. John O'Toole, for instance, wished to concentrate upon the value of audience participation in his research.[8] It can, however, be misleading, and might leave out some related but equally important findings.

If the pupils are the main subject of an evaluator's research there are some recognized features of different age groups' response to TIE programmes. Infants can be easily scared, they have no general knowledge on which to draw, and often have no real sense of history. TIE practitioners acknowledge Infant work as being one of the most difficult areas they have to tackle. Working with Juniors, however, can be immensely rewarding. This age group is much more able to become involved, physically and mentally. They are eager to learn, and therefore good at problem-solving. They also have a sense of group identity. Secondary school pupils' inhibitions can begin to effect their response to a programme, and to the evaluator! Physical participation is much more tricky to incorporate. To balance this, the age group is much more able to analyse, abstract and discuss the implication of the events in a programme and their own response to them.

What in fact are TIE teams and teachers looking for in a programme? Kathy Joyce sets out her criteria in her article "TIE in schools — A consumer's view-point":

1. Is the content worth presenting and how far does it arrest, inform, challenge and extend the audience (including the adults present)?
2. Is it well performed and presented, with good audience contact?
3. Is it performed to the right age-group and the most appropriate audience size?
4. How far does the company involve the teachers, or attempt to integrate its work into the curriculum?
5. How committed do the actors seem to the objectives of their work; and how open are they to discussion and criticism? Do they attempt to evaluate their work?
6. What unique contribution will this company make to the children's education?[9]

David Pammenter sets out his criteria for an effective TIE programme in his introduction to "Pow-Wow":

"Pow-Wow", although not a new programme remains a real challenge to the performer and participant alike, and the reason, I believe, is to be found in the honesty — the sense of purpose of the aim — the well formed structure of the piece — and the power of the programme — to make children take up and explore the truth behind an established myth.[10]

TIE teams often attempt some form of evaluation of their work. As discussed in Chapter 5 this is usually achieved through questionnaires and Teacher-Team meetings. Geoff Gilham, in his article on Theatrical Images, suggested that the teacher should question the pupils. This is a valid form of evaluation, but it has some of the same problems as emerged in the "Race Against Time" project: it takes time and is somewhat laborious, the questions must be carefully phrased, the pupils must be willing to participate, and the data must be collected by someone, and finally correlated. TIE teams have not the time or the resources to co-ordinate such research. Geoff Gillham's answer is not to construct better evaluation techniques, but to develop and use theory:

Correctly derived theory avoids the necessity of 'asking the kids' to evaluate our work. I say 'correctly derived' because theory can only be extracted from practice and, if it is to be correct, cannot exist just as a thing in our heads that we make up to justify what we do. Nor can theory be derived by just looking at the surface of things, or a random collection of facts.[11]

The Cockpit team, together with the other TIE company in ILEA, Greenwich, are beginning to find some answers to the problem of evaluating their work, and ensuring that it is properly used by schools. The Cockpit team are working closely with a small group of teachers from about fifteen schools. The team no longer books schools on a first-come-first-served basis, instead it plans to work with these fifteen schools over a series of programmes. Thus building up a strong working relationship with the teachers, who are involved in the decision on the subject-matter of the programmes, the form they should take and the nature of the follow-up material. The Cockpit policy statement explains the team's method:

> In order to realise in the classroom, the greatest potential of a TIE programme, we are building relationships with a limited number of teachers and schools and aim to develop with the teachers whole programmes of work around each programme.

The other London team, Greenwich TIE, has also developed this policy of much closer co-operation with a small number of schools (see Chapter 4). By working so closely and creatively with teachers both London teams are formulating theories about the work. Theories which are constantly evolving and changing, but which nonetheless provide some sort of framework.

This continuous co-operation with teachers makes the collection of facts about a programme, via questionnaires or interviews with pupils, less necessary. Evaluation need no longer be a separate process undertaken by someone outside the team, but becomes an integral part of the team–teacher relationship. The constant involvement with teachers and the continuing need for discussion on programmes, past, present and future provides an excellent flow of information on how the programmes have been received and used in schools. Evaluation is both summative and formative, in that the team–teacher meetings involve discussion on the effect of a programme just performed and this information then feeds directly into the planning of the next programme for the same age group or indeed for any age group.

Clear and apt criticism was difficult for teachers when their knowledge of TIE methods, techniques and philosophy was sketchy at best, and non-existent at worst. For those teachers who have opted to work much more closely with their local TIE teams, increasing familiarity with the ideas, problems and techniques involved in the TIE process will enable them to make more informed and helpful judgements. This increasing knowledge is of practical use to the team when these teachers become actively involved in programme preparation. In this they operate formative evaluation and can alter the nature of the work, see their own ideas used, and structure both the programme and the follow-up work.

Sue Bennion of the Greenwich team described how the teachers helped to shape the company's programme for the Junior age range, "Living Patterns" (described in Chapter 4, pp. 120–22):

> We had a number of meetings. It was a very long gestation period. We thought we would have to do something before the section on China, but talking to teachers really brought that home. The middle part of the programme came very much from teachers. We hadn't planned a three-part programme, but the teachers involved in our experimental project felt that a situation, a workshop, where kids could put right what they felt was wrong might be a good idea. China was offered to show an alternative system, and we stressed that the programme was not about China. Many teachers did work on China, however, and the material was useful.[12]

To avoid the danger of limiting the programmes and the co-operative work to just a few teachers over a long period of time, both TIE teams are ready to introduce other groups of teachers in the project when they can.

This new method of working has certainly reduced the usefulness of the questionnaires to teachers. These did provide some feed-back when teams were visiting schools on a one-off basis. Sue Bennion again:

> We haven't consciously abandoned questionnaires, but because of the way we work with teachers now they're becoming less important. Questionnaires were used because we didn't see teachers after programmes. With the projects we're now in constant and deeper contact with teachers, and so don't need a detached formal questionnaire.[13]

As Greenwich are still in the process of developing this method of working with teachers, and teachers are becoming involved in the whole process of preparing a TIE programme for schools, both sides are going through a learning process, and a sense that "they're all in it together". In spite of this struggle the method of work for both teams appears to be proving very valuable and worthwhile.

However, this move towards working with teachers, and using the concept approach (discussed in Chapter 4), has shifted the balance that TIE strives to keep between theatre and education. Sue Bennion noted a definite shift:

> During the last two years we've had a much greater drive towards education than towards theatre. This now needs to be re-dressed. It gets imbalanced, that's the nature of the medium.[14]

It is exactly this desire to balance both worlds, that has kept Theatre in Education out of either camp. By so doing it has retained a strong independence of spirit, an independence which has led teams to adopt a critical and innovative role in education, and prevented them from becoming an educational back-up resource under the control of the Local Education Authority.

This independence was helped by the fact that the majority of teams developed from repertory theatres, who were becoming aware of their role in the community. The nature of the funding for the Theatre in Education teams also aided their independence, the Local Education Authorities and the Arts Council both contributing in varying proportions. The late 1960s and early 1970s was a boom period for the economy, and consequently money could be found to finance new projects and allow them to grow.

The Arts Council appeared to assume that most of the new schemes they were funding would be geared towards theatre rather than education. The Report which initiated the financing of Young People's Theatre noted the Belgrade Coventry Theatre in Education work as "unique", and felt that the scheme "may be considered to fall more properly into the Enquiry's third phase of work".[15] This third phase was to place its emphasis on children's needs in Drama. A Report on Drama in Schools was produced by the DES rather than by the Arts Council. However, it was the Coventry scheme which actually produced the personnel to develop new Theatre in Education schemes. As the Belgrade, Coventry scheme had close links with education and was supported almost solely by the Local Education Authority, the people who left this scheme to begin others were trained to develop meaningful work for schools, not Children's Theatre. Thus a number of the new schemes backed by the Arts Council and the Local Education Authorities began to move away from theatre and entertainment towards education.

The theatre element was not lost, for it formed an essential part of the method of work in schools. The programmes frequently used actor–teachers in role, creating an "experience" with the pupils. These programmes utilized theatre: dramatic conflict, tension, creation and development of characters, plot structure, climax and plot resolution.

This use of theatre, and the fact of being small groups of 'performers' going out to meet their 'audience', linked Theatre in Education with Alternative Theatre. Theatre in Education appeared at the same time as the explosion of the Alternative Theatre movement. It was part of the rebellion against traditional theatre, and part of the social upheavals of 1968. It was part of the strong political element in Alternative Theatre with new companies and new writers showing "an increasing interest in the world of public as opposed to private affairs".[16]

This atmosphere of social and political criticism suited Theatre in Education personnel. The new profession of the actor–teacher was drawn from theatre people who found theatre irrelevant to present society, and teachers who were critical of the present education system, and from university students who wished to find a way of expressing their ideas about the world around them. Theatre in Education teams began to see themselves as innovators and questioners:

> Whatever the audience, there is amongst Theatre in Education teams a determination to see that teachers and kids alike shall have access to the liveliest, sanest and most challenging ideas around, through the medium that is most immediate, personal and yet most social — theatre.[17]

Unlike many Alternative Theatre companies Theatre in Education teams could develop their ideas, methods and beliefs in comparative security. Once established, many teams had a period of about 4–5 years of secure and increasing grant-aid. Whereas most Alternative Theatre companies relied heavily on box-office receipts, and those groups who received no Arts Council grants lived a very precarious existence, folded and were replaced by others.

Due to this security, and the development of group devising, policy-making and the constant stimulus of fresh subjects and challenges, many actor–teachers stayed in the profession for several years. They felt a commitment to the work, to the team and the area in which they were functioning. This accumulated experience and knowledge about Theatre in Education helped the movement to develop as a whole. It produced the Standing Conference of Young People's Theatre, the *SCYPT Journal*, the beginnings of an analysis of the process of work which Theatre in Education used and some long-standing and exciting Theatre in Education teams.

Although Theatre in Education established a fierce independence from the main-stream theatre and from education which led to some very effective work in schools, it has had repercussions. At a time of economic cutbacks, and drastic reductions in Local Authority spending, the independence of the teams places them in the greatest danger. In many cases their grants are separate funds not tied into salary payments by the Local Authority. An obvious sum of money to cut is that which forms a team's life blood for the year. The Arts Council, similarly pressured by cuts, cannot support a Theatre in Education team on its own, and its policy has always been to share support and to encourage LEAs to give money. Nottingham Playhouse Roundabout was an early victim of cuts in local government spending.

The parent repertory theatres do not appear to be able, or willing, to help their YPT teams. Since the end of "ear-marking" of funds for YPT by the Arts Council in 1974, there has been an actual drop of 10 per cent in the proportion of money spent by the parent companies on their YPT teams.

As Theatre in Education companies have refused to be part of either main stream theatre or education they are not protected by either of these areas. At a time of crisis a large umbrella organization can be very helpful, both for security and for the fighting of battles. Yet an organization like SCYPT has no protective power and no teeth as a pressure group. It has deliberately rejected this role, but in so doing it has made its members even more vulnerable.

For some teams, the answer to these financial pressures has been the broadening of the scope of the work, so as to draw on other sources of income. Companies' shift towards Community Theatre work may be partly due to a sense of commitment towards the whole community, but there is little doubt that the search for money to survive has become some companies' guiding policy. Introducing more adult work, or performances to children outside school hours, drastically reduces the amount of the work in schools, and its continuity. Although teams may still continue to do Theatre in Education programmes in schools when their schedule permits, this reduction in the amount of TIE work will obviously limit a team's effectiveness.

Although there are approximately ninety professional 'theatre' companies working with children in one form or another, less than half of the children of this country see even one performance a year. With only approximately twenty companies doing Theatre in Education, the proportion of children experiencing TIE is very small indeed.

Theatre in Education, as a method of working in schools, is in great danger of disappearing altogether. The economic cuts in the early 1970s meant the loss of companies like Theatremakers in Stirling and the Theatre in Education company at Exeter. The loss of companies had been counter-balanced by the starting of new ones with the help of the Man Power Services Commission. However, the point has now been reached where the MSC fund is being reduced, and the Local Authorities are having to implement stringent cuts. The Arts Council has insufficient money to meet its present commitments, let alone prop up companies who lose their Local Authority support. The next few years may well see other companies following Nottingham's fate; in fact Lancaster TIE has already fallen victim to the cuts.

Yet Theatre in Education has produced a very distinct way of working, a method of communicating ideas to a particular audience in a form that is relevant, understandable, yet exciting and often provocative. A method which uses both theatre and educational techniques and relies on the group's commitment, shared responsibility and ability to develop and learn themselves as the work progresses.

TIE makes a unique contribution to education. Teams are able to introduce themes and methods into a school which a teacher would find it hard to do as an individual. In its ability to motivate pupils to learn, and concentrate, and produce stimulus on many different levels, TIE offers something that the education system appears to destroy.

Criticism of the education system, both here and in America, emphasizes this destructive aspect. John Holt, in his influential book *Why Children Fail*, has this to say:

> We adults destroy most of the intellectual and creative capacity of children by the things we do to them or make them do. We destroy this capacity above all by making them afraid, afraid of not doing what other people want, of not pleasing, of making mistakes, of failing, of being *wrong*. Thus we make them afraid to gamble, afraid to experiment, afraid to try the difficult and the unknown.[18]

Theatre in Education can offer children a challenge in a context where being wrong is not relevant. They are involved in the "difficult and the unknown" without even realizing it is happening, and the experience is enjoyable rather than agonizing.

Obviously TIE cannot take on the whole of education, and its impact on the present system is limited. Yet as part of the development of the Arts in general, it has had a far greater influence than the present number of working TIE teams would lead one to expect. It had bred a new type of performer: an artist who is conscious of society, who wishes to question and change it, and wishes to have a real say in the choice and preparation of material; someone who has a sense of responsibility towards the group and towards the community in which he or she works.

As many of the Theatre in Education actor–teachers move on into mainstream theatre, Community and Fringe Theatre and into Education, they take with them the ideas, standards and attitudes of their TIE work. Although this statement is obviously difficult to prove the following quotes may at least provide some support: Edward Peel, actor and director and ex-Leeds TIE, ran the Humberside Theatre for a few years as Artistic Director. During an interview, he made this comment about the influence of Theatre in Education on theatre generally, and upon his own attitudes:

> It has produced a change in attitude in the theatre profession. There are a number of actors who are very much concerned with what kind of work they do. When I audition people I am as interested in the questions they ask me as in the ones I ask them. There are actors beginning to work in TIE or in the Fringe or in travelling theatre companies who are saying: "We are not just on this treadmill of Rep., West End, T.V. We are prepared to accept less money if we believe in what we are putting on." That, I think, comes as a result partly of TIE, now getting people who think, who question "What is the purpose of this play?"[19]

Or this quote, from an interview with Jean Bullwinkle and Bettie Ritchie at the Arts Council:

Jean Bullwinkle: TIE as it started in Coventry, is still going on in quite a small way, but it hasn't developed. I don't mean in the actual work but in the amount of work, but it has had an enormous influence on what is happening over all theatre.

Bettie Ritchie: It has had an influence on Main Theatre where Artistic Directors have taken TIE seriously. It has become integrated into companies at Newcastle and Leicester.[20]

Theatre in Education personnel have become Artistic Directors of mainstream theatres: Paddy Masefield at Worcester, and John Southworth at Ipswich. Some have moved into Higher Education: Stuart Bennett and Colin Hicks at Rose Bruford College, Gordon Vallins at Warwickshire College of Further Education; others, such as David Pammenter, went on to run Community Theatre groups, and David Hollman became a freelance writer for many different kinds of theatre.

Not only main-stream theatre has benefited, Children's Theatre has also gained. Many TIE teams present one or two Children's Theatre productions in the main house every year, just as the Coventry team does at the Belgrade (see Chapter 2). These productions have helped to raise the standard and improve the kind of subject-matter used in Children's Theatre generally. For instance, the Unicorn Theatre at the Arts in London has responded to TIE, and developed its own forms of audience participation and changed the nature of its subject-matter.

Theatre in Education's existence is under real threat, and it is doubtful, in the present economic climate, that the number of TIE teams will increase, or even remain static. Yet, on an optimistic note, Theatre in Education has had a far-reaching influence on the worlds of theatre and education, which the early pioneers in Coventry would, perhaps, have found it hard to imagine.

Notes

1. DES, *Actors in Schools*, HMSO, 1976, p. 49.
2. Belgrade TIE, *Rare Earth*, Methuen, p. 62.
3. Geoff Gilham, "The construction of theatre images", *SCYPT Journal*, no. 5, 1980, p. 10.
4. *Op. cit.*, p. 15.
5. Kathy Joyce, "TIE in schools — a consumer's viewpoint", *Learning Through Theatre*, Manchester University Press, 1980, p. 26.
6. See Chapter 5, p. 147.
7. David Pammenter, Introduction to "Pow Wow", *Theatre in Education, Five Infant Programmes*, P. Schweitzer (ed.), Methuen, 1980, p. 22.
8. See Chapter 5, pp. 156–58.
9. Kathy Joyce, "TIE in schools — a consumer's viewpoint", pp. 33–34.
10. David Pammenter, "Introduction to 'Pow Wow' ", p. 23.
11. G. Gilham, "The construction of theatre images", p. 15.
12. Sue Bennion, personal interview at GYPT offices, 7th January 1981.
13. *Ibid.*

14. *Ibid.*
15. The Arts Council, "The provision of theatre for young people", 1967, p. 18.
16. Peter Ansorge, *Disrupting the Spectacle*, London, Pitman, 1975, p. 56.
17. Tony Coult, "Viewpoint", *SCYPT Journal*, no. 1, 1977, p. 2.
18. John Holt, *Why Children Fail*, Penguin, 1977 (reprint), 1st printed 1964, p. 165.
19. Edward Peel, personal interview at Humberside Theatre, 21st June 1976.
20. Jean Bullwinkle and Bettie Ritchie, personal inverview at the Arts Council Offices, London, 26th June 1978.

Appendix A

Arts Council: Analysis of drama Grants and Guarantees, YPTS and TIE

Theatres	1968	1969	1970	1971	1972	1973	1974
Billingham	—	—	—	—	—	—	7000
Birmingham	500	500	500	375	—	—	—
Bolton	1550	4500	4750	6000	7000	7700	8500
Bristol Old Vic	—	1000	1000	750	750	750	—
Canterbury	530	400	400	—	—	500	550
Century	—	300	1000	2800	3600	—	—
Cheltenham	—	350	350	—	—	—	—
Chester Gateway	—	—	—	—	—	467	500
Chesterfield	2000	2000	2000	1500	1500	—	—
Colchester	500	400	400	400	500	1500	2000
Coventry	1000	2000	2000	2200	2700	3940	4500
Crewe	—	—	—	—	—	—	2250
Derby	500	500	500	—	—	750	1500
Exeter Northcott	2100	3000	4000	4200	6325	6600	7300
Farnham	750	750	1000	1000	1250	1340	1750
Greenwich	—	—	3835	2000	2450	3000	3300
Guildford Yvonne Arnaud	—	—	—	—	—	1500	1600
Harrogate	—	—	—	—	—	900	2000
Ipswich	2000	2000	2500	3000	3250	3575	4000
Lancaster Duke's Playhouse	—	—	—	—	—	5000	6000
Leatherhead	350	850	850	850	1000	1100	1250
Leeds	—	—	—	—	5000	7000	8000
Leicester Phoenix	1500	2000	1500	1600	2000	4000	7000
Lincoln	—	200	500	600	1000	1100	1200
Liverpool Rep.	1000	750	750	—	—	—	—
Nottingham	1000	2277	2000	2200	2700	2700	6000
Newcastle Tyneside	—	—	—	350	3025	5000	5500
Oxford Meadow Players	700	700	1000	750	1750	—	—
Richmond	500	—	—	—	—	—	—
Salisbury	980	1174	1000	1200	1500	2000	2200
Sheffield	5000	7000	7000	7000	7500	8250	9000
Watford	1320	1750	3000	3150	3950	4500	5000
Worthing Connaught	700	1500	2000	2200	2700	2700	3000
York	1000	1000	1000	750	1498	2000	2500

Theatres	1968	1969	1970	1971	1972	1973	1974
Scotland							
Citizens'	627	3000	5500	6000	6500	7000	8200
Dundee	—	1000	2290	3000	3500	5330	5500
Edinburgh	539	1000	2500	5000	5500	4344	14,994
Perth	—	—	—	2000	2750	3000	4000
Pitlochry	—	—	—	—	2250	3250	3750
St. Andrews	—	—	—	—	—	1500	2100
London							
Mermaid	1500	1500	1500	—	—	—	—
Specialist companies							
Educational Dance Drama	2500	3000	2500	3650	—	—	—
English Stage Co.	5000	4300	3690	3000	3750	3750	4000
Liverpool Everyman	18,500	18,000	18,000	23,000	25,000	29,000	36,000
Manchester Young People's Theatre	—	—	—	—	—	12,500	20,000
Polka Children's Theatre	—	—	—	—	2644	4250	5984
Scottish Children's Theatre	1260	700	—	—	—	—	—
Spectrum	—	—	—	—	—	2000	3000
Theatre Centre	8000	11,990	15,000	19,500	22,000	27,000	32,500
Unicorn	17,000	20,000	20,000	22,000	28,742	30,500	35,250
Community Theatre companies and Fringe							
Combination Ltd.	—	—	—	—	—	750	2000
Harbour Arts Irvine	—	—	—	—	—	—	10,000
Inter-Action	—	—	4000	4000	5650	6000	6500
Leeds Interplay	—	—	—	—	680	2000	2250
Oval House	—	—	—	—	—	—	150
Pioneer Theatres Ltd.	—	—	—	—	—	—	1000
Centres							
MacRobert Stirling	—	—	—	—	—	—	5000

Appendix B

Spread of Personnel From Coventry TIE
(D = Director)

(This list may not be complete or absolutely up to date, but even this information provides a clear picture of Coventry TIE's influence)

Coventry Team 1965–73   **TIE Companies in Britain**

1965–(year of joining Coventry)
Jessica Hill
Ann Lister
Dickon Reed
Gordon Vallins

1966
Gordon Wiseman   EDINBURGH (69–70) — COCKPIT (72–74, D.) —
                              GLASGOW (74–75, D.)
Rosemary Birbeck   (66–70, D.)
Frances Colyer   COCKPIT
Michael Jones   WATFORD (67–71, D.)
Alastair Ramage
Roger Chapman   BOLTON (68–70, D.) — LEEDS (70–76, D.)
Colin White
Victoria Ireland
Cora Williams   BOLTON (68–70, 70–75, D.)

1967
Paul Harman   EVERYMAN (73–75, D.) — MERSEYSIDE YPT Co. (78–D.)
Stuart Bennett   (70–72, D.)
Judith Warth

1968
Susan Birtwhistle   EDINBURGH (69–74, D.) — NOTTINGHAM (74–78, D.)
Anthony Kyle

1969
Roger Lancaster
David Pammenter   (72–77, D.)

1970
Roger Chamberlain   GLASGOW (73–74, D.) — COCKPIT (76–78)
Valerie Ann Lester
Grazyna Monvid   BOWSPRIT — LANCASTER (75–78, D.)
Keith Palmer   COCKPIT (75–78, D.)
John Prior   NORTHCOTT (73–74) — CARDIFF (74–)

1971
David Holman   BOLTON
Romy Baskerville   BOLTON — M.6 (78–)
Deborah Paige

1972
Mervyn Watson
David Frederick

1973
Orde Browne   BOWSPRIT (Greenwich TIE)
Sue Johnstone   M.6
Libby Mason
Clive Russell   BOLTON
Maggie Steed
Nigel Townsend   HUMBERSIDE (74–76) — CURTAIN (76–77) —
                     PLYMOUTH (79–D.)

Susan Bovell

Appendix C

Research on "Race Against Time"

Greenwich TIE Company

This Appendix includes the comments on, and breakdown of, the questions asked in my research; the most telling statements by pupils and teachers have been placed in Chapter 6.

Question:
What did you feel about role-play?

Breakdown

Twenty responses, some very long from seventeen interviews.

Most pupils commented on the job they got, and its grading, 1–3, or their inability to get work. They were concerned with these practical details rather than developing a personality for their role. The question brought out several levels of response:

1. The details of the role itself, family qualifications, job, grading, promotion and housing.
2. The pupil's reaction to the role — upset if it was a low-grade job or satisfaction if it was good.
3. The relation this alloting of roles played to the pupil's understanding of job hierarchy and the economic situation.
4. Introduction of the competitive element, seeking for a better job and house.
5. The pupil's emotional response to gaining promotion or losing a job, etc., and to the prejudice experienced.

Comment

The role play was a method to personally involve the pupils in the game, not a thing in itself. Pupils appeared to accept the roles quickly and play the "rules" of the game! By using these roles pupils began to understand the economics and hierarchy of job structures; the effect on them if the job was going well or badly (promotion or redundancy); how being a Saurition could

219

affect their job and housing possibilities; their feelings towards others who were doing better or worse than they were.

The pupils were given cards, which bore all the relevant details for role play. They were green cards for New Towners and blue cards for Sauritions.

Although, in the case of two schools there was a 2-month gap between the performance and the interview, and for one school a 6-month gap, the pupils had a very clear memory of the details of their roles, and the way they were involved in the action of the game.

Examples of pupils' comments
I was a foreman. I lost my job and felt fed up about it. I said I wanted a different house and more money. They started to shout at me. I got the sack, wasn't worth living. I felt it was silly, because I didn't have any money, or anywhere to live. I got £2000, when I finished going round the desks I only had £10 left and a grade 3 house.

(Pupil, Blackheath Bluecoat School)

I was a hotel owner and had £10,000 a year. Out of that I had to pay a mortgage. The way Mr. Ward put it, it made you feel like you were someone big, like you had the real position of that person.

(Pupil, Thomas Calton School, interview)

On the situation of the Sauritions
The people from Sauritious had lower grade jobs than the New Towners. In order for it to be a good job it had to be grade 1 or 2. Most people from Sauritious had grade 3 or 4.

(Pupil, Peckham School, interview)

We were promised good pay, good houses and jobs, but when we came over we couldn't get a house or a job.

(Pupil, Thomas Calton School)

Reaction to being in role
Acting in role just came naturally.

(Pupil, Samuel Peypes School)

In role when someone shouts at you your reaction is to shout back. In the end I took the child's point of view and just sat down and left it to others. If a New Towner came up to you, just told them to shut up and go away. I thought of the others as New Towners. People were saying we shouldn't have come and we're taking away all the jobs, and I'm arguing back saying we haven't got any jobs to take.

(Pupil, Kidbrooke School)

I was up in competition with someone else for a job and I got it, he didn't because he was a Saurition. I felt better!

(Pupil, Deptford Green)

Question:
What made you get involved?

Breakdown

The pupils' responses emphasized the fact that it seemed real or life-like (5 out of 17 responses). Two pupils commented that they were treated like adults, and four pupils said it was the way the team treated them in the situation they set up. Three commented on the introduction of the idea of the good life, and one thought it was the actual structure of the programme that made them get involved.

Comment

The structure of the simulation took the pupils through recognisable life-like activities. The actor–teachers were in role from the moment the programme started and therefore the pupils were thrown in the deep end, and immediately involved in the action. It was interesting that nearly all the pupils accepted this convention whether they had had a lot of drama or not. Of the schools visited five had Drama departments, and some facilities. Perhaps, as the pupils were given no choice it was hard for them to object. They could drop out of the simulation if they wished, and this did happen on occasions.

Examples of pupils' comments

I thought everyone was trying to build you up: this thing could happen to me. So when the argument came along we were shouting at each other. By giving you the sack they were showing you what it would really be like.

(Pupil, Samuel Peypes School)

It was the people who were actually doing it, they really went on at you. They made you angry because they really went on at you. You felt they were the real people.

(Pupil, Kidbrooke School)

We went into role straight away. They ordered you, didn't explain but straight into role . . . didn't want an explanation, as it came in sections.

1st pupil: Didn't get involved at first, but did as it went on.
2nd pupil: You get emotionally involved.
3rd pupil: Shirley, she was crying at the end when the Sauritions were on one side and the New Towners were on the other.

(Pupils, Kidbrooke School)

Question:
How and why did you react when things got difficult?
(This was asked in the context of the economic situation in year 3 and the loss of jobs.)

Breakdown

Many of the fifteen responses were quite long, and seven out of the fifteen said that they got very angry. One teacher expressed concern that had the pupils been pushed any further the situation might have got out of hand. Unfair discrimination was one of the major causes of the anger and frustration, and was also linked to failure in the competitive element of the game. Three of the pupils realized that the company were setting them up so that they would react. One pupil commented on the fact that although he got annoyed with the "characters", he always remembered that they were acting.

Comment

There were two very definite kinds of reaction to the question. One was descriptive, mentioning the loss of job and the problems involved, and the other was a strong gut reaction, usually of anger and frustration. Many New Towners began to blame the Sauritions for causing the trouble, these ideas were suggested by Mr. Ward, and hinted at by the actor–teacher working with the New Towners, and the Social Benefits officer.

There is no doubt that the majority of students did react to the situation in the way the company had intended.

Examples of pupils' comments
Description and realization of what was happening

1st pupil: I was a Doctor, they said the hospital closed down, and I lost my job. It was just to build up hatred. At the end practically everyone lost their jobs and were on Social Benefit.

2nd pupil: I went bankrupt. I was supposed to be a Headmaster, but they gave me a teacher's job, then I lost the job.

3rd pupil: I was a qualified mechanic and I lost my job.

4th pupil: I thought everyone was trying to build you up. I thought this thing could happen to me. So when the argument came along, we were shouting at each other. They made it into a real situation.

(Pupils, Samuel Peypes School)

Anger and frustration

In the third year my partner came over. I also got sacked from my job, because of the economic crisis. This made me furious because I seemed to be sacked just because I was a foreign person. Their reason for sacking me was because they didn't want just one foreign teacher they wanted a white person for no reason at all.

(Pupil in written work, Kidbrooke School)

It was very annoying. My partner went over first and got a job, then he got sacked from the job. I was annoyed, and I was sent from one place to another.

(Pupil, Deptford Green School)

Teacher's concern for the level of frustration the team built up
There were two or three points where the pupils got very involved. Two black kids who were playing immigrants got very angry. If the woman behind the Social Security desk had taken it any further she could have got bonked. The kids slammed down papers and walked away miles from anyone. It built up that degree of frustration.

(Teacher, Roger Manwood School)

Question:
Which side were you on in the discussion and why?
Breakdown
Eighteen responses, mostly fairly long.
Six groups of pupils out of the seventeen interviewed had physically changed sides during the discussion.
Six pupils said they realized that they had ended up on the wrong side, but did not change over.
Twelve of the responses revealed that the pupils had understood the true facts about the job and housing situation.

Comment
Most of the pupils had reasons for being on one side or the other. The fact that some of them realized that they were on the wrong side by the end of the discussion but did not move over was because they were afraid of losing their jobs or their houses. In some cases they were actually afraid of Mr. Ward.

From the Company's reports and the interviews it is obvious that the majority of classes participated well during the discussion and enjoyed the conflict. The team noted two performances where the discussion was difficult and slow. In one case this was because it was a remedial class, and the other because of some confusion in the school itself and a late start.

Examples of pupils' comments
Involvement in the discussion
There were two groups one bloke trying to say the Sauritions were to blame, and was against them. Other groups saying they came in (to the country). Found yourself getting angry, and arguing. Everybody concentrating and really getting it off the ground.

(Pupil, Blackheath Bluecoat School)

A view of the argument
1st pupil: We went into two groups. Shouting. One lot against and one lot for the Sauritions. They (the New Towners) said come in and get

jobs, but they (the Sauritions) said that they didn't have any. Others saying they shouldn't have them.

2nd pupil: Sauritions promised jobs and didn't get it, others in New Town promised the Good Life and they never achieved that. Both right on each side but different.

(Pupils, Blackheath Bluecoat School)

Being on the 'wrong' side and reasons for moving over or staying
I was a New Towner at the beginning, so I thought support what we are. Some changed over.

(Pupil, Samuel Peypes School)

He (Mr. Ward) offered me a first class house, which I took, and a top class wage of £10,000 a year. I had no problems of unemployment or being houseless because I had the 'good life'. When the Sauritions started to arrive it didn't bother me . . . when there were rumours of them coming to live in my area Mr. Ward persuaded me that they had to go. Even though they weren't bothering me. I felt compelled to stick up for my area and keep them out. Seeing as I had no worries of poverty I was just listening to Mr. Ward and eventually agreeing with him. Even though it was only a game I got really involved. Unfortunately I was on the wrong side. I should have been against him, but because of my situation in the 'good life' I wasn't.

(Pupil, in written work, Kidbrooke School)

New Towners were fed information that it was all their fault (i.e. the Sauritions). We stayed on the New Town side, because we felt that we would have a better chance of getting our jobs back.

(Pupil, Roger Manwood School)

1st pupil: They were all saying we took the jobs, but actually they all had the good jobs and houses. The business man, big man, blaming it on us (i.e. the Sauritions) and all the little people around him believed him. They all moved over and left him on his own.
2nd pupil: They all moved because everyone else did.
3rd pupil: No, because they realised everyone was wrong.

(Pupils, Crown Woods School)

Praise
(Peckham School, company visit in the autumn term).

Watching the simulation it was amazing the way it took out the Grade 1 and 2 people on one side . . . and others without jobs on different sides, and we actually did see kids, not primed to do it, getting up and saying "Oh we made a mistake we didn't realise that you didn't have jobs. I shouldn't be here", and they got up and changed sides. They were amazed at the way they had been manipulated. They had been hauled down the river . . . I think they realised how they'd been led and suddenly had to sit and think about what was going on. It was a very dramatic piece of theatre at the end.

(Teacher, Peckham School)

Question:

Why did the economic situation change?

Breakdown

Seventeen responses some fairly long.

Seven mentioned that the change was due to there being less money available, two actually mentioned inflation.

Seven thought that the change was caused by the Sauritions.

One thought it was caused by the bosses taking all the money.

One blamed it on the Government, taking too much money.

One did not give any clear reason.

Comment

Two of the groups who blamed the Sauritions for the change were third years, and they appeared to understand the economic base of the programme less well. About half the pupils I interviewed had some understanding of what actually caused the economic crisis in year 3 of the programme. In spite of the team's efforts and the facts revealed in the discussion at the end of the simulation, a large number of pupils were sure it was the Sauritions' fault. They may have stuck to this idea because it was being pushed by Mr. Ward, and mentioned by Liz and the Social Benefit's Officer.

Examples of pupils' comments

Response expressing two opposing points of view

1st pupil: Pay went down because the Sauritions were here.

2nd pupil: No because the country was coming to a bad state, and money dropped. We all had a decrease in pay. At that time the Sauritions were shipped out so we automatically thought it was the Sauritions who were causing it.

(Pupils, Thomas Carlton School)

Cause — "money dropping", inflation, etc.

No jobs, money was worthless, a crisis.

(Pupil, Charlton Boys School)

Inflation.

(Pupil, Roger Manwood School)

Government cut backs.

(Pupil, Crown Woods School)

The Government blaming the Sauritions:

1st pupil: The Government got so entangled in things, actually couldn't cope with it all. They blamed it on the Sauritions.

2nd pupil: Before we came over, they were happy. Whey we came over things were bad, so they had to blame someone. Blaming us for taking jobs.

(Pupils, Peckham School)

The bosses to blame
Not the Sauritions who were taking the jobs away, it was the people who own the firms who were benefiting. They got all the profits.

(Pupil, Deptford Green)

Question:
What did you think of the play?
Comment

This question was to open up discussion on the play's format and presentation. As the play was rather 'Brechtian' in style, the form and the use of song worried some of the pupils. The highest praise for the acting and mechanics of the presentation came from the fourth-year Drama option pupils. Nearly all the pupils seemed to have enjoyed the play, but they found it hard to analyse why.

Two of the characters, Mr. Wood and Mrs. Dexter, were criticized as stereotypes.

The Company's reports of their autumn tour noted restless audiences during the play in four schools, but in five schools there was good concentration. In one school the company felt that the songs had actually alienated the pupils. Where the restlessness occurred the company expressed concern that the play was too long.

Examples of pupils' and teachers' comments
I liked the way it was presented with the figures freezing.

(Pupil, Crown Woods School)

Brilliant acting, never forget that play it was so good.

(Pupil, Peckham Girls' School)

Criticism — songs
The music was funny, like it, but seemed funny.

(Pupil, Charlton Boys School)

The song were generally lost on the kids.

(Teacher, Roger Manwood School)

The ideas in the songs were too dense to grasp. Quite a few of the pupils were really startled by the songs but they didn't really listen.

(Teacher, Roger Manwood School)

Company's Reports on the Play
Lack of concentration, etc.
Student's reaction
They found most scenes long, interest waned towards ends of scenes. They were interested in the theatrical things, the freezes, spits, etc.

(of performance at Thomas Carlton School)

Students' reaction
The songs alienated them. They tried hard to concentrate, but it may have been too long. Young? They related p.m. to a.m.

Company's reaction
The company felt perhaps they were struggling to find kids in the p.m. performance . . . Some feeling that the performance was wrong for young people and that it was not up to standard.

(Performance at Woolwich Poly)
(Not one of the schools visited for interviews)

The Discussion After the Play

Question:
1. Did you get involved in discussion with the characters after the play?
(Question 2 asked during the discussion on this point.)
2. Did you use your own arguments or just the things you had learnt during the day?

Breakdown
There were fourteen responses to the first question, and twelve of these concentrated on the discussions with the two New Front officers.
Mr. Wood and his secretary Mrs. Dexter.
All the responses were long.

Comment
These questions produced lengthy replies. Like the role-play question the answers involved description of immediate experience rather than understanding of any abstract concepts.
It was the two extreme characters who provoked the most lively response.

Examples of pupils' comments
Coloured pupil: The lady who witnessed the murder, she was human. She didn't think anyone with coloured skin was different but when we had the N.F. man, when we put real things to him he'd shut up and sit back in his chair. Then he'd say, you're all the same you wogs.
C.R.: How did that make you feel?

Pupil:	Bad, made me want to punch him.
C.R.:	Could you argue with him and use what you had experienced in the morning?
Pupil:	Yes, we told him — it ain't because of the Sauritions. He said the population was rising and the country shouldn't bring in any more coloureds. I said, supposing you emigrated you'd want your family to come over too, and he said yes.

(Pupil, Deptford Green School)

Pupil:	We found out when arguing with Mr. Wood that he didn't want every immigrant to leave the country, just the black ones. We asked him about Australians, etc. . . . We told him he was biased about their colour. He said he would get round to Jews and Germans. We pointed out that he wasn't British because all the original Anglo Saxons had fair hair, and he blushed.
C.R.:	Did you use the arguments from the day, or your own experience?
2nd pupil:	Our own. He was saying their brains are smaller than white people. We said that was rubbish, not from the day, but from what we learnt before.
C.R.:	Did you talk to anyone else?
2nd pupil:	Mrs. Dexter, she was difficult, because she just followed Mr. Wood, and just went off the point.
3rd pupil:	We argued with her, because she said she had a black next-door-neighbour she liked.

(Pupils, Crown Woods School)

Other characters
1st pupil: We got a bit mad.
2nd pupil: We were arguing with the brother, just couldn't get through to him. Couldn't argue with him because he was disturbed.

(Pupil, Blackheath Bluecoat School)

Company's report on the discussion
   Out of the ten performances, the company noted six good discussions and no really bad ones.

Examples of comments on student's reactions:
Discussion good. They couldn't handle Orde's character though (i.e. Mr. Wood).

(First performance at Thomas Carlton)

Discussion very good, and balanced, mature, some opted out, but many really identifying and talking well.

(Performance at Deptford Green)

Honest in final discussion. Students seemed to be made to think even if there were no major conversions.

(Performance at Crown Woods)

Follow-up Work

Question:
What work did you do in the school as follow-up to the programme?
Breakdown
Twelve responses from pupils.
The teachers of the ten schools visited were also asked.

Out of these ten schools
Two did no follow-up work at all (West Greenwich and Thomas Carlton).
Two had one period of discussion after the programme and did no other work on it (Deptford Green, Crown Woods).
One class did some practical visiting to a court, related to their Social Studies (Samuel Peypes. The company were in the school for a week.)
One had a discussion and a class in Social Studies (Charlton Boys).
One did only drama work (Blackheath Bluecoat).
One did only written work (Peckham).
One did some written work and some drama work (Roger Manwood).
One did a full range of work, cross-curricular (Kidbrooke. The company were in the school for a week.)

Comment
Of the schools who did little or no follow-up work afterwards there seemed to be a desire to let the programme and not the school deal with the difficult subject of race and prejudice, and to let the pupils absorb the ideas from the programme in their own way.

To see what the pupils felt about following up I asked them what they would have liked to have done. This makes an interesting comparison and is dealt with in the next question.

Nine of the ten schools did deal with race in some form, again this is examined later.

In both Thomas Carlton School and Samuel Peypes I did not talk to all the groups who saw the programme, and therefore other classes might have done some follow-up work. In these two cases no information was available from teachers, due to difficulty in finding time to talk to teachers properly and the non-return of questionnaires.

Examples of comments from pupils and teachers
Reasons for doing no follow-up work — West Greenwich School

Head teacher: We have to be careful how things are approached and do so as
               a united group of people. We have problems but not because
               of colour.
C.R.:   Did you not do anything with the programme?
Teacher: We don't want to.
Head teacher: I'm not sure it's a good idea to hammer home they are
               different. We work together here.
C.R.:   Are the pupils aware of the race problem?
Teacher: A number of them are, but not in the school.

One discussion period

The teacher at Deptford Green preferred to use the programme as a one off, outside the curriculum. The pupils who saw it were from the Drama Class, fourth-year option, and therefore from a number of classes. There were also some Social Science pupils who saw the programme. Social Science does not do race until later on in the year. When the teacher does introduce the subject she may well use the Teachers' Notes provided by Greenwich TIE.

Crown Woods

The teacher wanted to use the programme as a discussion on drama, looking at the format and presentation. However, racism was of interest but not a subject she wished to develop. She has referred to the programme when discussing authority figures and when working on "Lord of the Flies".

Visiting related to Social Studies as follow-up
Samuel Peypes School

Of the two classes I spoke to one had done no follow-up, and the other had done some work in Social Studies. This consisted of a visit to Camberwell Court to see some of the cases that came up, and the pupils were much more aware of the colour problem when watching the cases. They had a number of lessons about "sus." and crime, myths and facts.

Discussion and a Social Studies class
Charlton Boys

The teacher could not attend the performance, and she is only there on a temporary basis. The school is closing down, and only the third year are in that section of the school. The teacher knew the team well and knew that the pupils had not seen much TIE work. She wanted the pupils to have the experience of a TIE programme, but as she was only there for two terms she did not plan to build the subject-matter or performance into any on-going work. The discussion period allowed the pupils to tell the teacher what happened.

The class in social studies consisted of discussion about coloureds in general and about immigrants. Also two lessons on the National Front and the Socialist party and the difference between the two (this information was from the pupils).

Drama work
Blackheath Bluecoat School
The drama teacher used the Greenwich TIE's Teachers' Notes and worked on the 'two blocks of flats' improvisation and developed it.

Pupil: Two housing estates — flats — one had facilities, the other didn't. We had to learn to share, but it didn't work out.
(Pupil, Blackheath Bluecoat School, Group A)

Pupil: Two lots of flats, one side was good, the other was smashed. Some of us were New Towners, some Sauritions.
(Pupil, Blackheath Bluecoat School, Group B)

Written work and social studies
Peckham Girls' School
No drama work was done partly because half term came after the programme and there were people in the school from Goldsmith's College and they were working with the class concerned. Some of the pupils came from Social Studies rather than the drama option class, but because they came from four different classes follow-up had to be in the form of individual talks on the programme.

The follow-up work for the drama class consisted of answering questions on "Race Against Time" on their worksheets and a discussion.

Written work and drama follow-up
Roger Manwood School
The drama teacher did improvisation work with the fourth years on the theme of immigration, and working generally on prejudice. One of the improvisations was videoed. For the small group of fifth year who had seen the programme, discussion and written work were the follow-up. The English teacher used the Greenwich TIE's Teachers' Notes with classes who had not actually seen the programme. One of the pieces he used was "The Arrangement in Black and White" by Dorothy Parker.

Full cross-curricular follow-up
Kidbrooke School
The company were in the school for a week.

Follow-up or related work was done in English, History, Geography, Social Science, Drama and Religious Studies.

The Religious Studies' department set out a course on the religious culture of ethnic minority groups, feeling that this was the best way that RE could contribute. They aimed at providing the pupils with an understanding of the different religious cultures:

Kidbrooke — drama follow-up
   In drama we did quite a lot of social situation work with third years. . . . Used basic conflict situation, used the idea of someone coming in from outside, the effect and response. Also used the Teachers' Notes — the idea of the East and West flats, and the idea of a youth club with another group joining.

(Teacher, in interview)

This concentrated follow-up can have its dangers:

Pupils' comments on the work done and their feelings
Kidbrooke:
1st pupil: There were classes going on in English, and Social Science about it.
2nd pupil: We talked about it in history.
3rd pupil: Did get a bit fed up with it, because everyone was saying what was it like.

Examples of follow-up work done after the first tour, summer term 1978
School visited for interview:

Peckham School
   Last term we got a lot more "mileage" out of the programme. Talked about their (the pupils') knowledge and experience of discrimination. We got them to discuss. Then we had another session on Colonial Background and why different people got here. Then what started to emerge was the kids' levels of racism. One group with a student had a marvellous one-and-a-half hour discussion.
   We refer back to the programme now with the fifth year who saw it last term. They use the programme, not the facts, but the impression — they are doing a project on the third world.

(Social Science Teacher, Peckham, in interview)

Follow-up after first tour in schools not visited for interview
St. Ursula's Convent
   I have used the same approach to other issues, several children have taken material to read and use in other subjects, English, Social Studies.

(Teacher, St. Ursula's Convent School,
Teacher's Questionnaire to Greenwich TIE)

Thomas Tallis
   The company visited the school for a week.
   Although the whole staff is committed to examining the curriculum for

racial balance, the presence of the programme was able to focus individual subject teachers on work to be done during, and following, the week. Considerable help was received here in the form of discussions with the team and the provision by them of a most effective collection of teachers' notes.

Extra materials and advice were provided by Crispin Jones from the Centre for Urban Education Studies.

The English drama time was used mainly for discussion and writing in-role essays on "My three years in New Town". The humanities' faculty concentrated on patterns of immigration in the world and over the centuries and our stereotyped views of different nationalities. Statistics, their use and misuse, were examined in maths, and in art pupils discussed the motivation and creation of propaganda posters. Our librarian, Jessica Yates, produced a booklet for each third year pupil listing and describing further reading stocked in the library.

This brief description of some of the work arising out of the week cannot adequately represent all our thinking and practice, but there is no doubt that our long term aims for the curriculum have been furthered by the concentration required for this week.

Two weeks later we held a follow-up discussion in the school during which the team showed slides of the programme and we talked about its effect.

(Maggie O'Connor, Head of Faculty at Thomas Tallis School,
Article in ILEA *Contact* Magazine, Issue 12, Vol. 7,
22nd September 1978, p. 34)

Question:
How would you have liked to follow it up?
Breakdown
Nine responses.
Four suggested that they would have liked to have made their own play up about the subject.
Two wanted some kind of discussion.
One group wanted to talk to people in the street about it.
One suggested a project.
One group was not sure.

Comment

There was definitely a feeling amongst the majority of pupils who did little or no follow-up that they would have liked to have done some kind of work on the programme, but not in the form of lessons. The suggestions to do a play came from the fourth-year drama option groups.

Examples of pupils' comments
On the need to do some kind of work
1st pupil: Better if we did some work.

2nd pupil: But not have it as a lesson.

(Pupils, Thomas Carlton School)

Do a play
1st pupil: Do a play, our own ideas, just once.
2nd pupil: I think we should have done more work on it, to make it stick in your head.

(Pupils, Blackheath Bluecoat School)

1st pupil: I'd like to do a play like they did, about it.
2nd pupil: Be a chance of saying more things. Give everyone your side of what you feel.

(Pupils, Peckham School)

Project
1st pupil: Find out more and do it in a folder as a project.
2nd pupil: See what people think about race as a project.
3rd pupil: We should have carried on otherwise it just goes out of your mind.

(Pupils, Charlton Boys' School, Group B)

Questions:
Did the programme change your ideas at all?
What was the value of the day for you?
Comment
   As these questions were concerned with the same thing, I have put the responses together. The majority of the pupils did have a definite opinion on what the programme had shown them. The actual effect on pupils appeared to be fairly similar although they expressed it differently, e.g. it made you think, or it made you more aware.

Summary of pupils' answers
Twenty-four responses in all from the two questions, all quite long.
The ideas were:
It made you think.
Can understand why white people are accusing us (coloured pupil).
Not change your ideas, but give them direction.
More aware.
See things better.
Realize immigrants are not taking jobs.
Feel more strongly.
Get the facts.
Did not say much before about prejudice, just repeated things heard.
Made things clear.
Learn about life and what is happening in the world.

It's wrong to be prejudiced.

Shows us what will happen when we leave school.

Made you embarrassed about thinking of any prejudice.

Made you more aware of what people will believe.

Made you think that you have to work hard at school so when you leave you can get a better job.

Showed us not to believe anything. Got to find out for yourself.

Showed you the other side.

It forced you to have an opinion.

Examples of pupils' comments
Made you think
1st pupil: It made you think. I've realised from that, that I've been against coloured people. It made me stop.
2nd pupil: . . . More aware of what's happening, should have noticed but I didn't. I'm more aware of what's happening when I listen to the news. When you see a swastika you're more aware.

(Pupils, Kidbrooke School)

Give ideas direction
1st pupil: It didn't change my ideas, but gave them direction.
2nd pupil: I had my own ideas.
3rd pupil: You can't be influenced by something like this.

(Pupils, Crown Woods School, Group A)

Repeated things before
I can see things better now, feel more strongly than before. I didn't say much before, but just repeated things. Now I see they're not true.

(Pupil, Roger Manwood School)

Learn about life
1st pupil: You learnt about life, and what's happening in the world.
2nd pupil: . . . Taught you about life, people losing jobs.
3rd pupil: How it affects us all.
4th pupil: More aware.

(Pupils, West Greenwich School)

Got to work hard at school
It made you think you've got to work hard at school, so when you come out you can get a better job.

(Pupil, Charlton Boys, Group A)

Find out information for yourself
It showed us not to believe anything. You've got to find out for yourself. You don't know if what people say is true.

(Pupil, Peckham School)

Pupils' written comments
Kidbrooke School (two pupils):
I learnt from taking part that there are many naive and ignorant people in the world who live on myth not on fact.

I have learnt a lot about prejudice and of the consequences it has, as in the play we saw. Also because of what the coloured people have to go through in the country of Britain.

Examples of pupils' comments from a questionnaire at Kidbrooke School — organized by the Drama teacher.

I've learnt that some people can be cruel and just shout cruel things without realizing.

I used to agree a bit with the National Front but I obviously didn't know about it. Now I don't agree with the N.F.

Everyone is the same, it doesn't matter what nationality you are.

I learnt that you should think before you blame.

Teachers' comments on the value of the day
From Teachers' Questionnaire (Greenwich TIE)
Question: Compare pupils' immediate response to their later reaction to the programme and the issues raised.
Answer (Teacher, Crown Woods School, after tour in summer term): The immediate response was very positive. Two boys in particular appeared to have modified their prejudices considerably and voiced what they had learned during the 'game', and the discussion, but had gone back to square one by the time we discussed the day or appeared to have done so.

Comment in interview from another teacher in Crown Woods:
It opened the kids' eyes to the problems of race, and made them aware of the capitalist situation — worker against authority.

Blackheath Bluecoat School — Teacher in written comment:
The long-term value seems hopeful. Much of our teaching is trying to "break" children into the outside world and give guidance as to how to operate in it, but the teacher can't be entirely successful because a school is not the real world. But Bowsprit (Greenwich TIE) can bring the real world into the Drama Hall in a programme of this kind.

Peckham School — Teacher in interview (Social Studies):
What I liked very much was having the Sauritions in another room. The kids saw immigration in to the country not as a great tide but as people trying to get in — reality.

Drama Teacher:

Also the reality of the situation they found themselves in. Better than watching a documentary. Very significant from the kids' point of view because it was actually happening to them.

Roger Manwood School — Drama Teacher:

It was a chance to air the theme, give them a gut reaction they could use and relate to.

English Teacher:

I certainly got a degree of optimism from the programme. People doing things kids could relate to.

Question:

Have you used the experiences or the facts in the programme?
Breakdown
Thirteen responses.
Five used the experiences and facts in arguments about prejudice with people outside school.
Two used the experience in arguments with their own friends.
Two might use the information when the occasion arose.
Four replies were not definite.

Comment

Three of the five examples of positive use of the programme were from pupils in the two schools who had the programme for a week. I visited them about 2 months after they had seen the programme and this time gap had allowed more opportunity than the 2- to 4-week gap between performance and interview of seven of the schools visited.

Examples of pupils' comments
My brother saw black boys mucking about and he started calling them all names, but there was a group of white kids who were much worse, smashing windows, and I said what are you going to say about them, and he said they're only having a bit of fun. We had this great argument about that and we wouldn't talk to each other for about a week, after seeing the programme I thought this is my chance. Wouldn't have done so before seeing "Race Against Time".

(Pupil, Kidbrooke School, Group A)

I argue with my older brother, he's very against white people. I argue its not always like that, did it before, but the programme helps because you can make points better after looking at the show. Argue about some thing but can make it come across to him better because you've got better points.

(Pupil, Samuel Peypes School, Group B)

Criticism of the programme

1st pupil: If you held any N.F. views then you would be out with (on the side of) the characters. So you had to play along with your part.

C.R.:   Did you all feel that you were being forced into playing a part?

2nd pupil: Yes you were being controlled, like pawns, in the game in the morning.

1st pupil: They wanted you to agree.

(Pupils, Crown Woods School,Group B)

(Group A also expressed similar feelings).

Samuel Peypes School

Pupil: I don't think it was a good idea for them to come to the school because it could start trouble.

C.R.:   Do you think it did?

Pupil: No, but it could have done.

(Pupil, Samuel Peypes School)

Other criticisms have been very specific and have been included in the appropriate section.

Question:

Do you think you learnt more from the programme than you would have done in a series of lessons?

Breakdown

Eighteen responses — all felt that they had learnt more through the programme.

Comment

The main reason given was that the programme was enjoyable and that to join in meant that they remembered more. It was learning by doing.

Examples of pupils' comments

I think if we had an exam in it we'd get full marks.

(Pupil, Kidbrooke School, Group A)

If we'd just had a series of lessons and not seen "Race Against Time" it wouldn't have had much effect.

(Pupil, Kidbrooke School, Group B)

Experience it. Feel it from a different point of view, you wouldn't get that in a lesson.

(Pupil, Deptford Green)

Enjoying yourself because you were actually acting it out. Get bored with a series of lessons.

(Pupil, Charlton Boys' School)

1st pupil: Yes, if studied by ourselves we wouldn't know what it was about.
2nd pupil: Everything was brought into one thing.
3rd pupil: If every lesson was like that it would be great.

(Pupils, Peckham School)

That was real learning, that was real work.

(Teacher's report of pupil's comment, Teachers' Workshop)

Teachers' comments

The programme was flashier than the classroom message, but in terms of reality it's doing the same kind of thing . . . It produced a day's entertainment that satisfied me because it raised some issues rather better than I could have done in lessons.

(Teacher, West Greenwich School)

It teaches them something different. The teacher's role is rather more wide-ranging. What the group did was to give the pupils an experience which they remember and can draw on.

(Teacher, Roger Manwood School)

There is only one of me. There's a great deal of difference doing a lesson if its just me. In drama kids need a certain amount of physicality, chairs, sets, etc., it helps. The detail aids their belief in the situation enormously, without it it's not as attractive.

(Teacher, Peckham School)

Teachers' Section

Why the programme was booked and by which department
Breakdown of the schools visited
The programme was booked by:
Four Drama departments: Blackheath Bluecoat, Kidbrooke, Deptford Green, Roger Manwood School.
Two Social Studies departments: Peckham, Samuel Peypes Schools.
Four English departments: Charlton Boys, Crown Woods, West Greenwich, Thomas Calton Schools.

Reasons for booking — Summary:
The company's responsible attitude to political and social issues (Blackheath Bluecoat).
A subject everyone is feeling strongly about (Kidbrooke).
TIE is a useful teaching tool (Deptford Green).
Wanted the pupils to experience a TIE programme (Charlton Boys).
As theatre criticism (Crown Woods).
An important subject not dealt with in the school (West Greenwich).

It fitted into the Social Studies Course, and useful as theatre and drama (Peckham School).

A different way to tackle the subject (Roger Manwood).

Teachers' comments
Blackheath Bluecoat School

The programme came at an appropriate time, after the N.F. demonstration in Lewisham, therefore it was a very sensitive area.

I had the programme in the school because Bowsprit (Greenwith TIE) have a responsible attitude towards political and social issues. They're aware of how vulnerable children are to the emotional impact of live performance and what a powerful effect outsiders have in a school.

(Written comment)

Kidbrooke School

I thought this was a great opportunity because it was a subject everyone was feeling very strongly about at the time. Also thought I could use this to show how useful a programme could be for different subjects.

(In interview)

Deptford Green School

I see TIE as a useful tool, and very useful to say something on more touchy subjects.

(In interview)

Charlton Boys' School

I realised that the school hadn't seen much of this kind of work, and I wanted the programme as an experience for the pupils.

(In interview)

Peckham School

I saw it last term when we went down to the Stage Centre. I thought it was very good in terms of timing, excellent the way it fitted into the course (Social Studies). When I found out that it was being done again I decided to use it again. Thought it had a mileage for Drama as well.

(Social Studies teacher in interview)

Peckham:

I must confess I was extremely keen on it, maybe for all the wrong reasons. I'm interested in theatre as an art form, and I know, having seen the way TIE companies work, what it was going to be like. I do a lot of talking to the kids about role play, improvised drama, scripted drama. I knew that the simulation would be a totally different experience for them . . . I wanted them to see all these different forms, so that when we looked at things in the theatre there were things we could readily refer to . . . I wanted them to be able to say whether it was more meaningful in terms of understanding more about the issue of race to actually take part in some things, as it was to sit and watch a play.

(Drama teacher in interview)

Roger Manwood School

I booked the programme because it was another, different way to tackle the subject.

(In interview)

Thomas Tallis School
(Not interviewed)

The general consensus was that we had more to gain than to lose. The way the programme took up the problem of discrimination and related it to race relations seemed a very positive approach and events in the last year in Lewisham and Greenwich, two of our catchment areas, made it clear that we ought to be doing something.

(*Contact*, Issue 12, 1978, ILEA, p. 34)

Organization and value of the week's performance in a school
Comment

The organization involved in having the company in the schools for a week was quite major. In the three schools that undertook it in the summer term; Kidbrooke, Samuel Peypes and Thomas Tallis, the staff were involved in drastic alterations of the timetable, and hours of discussion with other members of staff. However, the value of the week's presentation appeared to repay all their hard work.

Of the schools who had the programme for one day, two of those visited definitely wanted the company to come back for a week, and could see no major problems in organizing this (Roger Manwood and West Greenwich). One school would have liked the week, but could not take up the company's offer because the Head Teacher was worried, not about the timetable organization, but about the "readiness" of the pupils and the staff to cope with the programme for a week.

In the Teachers' Questionnaires two schools did not want the week, and another could see real organization difficulties.

The actual subject-matter of the programme was one of the causes of difficulty in booking both for one day and for a week.

Teachers' comments
Kidbrooke School — one week.
Organization

This was done with the Deputy Head to get all the teachers involved. The timetable was totally reorganized for the week. This was only possible with the third year. For the fourth-year it would be very difficult because they are all streamed. The subjects that became involved were: History, Drama,

English, Geography, Social Science and Political Science. All staff watched
the programme.

(From the Teachers' meeting)

Value

C.R.:   Was the week much better than the day?

Teacher: I think it was, we all talked to each other and all felt involved . . .
We needed to get so many teachers from different subjects
interested. Certain people have a sympathy and understanding
towards drama, but not very much knowledge. With the programme you could actually see what drama can do in any given
situation. I think it might help them to really appreciate the way in
which we're working.

(Drama teacher in interview)

Organization

Crown Woods School

Teacher had to see sixty-seven teachers to organise two classes because
they were fourth year all doing different subjects.

(Teacher, from interview)

Deptford Green School

It was just the Drama class that saw the programme. They take drama as
an option and are therefore a combination of a number of classes. There are
also some pupils from Social Science.

Peckham School

The Drama Workshop is on Thursday, she (Social Studies teacher) wanted
Thursday, so she said if my fourth years can take up your Thursday we'll
combine, so it was a thing of mechanics, effecting a combination between two
departments: English and Social Studies.

Thomas Tallis School (not visited for interview) — one week

Organization

First we had to persuade our colleagues that it was a good idea. One
advantage to us was that the week available from the team was in the summer
term, after examinations. With fifth- and sixth-form classes finished, there
would be more flexibility in the timetable in terms of staff available to help in
what we proposed, which was to follow Kidbrooke's example and have the
programme for a week. We made a written proposal to the Senior Staff
Conference, the management committee of the school, and included the
suggestion that each department could contribute to the week by organizing
work for their classes around the area of race relations. Some colleagues
immediately feared "overkill" — alienating the pupils if all their lessons
seemed to be on the same topic. Others felt that such an emphasis would be a

strain for the small number of black and Asian pupils in the school. Some felt that it was inappropriate to interrupt their syllabuses whilst others felt nervous about dealing with the whole matter.

These reservations were discussed at faculty and staff conference quite fully and a decision was made to go ahead.

. . . Our first problem was an organizational one. The team wished to work with only forty-five pupils a day but for contractual reasons could only work four and a half days in the school. This meant that we had to timetable two tutor groups for each day, thus going over their limit, but we relied on sufficient absence due to parental holidays at that time of the year. In fact, the over-large numbers did affect the team's work since a simulation depends on the complete involvement of all the pupils, and even five more put a strain on the team's energies.

After drawing up a timetable, faculties were asked to nominate staff to attend the programme all day with the pupils. As Sue Bennion pointed out, this was a bonus since it meant that staff movement to take other lessons was not necessary. However, this enthusiasm generated by the pupils after the first day attracted visitors of all ages whom, reluctantly, we had to discourage in case the concentration required by the simulation and the play was disturbed.

Value

However, the team's presence in the school all week did mean that pupils and teachers could check their experiences. This was particularly important for the part played by Orde Browne who, in both the simulation and the play, represented ultra-right wing views. Many pupils felt that the kind of person he appeared to be ought not to be allowed in the school, and so it was important that they were able to talk to him afterwards.

It was interesting that several fourth-year pupils who were known to hold views about "Britain for the British" came to speak to the team about their work on the basis of what they had heard from the third year. It was clear that it would have been a good thing if they could have joined the day and checked out their views in a more overt way, since normally they seek security in isolation. This programme would have given them an acceptable framework within which they could have examined their reasoning.

(*Contact*, Issue 12, 1978, IIEA, p. 34)

Roger Manwood School — one day
Value of a week
Drama teacher: It would be very good for the group to see the problems in a school.
English teacher: I was very impressed with their concept of taking the programme into the school for a week, very good, lots of rewards. Just being there meeting forty kids every day

would get so much dialogue going between the kids. It would be difficult for the teachers who are sensitive to kids at all to ignore. They would find it part of their lesson at some point even if it was deciding not to talk about it. They would have to acknowledge it was there. An interesting way to get involved in the school, and in that week the school would take the whole thing on and do follow-up work, which could happen as a matter of course.

(Teachers in interview)

Teachers' comments in Greenwich TIE Questionnaire

Crown Woods School — one day
Q5 b.
Question: For a whole week: "could you outline some of the benefits and/or problems?"
Benefits: Obvious — more possibilities of discussion; having the company around for the kids to talk to, etc.
Problems: General organization. To enable *one* group to do something different from their ordinary timetable for a whole day is hard enough, let alone several! Also we could have major problems in providing a suitable space for a week's continuous work.

Blackheath Bluecoat School — one day.
Q5 b.
Problems: Timetabling/class cover/rooms/time of year/co-operation of other staff.
Benefit: Of interdisciplinary enquiry, etc.

Company's comment on the value of presenting the programme for a week in schools

Not surprisingly with such co-operation, the team became part of the school. Having the team resident on the premises meant that many pupils who had questions, thoughts or problems to raise about the programme, could take these up with the actor/teachers the next day or even days later. There were other advantages, too, not directly related to "Race Against Time". The company were accessible as individuals to talk to the students about anything that came up. Several enquired how to join more of the activities and at Thomas Tallis the foyer was used to mount the GYPT mobile exhibition for the week following the programme.

Perhaps the best effect of the company's residence in a school for a week can be illustrated by the fact that at the follow-up teachers' meeting to discuss the programme's merits and otherwise, no less than eight teachers from one school attended. It is not unusual at these meetings to have less than eight from the schools the team have worked with!

(Sue Bennion, *Contact*, ILEA magazine,
Issue 12, pp. 33–34)

Whether the question of 'race' is taught or discussed in the school

Comment

Of the ten schools visited only one did not discuss or deal with race in any way (West Greenwich).

Five of the schools dealt with the subject in their Social Studies courses (Deptford Green, Peckham, Roger Manwood, Kidbrooke, Charlton Boys).

Two of the schools have a scheme of multi-ethnic education (Thomas Calton and Samuel Peypes).

Two schools bring up the subject as a matter of concern in any relevant subject (Blackheath Bluecoat, Crown Woods).

Teachers' comments
Samuel Peypes School

The school organized a full scheme of multi-ethnic education, but it leaned very heavily on history and geography and the pupils wanted to change it, so they were allowed to advise and suggest different approaches.

(Information from the SCYPT Conference, Sept. 1978.
Talk by Social Studies Teacher, Samuel Peypes)

West Greenwich School

We do not introduce anything divisive, I'm convinced this would be so (the subject of the programme).

(Head Teacher, in interview)

Roger Manwood School

Race is brought up as a matter of concern in English, Drama and Social Studies. A number of teachers are concerned with race studies. In the school we have come to be concerned with multi-ethnic education, and a large group are interested.

(Teacher in interview)

At *Peckham* and *Deptford Green* Schools "race" is dealt with by Social Studies during the summer term.

Has any cross curricular work been stimulated as a result of the programme?

From Greenwich TIE's Questionnaire:

Abbey School (not visited)

Inter-curricular communications not good here.

Crown Woods School

Never got cross curricular work going.

Blackheath Bluecoat School

Cross curricular approach difficult — depends on interested staff, inter-departmental co-operation.

(Written comment later):

An attempt to offer the programme to Religious Studies department. They declined yet again.

From interviews:

Peckham School

C.R.:   Did it help your departments to work together?

Social Studies
  teacher: Not really, we probably threw that one away.

Drama teacher: It has a lot of potential.

Social Studies: Everyone is working so hard, they are in blinkers. I was away after half-term on a school journey so that didn't help either.

Drama: The difference between what you want to do and should do is enormous.

C.R.:   Did it help the link between the departments?

Social Studies: Yes, but there are frustrations, always mucked up by irrelevancy — makes it impossible. I think that if we were sharing a programme again we would do more. We're now more aware of the potential and would plan in advance.

From interviews:

Kidbrooke School

There was a deliberate effort to get cross curricular work going and several departments were involved, and the work linked to the theme of the programme.

Teacher's comment on the chance of developing cross curricular work:

I think that comes out of relationships between each department. We talk about things. Each department has a lot of autonomy, but now instead of using a picture a department might let the pupils make up a play. See the intrinsic value.

Thomas Tallis School (not visited)

Planned cross curricular work here too, as described in the Follow-Up work section. English, drama, humanities faculty, maths, and art all used the theme of the programme.

Comment

In only two of the schools was real cross currricular work stimulated, and both these had the programme for a week. In the other schools timetabling and lack of staff co-operation or communication seem to present too many difficulties. However, if some of the schools who had the programme for one day have it for a week, I think that cross curricular work would be attempted in some form, e.g. at Peckham and Roger Manwood.

Research Material

Schools visited for interview
Kidbrooke Secondary
Samuel Peypes Secondary
Blackheath Bluecoat School
Thomas Calton Secondary
Deptford Green Secondary
West Greenwich Secondary
Crown Woods Secondary
Charlton Boys Secondary
Roger Manwood Secondary
Peckham Secondary

Teachers interviewed
Hiliary Randor, Drama Teacher, Kidbrooke School
Nigel Drew, Social Studies, Samuel Peypes
Liz Maidmont, Drama Teacher, Blackheath Bluecoat School
Maureen Cooke, Drama Teacher, Deptford Green
Mr. Osborne, English Teacher, West Greenwich
Mary Burnett, English Teacher, Crown Woods
Anne Tweddell, Drama Teacher, Charlton Boys
Dave Meacock, Drama Teacher, Roger Manwood School
Paul Patrick, English Teacher, Roger Manwood School
Daphne Such, Social Studies, Peckham School
Ann Lloyd, Drama Teacher, Peckham School

Written information
Essays on "Race Against Time" from Kidbrooke School.
Drama Teachers's Questionnaire to pupils on the programme — Kidbrooke School.

Greenwich TIE
Reports from the Autumn Tour, 1978 (Company's comments)
Teachers' Questionnaires from: (Summer Tour 1978)
Blackheath Bluecoat School
Crown Woods
St. Ursula's Convent School
Abbey Wood

Comment from Liz Maidmont, Blackheath Bluecoat School.
Contact magazine, Vol, 7, Issue 12 (22nd September 1978), ILEA.

Discussions
Sue Bennion, School's Liaison Office, GYPT, and with Greenwich TIE
Company.

"Race Against Time" Material
Teachers' Notes
Recording of programme at Kidbrooke School, June 1978.

Select Bibliography

General Background: Theatre and Education

Allen, John, *Drama in Schools, its Theory and Practice*, London, Heinemann Educational, 1979.

Ansorge, Peter, *Disrupting the Spectacle*, London, Pitman, 1975.

Armstrong, R. H. R. and Hobson, M., "Games and gaming/simulation techniques — a comparison". In Armstrong, R. H. R. and Taylor, J. (eds.) *Feedback on Instructional Simulation*, Cambridge Institute of Education, 1971.

Bates, T. and Robinson, J. (eds.) *Evaluating Educational T.V. and Radio*, The Open University Press, 1977.

Bolton, Gavin, *Towards a Theory of Drama in Education*, London, Longmans, 1980.

Bradby, David, James, Louis and Sharratt, Bernard (eds.) *Performance and Politics in Popular Drama*, Cambridge University Press, 1980.

Bradby, David and McCormick, John, *People's Theatre*, Croom Helm Ltd., London, 1978.

Brecht, Bertholt, *Brecht on Theatre*, translated by John Willett, London, Eyre Methuen, 1977 (first published 1964, Hill & Wang, New York).

Cook, Caldwell, *The Play Way*, London, Heinemann, 1914.

Courtney, Richard, *Play, Drama and Thought*, London, Cassells, 1974 (first published 1968).

Craig, Sandy (ed.) *Dreams and Deconstructions*, Alternative Theatre in Britain, London, Amber Lane Press, 1980.

Department of Education and Science, *Half Our Future*, Chairman: John Newsom, HMSO, 1963.

DES, *Education Survey, 2. Drama*, Chairman: John Allen, HMSO, 1967.

DES, *Children and their Primary Schools*, Chairman: Lady Plowden, HMSO, 1967.

DES, *Primary Education in Wales*, Chairman: Charles Gittins, HMSO, 1967.

DES, *A Language for Life*, Chairman: Sir Allan Bullock, HMSO, 1975.

Dewey, John, *Experience and Education*, New York, Macmillan Collier, 1963 (1st edition 1938).

Dodd, N. and Hickson, W. *Drama and Theatre in Education*, London, Heinemann, 1971.

Fines, John and Verrier, Raymond, *The Drama of History*, London, New University Education, 1974.

Goodman, Paul, *Compulsory Miseducation*, Penguin Education Specials, 1977 (first published USA Horizon Press, 1962).

Hamilton, D. *Curriculum Evaluation*, London, Open Books, 1976.

Hayman, Ronald, *The Set Up, An Anatomy of English Theatre*, London, Eyre Methuen, 1973.

Hodgson, J. and Banham, Ken (eds.) *Drama in Education, Annual Survey* Nos. 1, 2, 3, London, Pitman, 1972, 1973, 1975.

Holt, John, *How Children Fail*, Penguin, 1977 (first published London, Pitman, 1965).

Holt, John, *How Children Learn*, Penguin, 1976 (1st published USA, Pitman, 1967).

Innes, C. D. *Piscator's Political Theatre, The Development of Modern German Drama*, Cambridge University Press, 1972.

Illich, Ivan, *Deschooling Society*, Pelican 1978 (first published USA, Harper & Row, 1971).

Itzen, Catherine (ed.) *British Alternative Theatre Directory*, Joan Offard Publications, 1979.

Itzen, Catherine, *Stages in the Revolution*, Political Theatre in Britain since 1968, London, Eyre Methuen, 1980.

McGregor, L., Tate, M. and Robinson, K., *Learning Through Drama*, London, Heinemann Educational for the Schools Council, 1977.

Nagelberg, M. M. (ed.) *Drama in Our Time*, USA, Harcourt, Brace & Co., 1948.

Norman, Marshall, *The Other Theatre*, London, John Lehman, 1957.

Nunn, Percy, *Education, its Data and First Principles*, London, Edward Arnold, 1920.

Redington, Christine and Pickering, Ken, *Select Bibliography of Drama in Education*, London, British Theatre Institute, 1981.

Robinson, Ken, *Exploring Theatre and Education*, London, Heinemann Educational, 1980.

Ross, Malcolm, *Arts and the Adolescent*, Schools Council Working Paper 54, London, Evans/Methuen Educational, 1975.

Slade, Peter, *Child Drama*, University of London, 1954.

Stephenson, Norman and Vincent, Denis, *Teaching and Understanding Drama*, NFER Publishing Co. (Slough), 1975.

Taylor, John and Walford, Rex, *Simulation in the Classroom*, Penguin Papers in Education, 1974.

Wagner, J. B. *Dorothy Heathcote*, London, Hutchinson, 1979, USA.

Way, Brian, *Development Through Drama*, London, Longmans, 1971.

Witken, Robert, *The Intelligence of Feeling*, London, Heinemann Educational, 1974.

Journals

Gambit, Plays and Players, Theatre Quarterly, World Theatre.

Outlook (NADECT), *Plays and Players, SCYPT Journal, Teaching Drama* (ID) *Theatre Quarterly.*

Theatre in Education, Young People's Theatre and Children's Theatre.

Arts Council of Great Britain, *The Provision of Theatre for Young People*, Chairman: Hugh Willatt, Arts Council, 1966.

Arts Council of Great Britain, *Community Arts*, Chairman: Professor H. C. Baldry, Arts Council, 1974.

Belgrade, Coventry TIE, *Rare Earth*, London, Methuen Young Drama, 1976.

Bolton Octagon TIE Company, *Sweetie Pie*, London, Methuen Young Drama, 1975.

Chapman, Clair (ed.) *Theatre-in-Education Directory 1975–76*, London, TQ Publications Ltd., 1975.

D'Arcy, MacKay, Constance, *Children's Theatre and Plays*, USA, Appleton & Co., 1927.

DES, *Actors in Schools*, HMSO, 1976.

Gleed, B. and Good, T. *Community Theatre*, Drama Board Association Occasional Paper, February 1976.

Jackson, Tony (ed.) *Learning Through Theatre*, Essays and Casebooks on Theatre in Education, Manchester University Press, 1980.

Leeds TIE, *Snap Out of It*, London, Methuen Young Drama, 1973.

McCaslin, Nellie (ed.) *Theatre for Young Audiences*, London, Longmans, 1978.

O'Toole, John, *Theatre in Education*, London, Hodder & Stoughton, 1976.

Schweitzer, Pam, *Theatre-in-Education*, 3 vols. *Five Infant Programmes, Four Junior Programmes, Four Secondary Programmes*, London, Methuen Young Drama, 1980.

Ward, Winifred, *Theatre for Children*, U.S.A., The Children's Theatre Press, 1935.

Way, Brian, *Audience Participation*, Theatre for Young People, Boston, Walter H. Baker Co., 1981.

Webster, Clive, *Working with Theatre in Schools*, London, Pitman, 1976.

Index

Allen, John 37, 39, 88
Arent, Arthur 25
Arts Council 6, 28, 30, 40, 84–7, 96, ·100, 107, 108, 134–6, 209–11
Asquith, Peter 113, 159, 160

BEC 46, 50–1, 69, 80, 159
Benson, Frank 31
Berman, Ed 28
Belgrade Theatre, Coventry 28–9, 42, 70–2, 75
Belgrade Theatre
  Artistic Directors
    Bailey, Brian 43
    Jenkins, Warren 56, 59
    Richardson, Anthony 43–5
Bolton, Gavin 129
Board Games 5, 19, 159
Brecht, Bertolt 20–2, 24
British Children's Theatre Association (BCTA) 129
Brinson, Peter 125, 137
Bruner, J. 19

Café La Mama 27
Centre 42 27
Centre of Interest (project teaching) 15, 51, 91
Cheeseman, Peter 25, 26
Children's Theatre Companies
  Abroad
    Children's Educational Theatre, America 30
    Dansk Skolescene, Copenhagen 84
    Grips Theatre Company, Berlin 8
    Moscow Theatre for Children 30
    Rote Grütze, Berlin 8
    State Children's Theatre Company, Hungary 30
  Britain
    Argyle Theatre, Birkenhead 35, 38, 85

Arion Children's Theatre Company 85
British Dance/Drama Theatre 85
C.W.M. Productions 85
English Children's Theatre 35, 85
Glyndebourne Children's Theatre 37–8
Liverpool Everyman Theatre Company 85
Osiris Repertory Company 85
Parable Players 32
Pear Tree Players 33
Scottish Children's Theatre 32, 85, 91
Southern Children's Theatre 85
Unicorn Theatre for Children 85, 213
Welsh Children's Theatre Company 85
West of England Children's Theatre 34, 38, 85
Westminster Children's Theatre Company 85
Young Vic 37–8
Cobby, Maisie 34
Committee for the Board of Education 16
Compass Players 35–7, 38
Conference on Youth and the Theatre 38–9
Cook, Caldwell 17
CORT (Council of Repertory Theatres)
  YPTS (Young People's Section) 39, 87–8, 129, 130
Coventry, city of 42
Craig, A.T. 16

Devine, George 22, 37, 38
Dewey, John 14, 17
Drama Advisers
  Beloe, Cliff (Derby) 113
  Boylen, John (Peterborough) 107
  Greatorex, John (Powys) 135
  Hollins, Derek (Clwyd) 104

Mckechnie, Betty (Glasgow)   91
Morton, David (Leeds)   97, 99
Drama in Education   3, 16–19, 32, 38,
    52, 54, 85, 89, 90, 99, 112, 115,
    128–9
Duncan Macrae Memorial Trust   91, 137

Education Act (1944)   18, 35
Education Authorities (LEAs)   134, 135,
    137, 138, 142, 150, 209, 210
    Coventry LEA   42, 45
    Glasgow   32, 91
    ILEA, the   18, 100, 104, 105, 112, 136,
        163, 164, 192, 194, 207
    Ipswich   112
    Leeds   96
    Leicester   89
English, John   84
English Stage Company   22
Equity   85, 130, 133

Federal Theatre Movement   24, 30
Froebel   13, 17

Gaskill, William   22
Goodman, Paul   7
Greet, Ben   30
Gulbenkian Foundation (Calouste Gulben-
    kian)   125, 132, 133, 137

Herts, Alice Minnie   30
Hollingsworth, Catherine   34
Holt, John   7, 212

Illich, Ivan   7
Inter-Action   28
International Children's Theatre Festival
    (1971)   130

Jenner, Caryl   29, 35, 38, 39, 84, 87, 89,
    130

Laurent, Jeanne   26
Lee, Jennie   39, 84
Leeds Symposium (1974)   131
Lehrstücke, the   20
Life of Galileo, the   94
Littlewood, Joan   24, 27
Living Newspaper   24–5, 49
    Busman   24

It Can't Happen Here   24
One Third of a Nation   24–5
London Arts Lab   27

Man Power Services Commission (MSC)
    137–9, 211
Mary Ward Settlement, the   17
McColl, Ewan   24
Measures Taken, the   20–2
Mother Courage   72

National Council of Repertory Theatres
    (NCTYP)   39, 129–30, 133
National Festival of Young People's
    Theatre (1973)   130
National Youth Theatre   10
Nuffield Foundation   137

Odet, Clifford   23
Oh What a Lovely War   27
Old Vic, the   31, 33–4, 37
Open Space   28
Open Theatre   27
O'Toole, John   113, 156–8, 166, 205

Parnaby, Bert   116
Piaget   19
Piscator, Erwin   23
Planchon, Roger   26–7
Plater, Alan   72
Polka Company   130, 138
Project teaching   3, 15, 113, 121

Red Ladder   22
Red Megaphone   23
Regional Arts Associations   136, 138
Repertory Theatres
    Amersham Playhouse   35
    Bristol Old Vic   29, 89, 112
    Bolton   89
    Cheltenham   29
    Chesterfield   89
    Citizens' Theatre, Glasgow   89, 90, 92,
        127
    Citizens' Theatre, Close Theatre   92–3
    Colchester   29
    Dundee   89
    Exeter   89
    Farnham   89
    Greenwich   100
    Ipswich   89
    Key Theatre, Peterborough   107, 125

Leeds Playhouse   96, 97, 98
Lincoln   89
Marlowe Theatre, Canterbury   29, 89
Newcastle   213
Nottingham Playhouse   28
Phoenix Theatre, Leicester   89, 128,
   213
Salisbury   89
Victoria Theatre, Stoke on Trent   128
Watford Palace   29, 89
Artistic Directors
Blakemore, Michael   90
Havergal, Giles   29, 127
Hays, Bill   97
Hooper, Ewan   100
Masefield, Paddy   213
Peel, Edward   128, 212
Southworth, John   213
Reports
   Actors in Schools   202
   Drama (DES) (1967)   18, 85, 209
   Drama in Adult Education (1926)   17,
      18
   English (1921)   17
   The Primary School (1931)   15
   Children and their Primary Schools (1967)
      16
   English in Secondary Schools (1959)   16
   Half our Future   19
   Handbook for Teachers, the (1937)   18
   Provision of Theatre for Young People, the
      (1966)   30, 40, 85, 209
   Secondary Schools (1947)   18
   Teaching of English in England, the   31
Robinson, Ken   143, 152
Rousseau, Jean Jacques   13
Russia's Day   23

Scottish Arts Council   91
Señora Carrar's Rifles   24
7.84 Company   22
Simulations   5, 19, 76–81, 117, 122, 152,
   153, 162, 170
Slade, Peter   18, 32–3, 38, 58, 80
Stafford Clark, Max   27
Standing Conference of Young People's
   Theatre (SCYPT)   11, 118–9, 121,
   125, 128, 131–3, 210, 211
SCYPT Journal   133, 210
Swedish Education Television and Radio
   Service   155

Théâtre de la Cité   26–7
Theatre in Education (TIE), Abroad
   Magpie TIE Company, Adelaide   9

Marmeille Theatre of Quebec, La   9
Rochester project   8
Theatre in Education (TIE) and Young
   People's Theatre (YPT), Britain
Companies
   Aberdeen   34, 104, 135
   Action Pie (South Glamorgan)   138
   Belgrade, Coventry   2, 22, 26, 40,
      45–82, 95, 111–2, 115, 118, 129,
      130, 131, 135, 145, 149, 156,
      200, 209, 213
   Billingham Young People's Theatre
      95, 128
   Bolton   95, 115, 130, 142
   Citizen's Theatre for Youth, Glas-
      gow   90–5, 103, 127, 138
   Clwyd   103–5, 135
   Cockpit, London   95–6, 104–5, 115,
      118, 122, 135, 143–4, 200, 203,
      207
   Curtain, London   104, 143–4, 151
   Derby   95
   Dundee   127
   Easterhouse, Glasgow   138
   Edinburgh LEA   5, 135
   Edinburgh, Lyceum   3, 95
   Exeter   211
   Flying Phoenix, Leicester   16,
      89–90, 112
   Gateway, Chester   90, 92
   Greenwich Young People's Theatre
      (GYPT), formerly Bowsprit
      99–103, 104, 105, 114, 119–22,
      128, 135, 136, 149, 150, 156,
      162, 164, 200, 207, 208
   Harlow Community Theatre   138
   Harrogate   127
   Ipswich   112, 128
   Key Perspectives, Peterborough   96,
      107–8, 118, 128
   Lancaster   104, 151, 152, 211
   Leeds   95–9, 103, 128
   Liverpool Everyman Priority Theatre
      Project   43, 137, 138
   Marlowe Mobile, Canterbury   95
   M.6   127–8
   Medium Fair, Exeter   138
   Merseyside Young People's Theatre
      138
   Northumberland, Theatre in Schools
      137
   Phoenix Theatre, Leicester   138
   Plymouth   138
   Roundabout, Nottingham   11, 127,
      139, 210, 211
   Serpent Theatre Company, Essex
      137

Sidewalk Theatre Company 106
Solent Theatre Company 137
Theatre Centre 39, 85, 137
Theatremakers, Stirling 211
Wakefield Drama in Education 138
York Young People's Theatre 202
Personnel
Baskerville, Romy 115
Bennett, Stuart 57, 58, 63, 80, 81, 111, 113, 114, 127, 213
Bennion, Sue 122, 195, 208
Birbeck, Rosemary 54–6, 57, 68, 113
Birtwhistle, Sue 95, 113–4, 128
Chapman, Roger 96–7, 127
Davison, Alec 105
Gillham, Geoff 100, 203, 206
Forder, David 43
Harman, Paul 43, 138
Hawksley, Fred 126
Hicks, Colin 213
Hollman, David 213
Leech, Peter 90
Mitchell, June 101–2
Newton, Derek 43
Pammenter, David 81, 126, 205, 206, 213
Reed, Dickon 56
Steed, Maggie 160
Vallins, Gordon 42–9, 55–6, 64, 213
Vine, Chris 117, 119, 134, 139
Wiseman, Gordon 56, 95, 114
Wyatt, Stephen 160
Programmes
Belgrade, Coventry TIE
Actor and his Work 72
Adventure 70
Baldur, the God of Light 50–2
Balloon Man and the Runaway Balloons 47–8, 50
Cocoa Tree, the 62
Conflict in Coventry, the 65, 95–6
Emergent Africa Game, the 21, 79–80
Example 96, 105
Excursion 72
Frozen Lands, the 59, 65
Great Fire of London, the 73, 80
High Girders 48–9
How the Rain came to Hweng Chow 60
Ice Station Zero One 96
If it was not for the Weaver 73–5, 80, 114
Ifan's Valley 4
Industrial Revolution, the 69

Journey of the Running Deer Tribe 58–9
Kenny's Comic 58, 63
Lunt Fort at Baginton 65–8, 69, 114
Mother Courage (Courage in War) 72
Mysterious Wanderers (or the Gypsies) 60–2
Navvies, the 117–8
Noah and the Animals 59, 80
Noise, Noise, Noise 52–4
People Matter More than Plans, Councillor Kean 76–9
Person 59
Penhale 117
Pinocchio 59
Pow Wow 5, 22, 96, 114, 118, 145–9, 153, 202–6
Princess and the Fisherman 58
Rama and Sita 62
Rare Earth 3, 82, 116, 118, 159–61, 202–4
Recital of D.H. Lawrence (As Far as I'm Concerned) 72
Rise of Hitler, the 117
Secret of the Stone 48, 51
Secret of the Sun 70
Siege of Kenilworth, the 64
Slavery 69
Story Making 62
Teeth 56
Ugly's Trust Abused 82
What on the Landing, the 72
Citizens' Theatre for Youth
History of Scottish Coalmining (Dusky Diamonds) 91
Landor Brothers, the 92
Modern Drama 91
Responsibility of the Scientist (Life of Galileo) 94
Clwyd DIE
Doctor Drip 105
Fire of London 105
Henry V 105
Tempest, the 105
Cockpit TIE
Coriolanus 149
Marches 6, 105, 117
Ways of Change 123, 203
Edinburgh LEA TIE
Opportunity Strikes 3
Edinburgh, Lyceum TIE
Blew Blanket, the 95
Greenwich Young People's Theatre
Living Patterns 19, 121–2, 156, 205
Race Against Time 11, 19, 117, 119, 123, 144, 150, 156, 162, 164, 168–200, 203–6

Unemployment 6, 119, 123
Lancaster TIE
Travellers 118, 151
Leeds TIE
A Place to Live (Quarry Hill Flats) 25, 99
Tynewear TIE
Labour for the Lord 26
Theatre of Action 24
Theatre Workshop 27
Tyler, Gerald 35

Unity Theatre 23, 24

Vygotsky, Z. 19

Waddell, Bertha 32, 85, 91
Waiting for Lefty 23
Walton, John 163
Ward, Winifred 30
Way, Brian 18, 33, 34, 38, 47, 58, 59, 80, 84, 85, 89, 111, 129, 130
Welsh Arts Council 138
Wesker, Arnold 27
Workers' Theatre Movement 24

Young People's Theatre Panel (Arts Council) 87, 107